THE CONSTRUCTIVE THEOLOGY OF BERNARD MELAND

Postliberal Empirical Realism

AR

American Academy of Religion
Studies in Religion

Editor
David E. Klemm

Number 69
THE CONSTRUCTIVE THEOLOGY OF
BERNARD MELAND
Postliberal Empirical Realism

by
Tyron Inbody

THE CONSTRUCTIVE THEOLOGY OF BERNARD MELAND

Postliberal Empirical Realism

by
Tyron Inbody

Scholars Press
Atlanta, Georgia

THE CONSTRUCTIVE THEOLOGY OF BERNARD MELAND

Postliberal Empirical Realism

by
Tyron Inbody

© 1995
The American Academy of Religion

Library of Congress Cataloging in Publication Data
Inbody, Tyron

    The constructive theology of Bernard Meland : postliberal empirical realism / by Tyron Inbody.
      p.   cm. — (American Academy of Religion studies in religion ; no. 69)
    Includes bibliographical references.
    ISBN 1-55540-989-X (alk. paper). — ISBN 1-55540-990-3 (pbk. : alk. paper)
    1. Meland, Bernard Eugene, 1899–1993. 2. Empirical theology. 3. Process theology. 4. Chicago school of theology. 5. Theology, Doctrinal—United States—History—20th century. I. Title. II. Series: AAR studies in religion ; no. 69.
BX4827.M45I52 1995
230'.092—dc20   94-17816
                                  CIP

Printed in the United States of America
on acid-free paper

Contents

Preface ix

| 1 | Fifty Years of Religious Inquiry: Meland as Embodiment of the Chicago School | 1 |

I. Foreign Born Parents: 1899-1920   5

II. Crusading Days: 1920-1925   10

III. End of Modernism: 1925-1929   13

IV. Between Modernism and the New Realism: 1929-1936   20

V. A Time of Incubation: 1936-1945   22

VI. A Constructive Theologian: 1945-1964   31

VII. From the Summit View: 1964-1993   39

| 2 | Experience in the Radical Mode: Meland as an Epistemologist | 43 |

I. From Mystical Naturalism to the Appreciative Consciousness   46

II. The Appreciative Consciousness   51

III. Cognition Within the Appreciative Consciousness   55

IV. Frames of Meaning and Fundamental Notions   60

V. Language and Reality   65

| 3 | Experience and Culture: Meland as a Theologian of Culture | 75 |

I. Naturalism and Emergence 76

II. The Idea of Spirit 81

III. Experience and Culture 86

IV. Faith and Myth 92

V. Relativity and Relativism 100

| 4 | Meland as a Process Theologian | 109 |

I. Three Types of Process Theology 109

II. Meland's Orientation Toward the Process Vision 113

III. Meland and Process Metaphysics 117

IV. Meland as a Process Thinker 126

V. The Absolute and the Relative in Metaphysics 133

| 5 | Meland as "A Rebel Among Process Theologians" | 143 |

I. The Limits of Metaphysics 145

II. Radical Empiricism and Rational Empiricism 148

III. The Principle of Limitation 155

IV. Coherence and Dissonance 164

| **6** | Meland's Naturalistic Interpretation of God | 175 |

I. God as a Constructive Idea	177
II. The Religious Meaning of the Concept of God	179
III. The Realistic Meaning of the Concept of God	180
IV. God as a Designative Image	186
V. The Ambiguity of God	189
VI. Meland on God and Evil: An Evaluation	192
VIII. Meland and the Future of Empirical Theology	199

| **7** | Postliberal Empirical Realism | 205 |

I. Postliberal Theology	206
II. Empirical Theology	215
III. Realistic Theology	220
IV. Constructive Theology	222

Complete Bibliography of Published Writings — 235

Index — 249

Preface

This book is written to meet a need. There is no comprehensive introduction to the context, idiom, and scope of the fifty years of religious inquiry of Bernard Eugene Meland available today. Such a study is important for three reasons.

1. Bernard Meland offers a postliberal theology that is an alternative to the theology that commonly goes under that name in contemporary discussion. Instead of offering a postliberal theology which continues the Barthian revolution from the mid-twenties through the mid-sixties, represented today by "the Yale School" of Hans Frei and George Lindbeck, he offers a postliberal theology that grows directly out of the revolutions within liberal theology itself during the same period, represented currently by the various forms of process theology and revisionary theology growing out the Divinity School of the University of Chicago.[1]

2. In his thought Meland gathers the developments which occurred throughout the three distinct phases of "the Chicago School of Theology," beginning with the socio-historical period under Shirley Jackson Case, Shailer Mathews, and G. B. Smith, moving through the philosophical season under Henry Nelson Wieman and Bernard Loomer, and culminating in the theological phase following WWII under Daniel Day Williams and his own work.[2] Unlike any other member of

---

[1] For an analysis of the options in the contemporary postliberal situation from the point of view of the Yale School, see Hans Frei, *Types of Christian Theology* (New Haven: Yale, 1992); for such an analysis from the point of view of the Chicago School, see David Tracy, *Blessed Rage for Order: The New Pluralism in Theology* (New York: Seabury Press, 1975). An excellent comparison of these two schools can be found in Edward Oakes, "Apologetics and the Pathos of Narrative Theology," *Journal of Religion* 72 (January, 1992) : 37-58.

[2] For histories of the Divinity School of the University of Chicago, see Charles Harvey Arnold, *Near the Edge of Battle: A Short History of the Divinity School and 'The Chicago School of Theology' 1866-1966* (Chicago: Divinity School Association, 1966), and Bernard

the Divinity School, either student or faculty, Meland's thought embodies the range of themes developed throughout the three phases of empirical theology in the Divinity School from 1906-1966.

3. Meland represents a distinct version of process theology, namely, empirical theology, which is making a strong resurgence in the last decade among a new generation of philosophers of religion and theologians.[3] As a major representative of the empirical movement within the process school, especially from the time of his return to the faculty at Chicago in 1945 through his retirement in 1964, he develops his own emphases within process thought which make him a distinctive kind of process theologian. During the fifty years from 1929 to 1979, his empirical brand of process thought is developed in 13 books, 152 published essays, two edited books, and at least 50 other articles which can be accounted for but have not yet been published.

This book, then, offers the first comprehensive study of the scope of the theology of Bernard Meland. There have been other studies of his thought, but none of these is comprehensive. J. J. Mueller's study, *Faith and Appreciative Consciousness: The Cultural Theology of Bernard Meland*,[4] focuses almost wholly on his trilogy in methodology, and ignores the first thirty years of his writings. Delores Rogers's study, *The American Empirical Movement in Theology*,[5] is somewhat broader in

---

Meland, "The Empirical Tradition at Chicago," in Bernard Meland, ed., *The Future of Empirical Theology* (Chicago: University of Chicago Press, 1969), pp. 1-62, and Tyron Inbody, "History of Empirical Theology," in Randolf Crump Miller, ed., *Empirical Theology: A Handbook* (Birmingham: Religious Education Press, 1992), pp. 11-35. For a discussion of the current reconstitution of that tradition within the Divinity School, see Jerald C. Brauer, "A History of the Divinity School: Creatively Out of Step," *Criterion* 29 (Autumn, 1990) : 12-17.

[3] Two major milestones in publications represent the revitalization and continuing significance of the empirical wing of the process movement in theology. The first is the volume published from the conference celebrating the one hundredth anniversary of the Divinity School, *The Future of Empirical Theology*, ed. Bernard Meland, and the recent *Empirical Theology: A Handbook*, ed. Randolf Crump Miller. The work of this brand of process thought also continues in the academy through the Highlands Institute for American Religious Thought, the Pragmatism and Empiricism in American Religious Thought Group of the American Academy of Religion, and the *American Journal of Theology & Philosophy*, which has been published since 1980.

[4] J. J. Mueller, *Faith and Appreciative Consciousness: The Cultural Theology of Bernard Meland* (Washington: University Press of America, 1981).

[5] Delores Joan Rogers, *The American Empirical Movement in Theology* (New York: Peter Lang, 1990).

scope, and includes a concurrent study of Mordicai Kaplan, but it also ignores the earlier period of the development of Meland's thought.

In addition to the two monographs, four journals have devoted entire issues to Meland, viz., *Quest*,[6] *Criterion*,[7] *Journal of Religion*,[8] and *American Journal of Theology & Philosophy*.[9] Also there have been three conferences featuring Meland's work: 1) "Fifty Years of Religious Inquiry," a meeting of the Indiana Academy of Religion at Purdue University on March 31, 1979, 2) "Meland and the Future of Theology," a working scholars conference held at Purdue University in October, 1982,[10] and 3) "Wieman and Meland: Apostles of Creative Naturalism," a symposium held at Park College, April 11, 1986. Finally, beyond the two books, the special issues of the journals, and the conferences, his thought has been significantly commented upon and influential in the constructive work of such scholars as Nancy Frankenberry, William Dean, Clark Williamson, and Jerome Stone.

This study attempts to present Meland's thought in its context, its distinctiveness, its development, and its broad scope. Beyond that, there is a deliberate effort to move him into our context and to understand his issues and themes as they bear upon the contemporary discussion in theology. This intent should be apparent from the start, as the reader discovers in the table of contents a chapter on Meland in his context (one) and a chapter on Meland in our context (seven).

As the author of a comprehensive book on Meland, I could offer either a synthetic interpretation of his thought or an organic account of his concerns. If my task were the former one, I would attempt to create a mosaic of the deposits of insights Meland contributes to theological discussion, some of the facets, endowments, continuities and discontinuities, and the fabric of his thought throughout his lifetime. If my task were the latter, I would attempt to get at his intent and to account for his decisions in pursuing the inquiry he pursues, his considered judgments, and what he means to convey.

---

6 *Quest* 8 (August, 1964).
7 *Criterion* 3 (Summer, 1964).
8 *Journal of Religion* (October, 1980).
9 *American Journal of Theology & Philosophy* 5 (May-September, 1984).
10 Larry Axel published a review of this conference, "Bernard Meland and the Future of Theology," *Criterion* 22 (Spring, 1983): 16-21, and the papers of the conference were published under the title "Bernard Meland and the Future of Theology," *American Journal of Theology & Philosophy* 5 (May and September, 1984).

I have chosen the former task. I do this, in part, because Meland himself is keenly aware of the fact that what interpreters see in his thought may not be identical with what he intends. An author may or may not be aware of her own elan as she experiences it and understands it throughout her probings and formulations. But no interpreter can or needs to get at the intent of another author. The products stand on their own, and present a reservoir of contributions to the ongoing theological discussion. A synthetic view, then, is more a comment on the various insights and formulations Meland offers to the discussion along the way than a privileged awareness of the efforts that go into the twists and turns of his life project. It is more a summation of what Meland's total effort comes to as it contributes to our own postmodern situation than a statement of what his motivations and internal workings are.

In addition to a presentation of his major themes, the study is also my interpretation of the contribution of his work to theological discussion today. Interpreters may see something from a synthetic point of view that the author does not intend or see. Besides, once the author has put out into the public domain his own ideas, he no longer owns them but they become part of the grist for the discussion. Intent and ownership are sacrificed to the larger discussion. One hopes that Meland might recognize his own thought, and perhaps even intent, in what I write about him, but what I offer is my interpretation of the significance of his work for the ongoing theological discussion. If such a study succeeds in sizing up the whole of his contribution, it might have considerable value, both as an interpretation of the author and a contribution to the ongoing theological discussion.

I hope the study is not judged by whether or not it gets inside Meland's head, but primarily by whether it is a useful guide for interpreting the scope of his writings and their contribution to the contemporary theological discussion. At the same time, the reader may be curious, and might even benefit by learning a bit, about my own relationship with Meland. When I matriculated at the Divinity School of the University of Chicago in the fall of 1965, I took three courses from Meland, two in the history of liberal theology and one in theological method. Although officially Meland had been retired for one year, he continued to teach courses in retirement. Subsequently (1973), I wrote my dissertation on the thought of Paul Tillich and Bernard Meland as they respond to the problem of cultural relativism for theology. The work on that dissertation provides some of the ground work for two of the chapters in this study.

I also have had the good fortune of my school, United Theological Seminary, granting me a semester sabbatical in which I could read uninterrupted the entire Meland corpus as research for a major paper for the conference at Purdue in 1982. In addition, some of my research and writing during the last decade has been devoted to understanding Meland better and employing his sensibilities and general orientation in my own constructive work.

At a more personal level, Meland's thought provides me with a major resource for the formulation of some of my own religious and theological convictions. Although he did not create the religious sensibilities which still shape my life, he succeeds more than anyone else is expressing and giving shape to them.[11] Although I am not uncritical of some of Meland's thought, especially with respect to problems inadequately explored for our postmodern context or assumptions still located within the liberal tradition that have become highly problematic in our context, I am grateful to him for his success in providing some of us with a way to understand the relation of religious sensibilities and theological construction that still informs our work more than any other single theologian.

Chapter One is an intellectual biography of Bernard Meland. It introduces the reader to him, sets his life and thought in his own context, introduces the key ideas that will be developed in the following chapters, and traces the development of his thought through its various phases. Chapter Two describes Meland's empirical epistemology, introducing his mystical naturalism, his concept of the appreciative consciousness, and his idea of the relation of experience and language. Chapter Three relates his empiricism to his concept of culture, focusing primarily on his understanding of the relation of faith and culture and on his idea of relativity. Chapter Four presents Meland as a process theologian, while Chapter Five describes ways and reasons he is critical of some of the recent developments in process theology. Chapter Six shows how his empirical orientation in theology works out in his concept of God. Finally, Chapter Seven presents Meland in our context, describing how

---

[11] See my essay, "Religious Empiricism and the Problem of Religious Adequacy," in Michael Shermis, ed., *The Writings of Larry E. Axel: Studies in Liberal Religious Thought* (Lewiston: The Edwin Mellen Press, 1992), pp. 247-260.

his empirical realism is postliberal. Readers who are unfamiliar with Meland's theology and want to begin by placing him in the context of contemporary theological discussion may want to begin by reading Chapter Seven.

I find it impossible to acknowledge adequately the people who have contributed to my understanding of Meland's thought over the last twenty five years. Instead, I express my gratitude to those who read substantial parts of the book and made valuable suggestions for improvement: Nancy Frankenberry, Jerome Stone, and William Dean. Jennifer Jesse and Les Muray also read parts of early drafts. Our faculty secretary, Ann DeHays, typed some of this material onto a disk for me. Daniel Eppley read the entire manuscript in its next to final form and offered many valuable suggestions for improvement. The generous sabbatical program offered by my institution, United Theological Seminary, provided me with time to write and rewrite much of this text. Finally, and most important, I want to express here my deep gratitude and affection for my wife, Fran, who has graciously encouraged me in this project since it began years ago in graduate school. She contributes to my life even more than she knows a deeper appreciation and understanding of the graces which emerge from the rich range of "lived experience."

1

Fifty Years of Religious Inquiry: Meland as the Embodiment of the Chicago School[1]

"Bernard E. Meland, in the span of his professorship and in the task to which he set his mind, is a personal summary of the work of [the Divinity S]chool. In him is represented the axis upon which theological reflection in our time has turned."[2]

"I speak also as one for whom time is of the essence. Yet the measure of my days in [the Divinity School] by no means gives the measure of my concern for the work of this school, for each of you, and for all of us together in this theological community. For in ways I find difficult to explain, I find that, to myself, I am the Divinity School. Its history is the

---

[1] Bernard Meland provided four autobiographical statements between 1944 and 1979: "Confessions of a Frustrated Theologian" (1944), 11 pp; "Towers of the Mind" (1946), 81 pp; "Some Autobiographical Reflections Bearing on Works Preceding Faith and Culture" (1969), 20 pp; and "Fifty Years of Religious Inquiry" (1979), 44 pp. Unidentified quotations in this chapter are taken from these four statements. In addition, there are twenty-two boxes of unsorted letters and papers in the Meland archives at the Regenstein Library at the University of Chicago. Finally, Betty Jean Hodge, a niece, has been helpful with some details of Meland's biography.

[2] This is a citation from the Board of Trustees of the Baptist Theological Union when Meland was honored as Alumnus of the Year. *Alumni* (November, 1970), 4.

history of my own theological pilgrimage; hence the Divinity School is very much in me."[3]

The Divinity School of the University of Chicago has been at the forefront of liberal theological thought in the United States since the Baptist Theological Union became part of the University of Chicago under William Rainey Harper in 1892. Throughout the twentieth century "the Chicago School" has been "creatively out of step" with other American theological institutions.[4] No person embodies the ethos of the Divinity School or the phases of its development throughout the middle half of this century more completely than Bernard Eugene Meland. As a student and eventually as a faculty member, his career depicts the University's commitment to creative scholarship independent of class rank and privilege. A son of immigrants to a small town outside Chicago in the late nineteenth century, he becomes a significant voice in one of the four or five most influential divinity schools in the United States. Whereas the predominant response to the collapse of liberal theology in the late twenties and early thirties is the neoorthodox theology of Karl Barth and Reinhold Niebuhr, Bernard Meland's response is to enrich and revise liberal thought in the light of these cultural changes. Each phase of his thought is an effort to reconstruct liberalism in a postliberal era.

From 1929 to 1979, Bernard Meland embodies the issues, the resources, and the developments within the Divinity School. He writes 13 books, edits two, and publishes 152 articles throughout this half century.[5] His writings, however, are difficult to read; his mode of expression is unconventional, even eccentric and esoteric. That is the way he writes, and that is the way he is to be read if he is to enlighten us about ranges of our experience that are often ignored by more precise authors. His constructive essays are usually extended soliloquies instead of logical arguments. One frequently has the feeling of eavesdropping on the musings of a poet or a mystic. If others can benefit from reading

---

[3] Bernard Meland, "A Long Look at the Divinity School in Its Present Crisis," *Criterion* I (Summer, 1962), 30.

[4] Jerald C. Brauer, "A History of the Divinity School: Creatively Out of Step," *Criterion* 29 (Autumn, 1990): 12-17.

[5] Well over fifty unpublished essays have been located. The twenty-two boxes of letters and papers in the archives at Regenstein Library at the University of Chicago have yet to be indexed.

these musings in printed form, they are invited to "listen in" for their own benefit.

Meland resists being a technical thinker and precise writer. The reason is not that he is lazy or a shabby thinker, but because his conception of the object of theology, namely, "the more," is not accessible to definitive formulation. He is a keen observer of lived experience who attempts to convey the depth and complexity of the world as faithfully as he can, even if it is at the expense of razor-sharp clarity. No theologian describes lived experience in its depth and richness more faithfully than Meland. Experience to him is more a medium of disclosure than a ground of cognitive certainty. Clarity at the expense of the rich fullness of experience leads to the trivialization of life and thought.

His manner of writing tends more toward rumination and illustration than toward analysis. Thus to the more technical, concise thinker and writer, his style is cloudy, mystifying, bewildering, vague, and above all elusive. However, to those who are willing to let the mist settle and then lift, his thought is rich, complex, nuanced, suggestive, even poignant. Readers can be prodded, tempted, or even seduced into seeing new configurations of reality. Many of his students have repeated in one form or another the comment of Joseph Sittler, his colleague in theology, on listening to Meland: When Meland begins to talk a gentle mist descends upon the room. Shortly, it envelopes everything in a dense fog. The fog always lifts, but when it does all the furniture has been rearranged.

The form of Meland's theology, then, is more poetic than philosophical. His constructive theology exhibits more the form of a musical symphony or an artistic photograph than a philosophical treatise or a systematic theology. Indeed, Meland compares the structure of theology more to the symphonic structure than to the logical treatise.[6] But that suggests only part of the significance of this analogy for understanding Meland's theology. If constructive theology is analogous to the symphony, the question for understanding Meland is what kind of symphony? Is it close to the classical symphony, with its style of gaiety or serenity? Or does it exhibit struggle, the tragic, pessimistic, lyrical and dark pathos of the romantic symphony, as in

---

[6] Bernard Meland, "Interpreting the Christian Faith within a Philosophical Framework," *Journal of Religion* 33 (1953): 87-102.

some of Beethoven's symphonies? Or is it, like Mozart, combining both classical gaiety and moments of dark pathos, as in the "D Minor Concerto" or "Don Giovanni" or his unfinished "Requiem"? Or does his work reflect the atonality and dissonance of the postmodern symphony, like Schoenberg's "Five Pieces for Orchestra," where one learns not to expect melody and harmony but rather a wide range of tonal colors available on the palette of the orchestra? If one is going to follow out this analogy, Meland's symphonic theology moves between the romantic and the postmodern. Lyricism and dissonance mix to reflect both romantic and postmodern sensibilities. Much as we can sense Mozart's link to the romantic future in music, we can sense Meland's link to the postmodern future in theology.

If one applies as analogy the visual arts, and particularly photography, instead of music, his constructive theology expresses more of what the photographs of Ernst Haas's *Creation*[7] or Eliot Porter's and James Gleick's *Nature's Chaos*[8] or John Briggs's *Fractals: The Patterns of Chaos: Discovering a New Aesthetic of Art, Science, and Nature*[9] express than of what representation photographs or the advocacy photographs of Dorothea Lang and Walker Evans express. Like Haas, Porter, and Briggs, Meland seeks more to exhibit the subtle patterns amidst the chaos of nature than to represent objects or advocate moral positions. Porter's and Briggs's photographs are stills of nature, which, upon first glance, appear not to be orderly at all. But when viewed in detailed sections they suggest a tension between order and chaos. In commenting on the photographs of Porter, James Gleick, the author of *Chaos: Making a New Science*,[10] says, "The rivers, the clouds, the snowflakes of our usual perceptual tool kits miss much of nature's true complexity: the intricate recursion, the convoluted flows within flows within flows.... The essence of the earth's beauty lies in disorder, a peculiarly patterned disorder, from the fierce tumult of rushing water to the tangled filigrees of unbridled vegetation."[11] Nature, then, is rarely a static and balanced harmony, but rather a weaving, lurching, animating

---

[7] Ernst Haas, *Creation* (New York: Viking Press, 1971).

[8] Eliot Porter and James Gleick, *Nature's Chaos* (New York: Viking Press, 1990).

[9] John Briggs, *Fractals: The Patterns of Chaos: Discovering a New Aesthetic of Art, Science, and Nature* (New York: Touchstone Books, 1992).

[10] James Gleick, *Chaos: Making a New Science* (New York: Viking Press, 1987).

[11] Porter and Gleick, *Nature's Chaos*, pp. 11, 14.

movement. The photographer examines "fractal relationships" and "fractal patterns," patterns that seem annoyingly random but reflect a sense of hidden connections. Gleick says Porter's task is "to investigate the morphology of the amorphous." This apt phrase — the morphology of the amorphous — describes as well as any the task Meland sets for himself when he attempts to provide a theological account of the rich range of lived experience.

We are about to launch the study of a constructive theologian who speaks out of and to the liberal tradition in theology but revises that tradition to such an extent that he can only be called a postliberal theologian. Thus, those who are influenced by Meland's thought are prepared to have much sympathy with and at the same time to be critical of some of the developments in postliberal theology. The intent of this study is to show how a theologian shaped by the liberal tradition in theology advances the conversation about the meaning and shape of postliberal theology. Although liberalism seems to be a dead term today in theology, it possesses resources for both criticism of and advance toward a genuinely postliberal theology. A revision of liberalism through critique and reconstruction characterizes Meland's agenda through every twist and turn. My intent here is to offer a synthesis of his thought with an eye to its contribution, both actual and potential, to the contemporary search for a postliberal theology.

I. "FOREIGN BORN PARENTS": 1899-1920

Bernard Eugene Meland was a son of "foreign born parents." His mother and father came from Norway, part of a large community of Norwegians who emigrated to America during the 1880's and 1890's. A considerable group of Norwegians, many with the name Meland, settled in northern Minnesota, some in Iowa, and a few in Pullman and Kensington, Illinois. His father, Erik Bernhard Meland, was born February 13, 1871, in Haugasund, a seaport town on the southeastern coast of Norway; his mother, Elizabeth Hansen Meland, was born in Bergen. Both parents came to America when they were young (Erik was sixteen, Elizabeth was four). Following two years of service in the Norwegian navy, Erik was offered an opportunity to join several other countrymen in filling the immigration quota after another ticket holder had died. It was such an honor for a town to have an immigrant to the

United States that Erik felt compelled to come. He went directly from Ellis Island to Pullman to live with his uncle.

Since Erik Meland had not completed his schooling and had to go to work immediately, he actually stepped backward in the economic and social scale when he arrived in America. He began an apprenticeship in cabinet making in the Pullman Car Works in 1889, and worked there for 40 years. Unlike many of his family in Norway, who had been educators, bookdealers, owners of fisheries, and one a painter of renown, most of the family who came to this country were factory workers, though a few were farmers. As a result of the Pullman strike of 1894, Erik went to work in the Wagoner Car Works in Buffalo, New York, where he met Elizabeth Hanson, whom he married in 1897. He also helped build the staircase at the Vanderbilt Castle, now known as the Biltmore House, in Asheville, North Carolina. With the exception of that brief interim, however, he spent his entire career until 1930 with the Pullman Company as in inside finisher of Pullman cars and a cabinet maker. Bernard described him as a quiet man who expressed himself best through the work of his hands.

Eight children were born to the Melands, two of whom died in infancy. Born June 28, 1899, Bernard lived with his six sisters and brothers in the Chicago suburb of Pullman near the Pullman Car Works. His recollections of his early years at home express complementary inclinations toward city and country, factory and farm, community and family, and nature and the church, reminiscent of Tillich's *On the Boundary*.[12] While living in Pullman, Bernard frequently visited his grandfather's farm in Allegan, Michigan, and worked on local farms in the area. He began working on the farms in the summer at age ten and continued throughout high school. Being one of the smallest members of the crew, he was always put on the stack to catch the straw as it came out of the shoot to pile around the loft.

Images of the farm from his boyhood years shaped his "mystical naturalism." They also helped form a tragic sense of life. In a 1946 vesper service he spoke of the October scenes of harvest in the Midwest as "the bitter fruit of autumn.... To this day, when I think of late autumn, I feel the sharp wounds and the ache of chill that has settled deep inside." The autumn, he said, is easily the earth's hour of triumph and

---

12 Paul Tillich, *One the Boundary: An Autobiographical Sketch* (New York: Scribners, 1966).

culmination, yet no beautiful thing lasts. "Curiously enough, dwelling upon these autumn scenes, the mind inescapably moves toward the tragic sense of life."[13]

In 1910 the family moved from Pullman to Homewood, a semi-rural region 23 miles south of Chicago. Rising at 5:30 in the morning to milk two cows, Bernard delivered the milk on the way to the train (a mile away), and then rode four miles to school. After school he worked in the fields and did the chores. Throughout his life Homewood was "home."

The Meland family lived with meager resources. Contrary to the common assumption about immigrants to America, immigration for his family meant a set back economically and culturally from which most of them never recovered. In his perception his boyhood years were spent in an atmosphere of privation. He described his family as "people on the margin." There was always a sense of the "pinch of poverty." Illnesses and other demands kept the family at the economic boundary line. As a result, he had a distinct sense of coming from a worker's family. "Before I went to high school I knew no one except working people.... They were *we!*"[14] All the children worked whenever the opportunity arose. The impact of this early experience produced a "class attitude" during his youth, as he came to look upon himself essentially as "a manual person."[15] This self-perception shaped his early responses so thoroughly that when he was encouraged by teachers to go on in his studies, he believed that he was destined to be a laborer. The workers he knew were socialists in politics, a fact that surely helped shaped his sympathies for "social Christianity" during his college, seminary, and early graduate school years.

The sense of deprivation, however, was offset by a communal and family life rich in tradition and ritual. The lives of many in the

---

[13] Bernard Meland, "Inner Harvests," *The Chicago Theological Seminary Register* 36 (1946), 13.

[14] Bernard Meland, *America's Spiritual Culture* (New York: Harper & Brothers, 1948), pp. 51f.

[15] There is some discrepancy between Bernard's report about the family circumstances and the current family mythology. His picture is offset by the claim that there was no sense of poverty or marginality in the family, that there was always food and a great sense of well-being, and that the home was a center of stability. It is possible that since Bernard was older he saw more, or that he always felt his family was inferior to the family of Margaret, his wife, whose family he held on a pedestal.

Norwegian community centered around the lodge and the church.[16] The impact of his community and family on his theology is conveyed in his notion of the power of myths, rituals, and traditions in the "structure of experience" of a people. The endurance of his parents under strain also shaped his conviction about the tragic sense of life and the resources of hope amidst that tragedy. In an essay he wrote when he was 42 years old, he reflected upon their lives as "the triumph of hope over experience."

> This fact has impressed itself upon me many times as I have pondered the experience of two people whose lives I know well. They are of the genus whom Carl Sandburg describes as having "storms in their blood, seeking peace." All their days they have striven for a margin of material resources with which to find a degree of release from anxiety and the pinch of poverty. Yet physical want has never been their most conscious concern. Within their meager worldly estate they have sought to inherit the world's most precious goods, not directly, but through their children. Like many foreign-born parents, they had hoped to realize through the children what they, themselves, only faintly apprehended in their wistful moments: the culture of the competent mind and of the aristocratic spirit. Yet dreams have not been kind to them, and their hopes have been only meagerly realized. Tragic turns more devastating than death or bankruptcy came into their path. Only the mirrored pain of an inward aching in eyes now grown languid with longing remains to recall those shattered dreams. Despite this deep draught from the cup of failure, they have lived on expectantly — not with the zest that once marked their efforts, but with sufficient heartiness of spirit to make their company genial and reassuring. These two lives are not singular in their experiences. What I see in their conquered defeat, thousands, who are thoughtful, will sense in other lives. It is the expression of a universal phenomenon in the midst of life — the triumph of hope over experience.[17]

His strongest surviving memory of family life and worship was its festive character. The Meland family was part of the Norwegian Lutheran Church for the first eight years of his life. His earliest recollection of religious interest was at age four in the Lutheran Church

---

[16] The family remained very close throughout the years. There were many family gatherings, at which Bernard was never eulogized because he was a theologian at the University of Chicago. He was "just one of the members," described by a niece as her "loving uncle."

[17] Bernard Meland, "The Tragic Sense of Life," *Religion in Life* 10 (1941), 213.

in Roseland on the south side of Chicago, a Norwegian community. The dramas of the Bible formed the earliest childhood images of which he had any conscious recollection. "I do not know a time in my personal history when this imagery did not shape what thoughts I had concerning the beginnings of life and my own destiny.... In this respect I was literally a child of the Christian community, whose mind and spirit was cradled and nurtured by its formative myth."[18] Childhood and Christian faith were inseparable in the experiences that formed his personal identity.

His memory of his childhood religious faith was somewhat disrupted by the move of his grandfather, and the family with him, to leave the Norwegian Lutheran Church and join the Millennial Dawn or Russellite movement, which was founded by Charles Taze Russell and J. F. Rutherford, and subsequently became known as Jehovah's Witnesses. Although his mother and father were ill at ease with this group, they went along out of loyalty to the grandfather.

When the family moved to Homewood, however, they found only two churches in the community, one German Lutheran in which only German was preached and sung, the other a Presbyterian Church. So by circumstance more than conviction he became a Presbyterian. Although his relationship with the Presbyterian Church culminated in his ordination as a Presbyterian minister, he acknowledged the persistence of the Lutheran heritage in his thought and sensibilities. Subsequently, not much was ever made in the family mythology either about the Russellite episode or about the Lutheran background. The family always thought of themselves as "a Presbyterian family."

Meland graduated from high school in 1916 as a fully accredited professional stenotypist and became a stenographer in the Forsyth Auto Manufacturing Company in Harvey, Illinois.[19] Business, too, had its lure, as he had made steady progress in this field as well. He worked the better part of four years in the office of this automobile manufacturer, working his way from stenographer, to bookkeeper, to chief clerk.

---

[18] Bernard Meland, "Interpreting the Christian Faith within a Philosophical Framework," *Journal of Religion* XXXIII (April, 1953), 89.

[19] Typing remained his avocation. He earned money during college and graduate school typing manuscripts. He typed for Professors Willoughby and Wieman (*Methods of Private Religious Living* and numerous articles), doctoral theses (including his own), and the manuscripts for all of his own books. He even referred to himself as "a professional typist." Letter to Larry Axel and Lori Krafte-Jacobs, 19 May 1984.

Awareness of the significance of his temperament for his theology erupted occasionally in his writings.[20] His association with the out of doors, beginning with his work on the farms, developed into a love of nature. This love was so deep that he decided at one time to become a forest ranger. He made application to the Michigan Agricultural College, but in 1917 the war interrupted his plans. Three months at the University of Illinois turned his future in another direction. However, this desire persisted as late as the spring of 1943 when he inquired to the Department of Agriculture about the possibility of someone his age becoming a forest ranger. He had become "nature's child without a protest."

II. "CRUSADING DAYS": 1920-1925

In 1920 Meland enrolled in Park College, a Presbyterian school near Kansas City, Missouri (attended earlier by Henry Nelson Wieman). The year before he had taken five undergraduate courses at the University of Illinois, and in the summer quarter of 1922, three courses in the college at the University of Chicago, all of which transferred to Park. Bernard recalled that his grandparents did not want him to go to college because it was the surest road to hell. One Sunday afternoon they drove over to try to persuade his parents not to send him college. At Park he majored in English literature and writing. In addition to his major, he also excelled in physics, sufficiently to be urged by the chair of the department to pursue graduate work in this field. He graduated from Park College on June 4, 1923.

Surprisingly, college was not immediately the major influence on his religious thinking as it was for many religiously sensitive students. At least for the first year and a half at Park he continued to espouse a sort of modified evangelical fundamentalism. Gradually, however, this enthusiasm underwent a transformation, or a transference, from pietism to the social gospel. The key to this transition was his study of sociology during his senior year, which in that day was largely the

---

20 "You will have decided by this time from my remarks that I am not the best spokesman for the topic I have been assigned. There is too much of the subjectivist speaking in me. Or, to put it differently, the inner landscape of memory and brooding, with its coloring and circuitous paths, make too great a claim upon me to permit a propositional faith." "Interpeting the Christian Faith in a Philosophical Framework," 89.

ethical study of society and social institutions. He was introduced to the social prophets, including Shailer Mathews, thereby initiating him into the socio-historical method of the early Chicago School. During his senior year at Park he even planned to enroll in the Divinity School following graduation. The University of Chicago was not unknown to him, as he had registered for a course in Latin hymnody on the Quadrangles during the summer of 1922.

His intention to enroll in the Divinity School, however, was temporarily interrupted by an invitation to become assistant to the minister at the University Presbyterian Church in Urbana, which provided him the opportunity to do graduate study at the University of Illinois. There he took a seminar the first semester in sociology under E. H. Sutherland, whose book, *White Collar Crime*, was well known among sociologists for its "differential association" theory of criminality.[21] At a time in his life, then, when he was in "the uncertain state of mind," he escaped disillusionment not by the spirit of wonder and awe but by sociology, which he continued to study the second semester. His perplexity during this period of transition, then, was sublimated into the novelty and enthusiasm of the social gospel and sociology.

In addition to his interest in nature mysticism and sociology, a third sublimation occurred during this period of perplexity. In 1923-1924, while assisting the minister of the University Church and pursuing graduate study at the university, he registered for a course the second semester in philosophy and was introduced to Josiah Royce and William James. As his study of sociology began to wear thin, he was attracted to the absolute idealism of Royce. With his "incurable evangelical turn of mind," he found Royce more appealing than James, at least enough to turn away the doubts and misgivings that had crept into the corners of his mind.[22] A new philosophical interest was developing. But two facts

---

[21] Don Martindale, *The Nature and Types of Sociological Theory* (Boston: Houghton Mifflin, 1960), pp. 203-205.

[22] His earliest encounter with Royce was not altogether enlightening. In a letter to Margaret, written while the Assistant at the University Presbyterian Church, he says about Royce's *Religious Aspects of Philosophy*, "Hour after hour I tried to inhale knowledge which Brother Royce seemed to have stored away in the volume. Let me tell you how hard I had to work to get this stuff — I read the 400 pages over once — fairly carefully; but I lifted my eyes away from the last page dazed — swimming in doubts — about everything, leave alone having any knowledge of Royce's philosophy."

are worth noting. First, his introduction and interest in philosophical problems was fairly late in developing, and second, the early stages in that development disposed him toward the philosophy against which the Divinity School was in revolt.

Meland's primary interest, though, was in the social gospel movement, which was simultaneously an alternative to the evangelical faith he was abandoning and a channel for his persisting evangelical zeal. In the late twenties a youth movement had begun to take shape in this country, as happened in other parts of the post-war world. Meland's transference of fervor from evangelical piety to the social gospel made him a natural candidate to save the world and remake the church. He helped organize the National Presbyterian Student Association in 1924 and became its first president from 1924-1925.

On April 9, 1925, the *Chicago Tribune* reported on a "new demonstration of what has been termed the youth movement" that was held in Ann Arbor, Michigan. It represented various Presbyterian colleges across the country, registering some 60,000 students for a three day convention. The program centered on the attitude of the present generation toward war, industry, race relations, internationalism, and modernism verses fundamentalism. Meland, by then a student at McCormick Theological Seminary during 1924-1925, was chair and presiding officer of the convention. He frequently had other opportunities to decry the state of the nation and the church, and he fell into this role with great fervor, preaching in Urbana and on the circuit on such topics as "War Is Sin!" and "Toward a Christian Social Order."

He preached especially against "the establishment" in the churches. He was so effective in a national radio broadcast that a speech he had been scheduled to give before the Presbyterian Club at the University of Chicago was cancelled. Crediting his spirited oratory to his glands, to the reactions of a sensitive youth, and to the effervescence of a superficial mind, he was effective in his round of barnstorming appearances. This tour climaxed with an invitation to address the meeting of the General Assembly of the Presbyterian Church in the spring of 1925. When in route to New York to confer about the meeting, he was stricken with a virulent case of blood poisoning so serious that the family expected him to die. Nevertheless, he wrote his speech in bed with a high fever and it was read by proxy before the thousands gathered at the General Assembly. This was the climax to his year of crusading.

In 1925 while Reinhold Niebuhr was still a pastor in Detroit, Meland prevailed upon him as Program Chair to be the principle speaker at the Interdenominational Student Conference in Evanston. His esteem for Reinhold Niebuhr as a social critic, which continued throughout the 30s and beyond, dates from this period. There was a picture of Niebuhr and Meland in the *Chicago Daily News* on December 30, 1925. However, Meland's distaste for his own Huey Long exhibitionism had been gathering for some time. By the time of the Interdenominational Student Conference, his reaction to bombast and shallow criticism was complete. He announced to his associates at the end that he was going to leave the circuit.

III. "THE END OF MODERNISM": 1925-1929

In the fall of 1925 Meland enrolled in the Divinity School of the University of Chicago, after completing one year at McCormick.[23] During these years he saw Swift Hall rise from the ground, block by block, then Bond chapel, followed by Rockefeller Memorial Chapel. Though Mathews praised him for his work as Program Chair of the Interdenominational Student Conference, Bernard's reaction to his crusading years was so intense and thorough that he felt like he had entered a monastery. These years were "the best years of my life up to that time." The world of history opened up to him in Goodspeed Hall, and he became ravenous for the nourishment of books and reflection.

Meland was a student during one of the most important periods of transition in the Divinity School. He came "under the spell of two quite different orientations in religious thinking," the modernism of his early graduate years, and the emerging postliberalism of his late graduate years. When he matriculated, modernism, with its socio-historical method of inquiry and its pragmatic orientation, had reached its zenith. By the time he graduated, both Gerald Birney Smith and Wieman, even though they continued the empirical method and the scientific outlook, had brought a new perspective to religious inquiry. Meland's graduate

---

[23] Among the distinguished group of students who entered Chicago with him were Wilhelm Pauck, Gregory Valstos, John Knox, Benjamin Mays, Henry Steele Commanger, John Wilson, Herlee Creel, and Joseph Schwab. Bernard Meland, "Reminiscences and Reflections Concerning Wilhelm Pauck's Years in Chicago," *Criterion* 21 (Spring, 1982), 3.

work straddled this critical transition period in the Divinity School. His career embodied the subsequent developments in the Chicago School of Theology throughout the second and third quarters of the twentieth century.

During the early years of his graduate study, his experience of grappling with the socio-historical approach to Christianity as employed by Mathews and Shirley Jackson Case[24] stimulated him beyond anything he had encountered to this point. He had been introduced to both through his earlier study of sociology. However, the air of pragmatism breathed in those days by everyone in the Divinity School was new to him and was never adopted by him in the modernist manner. Although pragmatism and the socio-historical method influenced his thinking, psychology, anthropology, and history of religions, especially the study of archaic peoples and the early stages of culture, proved to be more determinative of his thinking.

The most singular influence on Meland during his graduate years was Smith.[25] Smith was a pivotal figure at Chicago during the transition from the socio-historical orientation of Case and Mathews to the philosophical orientation of Wieman. Especially influential for Bernard was a series of seminars Smith offered which introduced Bergson and the literature of emergent evolution to his graduate students. Smith had discerned the collapse of the modernist method. As sociology became more and more "a new science," it offered less and less support for the social agenda of the modernists.[26] Consequently, modernism was cut adrift. Smith himself was moving toward the new vision of science shaped by relativity theory. But especially important for Smith were his efforts to try to understand our relation to "this mysterious universe." Smith's own thought, then, was more a symptom

---

[24] For a study of Case and the Chicago School, see William Hynes, *Shirley Jackson Case and the Chicago School* (Chico, CA: Scholars Press, 1981).

[25] Although Meland had been introduced to Mathews' thought in undergraduate school, and began his study at Chicago by taking Mathews' "Systematic Theology I" in the autumn of 1925, he took a total of five courses from Mathews. However, beginning in the spring of 1926, he registered for Smith's "Christian Ethics," and subsequently took a total of 11 courses from Smith.

[26] Delwin Brown, "The Fall of '26: Gerald Birney Smith and the Collapse of the Socio-Historical Framework of Theology," *American Journal of Theology & Philosophy* 11 (September, 1990): 183-201.

of the need and a quest for new resources based in the new science and in mysticism than a solution to the crisis of modernism.

Smith became Meland's advisor in 1926. The impact of Smith on his graduate work at Chicago can scarcely to overestimated. Amidst all the twists and turns which came in Meland's thought, the themes of creatural stance, mystical naturalism, elementalism, wonder, and appreciative response emerged under the stimulus of G. B. Smith. These themes underlie Meland's thought and shine through every stage of development. He says, "As I have approached the terminal years of my half century of religious reflection, I have come to see that the nub of my orientation and procedure in religious inquiry has been what I now choose to call *the creatural stance*." Smith was the Chicago School member who introduced that theme to empirical inquiry.

Equally important in the development of Meland's mystical naturalism and his own search for the objective theme in religion (realism) was the impact of his 1928-29 year in Germany as an American-German Exchange Fellow at the University of Marburg.[27] During the spring of 1929 he visited the theological seminary in Wittenberg where Luther had taught, and Roman Catholic masses in Milan, Florence, and Marburg.[28] Prior to his exam that spring, he had studied under Frederick Heiler and Rudolf Otto at the University of Marburg, an enterprise cautioned by Mathews and Wieman but encouraged by Smith. Otto's understanding of religion as a distinctive awareness or apprehension transcending both reason and moral good had a lasting influence on Meland's thought, although he consistently remained reticent about efforts to correlate his work with Otto's numinous theology.

Nearly oblivious during his study in Germany, however, to the "crisis theology" on the Continent and to the surging importance of Karl Barth, Emil Brunner, and Paul Tillich, he spent his time studying the liturgical renaissance led by Heiler, a Lutheran convert from Roman Catholicism, as well as Otto, the foremost theologian and mystic. The

---

27 Travel influenced his thought throughout the years. He and Margaret traveled in the United States and Mexico, in northern Europe and along the Mediterranean coast in Italy, and Greece, in northern France, Egypt, West Africa and the Middle East, as well as in Southeast Asia, particularly India, and the Far East. "Statements in Tribute to Margaret McClusky Meland," 6.

28 Bernard Meland, "The Range of Our Dedications," *The Divinity School News* 14 (November), 1.

results of his study eventually constituted the first half of his first book, *Modern Man's Worship*.[29] Although that book was oriented toward the American context, reflecting the renewed mood of worship in America and Meland's own realism, the first half was nevertheless a notable diary on the liturgical renaissance in Germany.

Both the study in Germany and Smith's untimely death gave shape and urgency to his orientation in thought which Smith had stimulated prior to his year abroad. Upon his return, "I recalled, too, at this moment the crushing confusion of frustration and renewed responsibility that fell upon me when, as I came to the Dean's office to arrange for my orals, I was told that G. B. Smith had died."[30] Meland had became so identified with and devoted to Smith that his death was not only the loss of a personal friendship but also of personal orientation. It caused Meland to think for years of his own work as a continuation of Smith's work, even to the point of classifying himself along with Smith as a "mystical naturalist" in *American Philosophies of Religion*.[31] What was new in Meland's reconception of liberalism following the collapse of modernism was his sense of exploring "the mysterious universe." *Modern Man's Worship* developed the theme of being "at home in the universe," and throughout the entire decade of the thirties a series of articles in a variety of journals carried forward his theme of mystical naturalism.

When Wieman came to the Divinity School in 1927 near the end of Meland's course work, he represented a distinct break with the early Chicago School. Wieman retained an empirical orientation in theology, but he represented a philosophical rather than an historical approach to experience. The primary influence of Wieman on Meland during his last months at Chicago, however, was in expanding his sense of perceptual awareness. Many of the phrases in Wieman's early books pointed to a horizon of meaning that accompanies every perceptual event and eludes abstract concepts. There was a mystical quality to Wieman's perception which was an accompaniment instead of an alternative to his critical inquiry. Despite Wieman's increasing insistence that the language of inquiry should be emptied of emotive coloring and reduced to cold abstract terms in the interest of precision, his vocabulary early on was

---

29 Bernard Meland, *Modern Man's Worship* (New York: Harper, 1934).
30 Meland, "The Range of Our Dedications," 2.
31 Henry Nelson Wieman and Bernard Meland, *American Philosophies of Religion* (Chicago: Willet and Clark, 1936), pp. 291-295.

loaded with biological and mystical terms. Sympathetic to Wieman's claim that knowledge of God must be an immediate datum, Meland's early response to Wieman was based on his belief that Wieman held the two projects of awareness of depth and scientific clarity together as indispensable to one another. Initially he considered Wieman's thought a way to continue to develop his own mystical naturalism and the intuitions that he had discovered in Smith's seminars.

Wieman continued to influence Meland after he left Chicago, although that influence was more verbal than structural. The extent of Wieman's influence was evident in the fact that when Meland presented his theological statement for his ordination examination before the Chicago Presbytery, his sentences were packed with Wieman's words. Although Meland had begun his theological studies at McCormick, he transferred to the Divinity School at the end of the first year. He received his B.D. from the Divinity School in the spring of 1928. He returned to McCormick to appear before the ordination board of the Presbytery along with the other graduates who had completed their studies at McCormick. The latter had carefully formulated their statements so as to disguise any liberal doctrines. Meland, however, came to the examine after his study at Chicago wholly unprepared for such restraint. After listening to his colleagues, he nearly decided to withdraw his statement before the examination began.

After reading his paper before the Presbytery, a gentleman in the front of the audience asked Bernard if he believed in the virgin birth. He answered by describing the context in which the concept had arisen, whereupon the gentleman asked for a straightforward answer. Meland answered, "No! In the sense in which the gentleman conceives the matter, I do not." After a round of further questioning, the man arose and moved that Meland be denied further examination. The motion lost for lack of a second. In the closed session that followed, the same man made two further motions for denial, but each again lost for lack of a second. Thus Bernard Meland was ordained through the hush of the assembly. Apparently, he had been saved by the zeal of his examination sermon. He was ordained and he maintained his orders in the Presbyterian Church throughout his life.

In addition to providing him with a language, Wieman's insistence on the "objectivity" of God (realism) began to nudge Meland beyond the conceptualism of Ames and Mathews. Although this shift was not obvious in Meland's early article on God, the objective mood was present in his earliest publications. He believed, though, that in his effort to elaborate the datum of experience in terms of some specific behavior, Wieman soon fell back upon a ground which was no more specifiable than that which Mathews and Ames offered. So Meland left the Divinity School deeply affected by the realistic mood of Wieman but still inclined in his early writings toward the conceptualism of Mathews and Ames.

Many philosophers and theologians around the country in the early thirties assumed that Meland and Wieman spoke with one voice, in part because they worked within an empirical method, in part because of Wieman's glowing review of Meland's first book, in part because Meland became known as an interpreter of Wieman's thought, and in part because of their close personal and professional association, most notably on their writing of *American Philosophies of Religion*. However, early on Meland was critical of Wieman. The most fundamental difference was that Wieman believed one eventually had to make up one's mind whether to hold in tension the manageable and unmanageable modes of religious inquiry or singularly to pursue the manageable course. Wieman had announced in his first book that his life project was to devise a scientific means of apprehending the meaning of God, and he pursued it singlemindedly. Meland, however, believed that Wieman overstressed criteria. Instead, he chose Smith's earlier suggestion to venture boldly and imaginatively toward understanding our relation to this mysterious universe. This decision committed Meland to keep the appreciative consciousness and the pursuit of precision in juxtaposition.

Wieman chose singlemindedness, and Meland chose juxtaposition.[32] On that decision hinged the fundamental divergence between these two Chicago theologians. The fact is that they worked in somewhat different orbits of meaning. Wieman's decision was clear as early as *Religious Experience and the Scientific Method*; Meland's course was apparent as early as his graduate work with G. B. Smith and *Modern Man's Worship*.[33] From first to last Meland was bent on keeping the

---

[32] Ironically, though, one of the stimuli and directions for Meland to pursue in his own course had been suggested in the earlier books of Wieman.

[33] Insofar as there was a "formal" break between Wieman and Meland on this decisive point, it occurred in Wieman's home one summer evening in 1934 while they were working on a chapter for *American Philosophies of Religion*.

appreciative and the analytical in juxtaposition if not correlation in so far as that was possible. Wieman provided an explicit language for Meland, and he also served as a catalyst for Meland's own decision. Early on, though, Meland decided to follow the path of appreciation and analysis instead of the path of sheer clarity. All of the turns and twists of the fifty years of religious inquiry were shaped by that decision.

The issue between conceptualism and realism, he came to see, was also a metaphysical issue between Kantianism and radical empiricism. In his early essays he employed a Neo-Kantian perspective which had been unwittingly appropriated through the early Chicago School, especially Ames and Mathews, by means of the early developments within pragmatism. The radical empiricism of James's later work with his notion of experienced relations and Whitehead's empiricism with his concept of the structure of events had not yet made their impact on Meland's thinking. Relations and structures within radical empiricism were not seen as functions of the mind but realities in experience which are real data to be described. When he left the Divinity School in 1929, he had a strong sense of leaving behind the philosophical assumptions of the socio-historical method and its modernist orientation.

In fundamental ways, however, Meland never abandoned the socio-historical perspective. He never could participate fully in the ahistorical kind of the metaphysics advocated by Wieman, Charles Hartshorne, and Bernard Loomer which reigned in the Divinity School when he returned in 1945. It never occurred to him to discuss any theological idea or period, past or present, without uncovering its context, ethos, and formative imagery. He simply had no idea how else to proceed to understand an idea or period, and he learned that orientation from the early Chicago School.[34] "While the notion of the structure of experience, as I develop it in *Faith and Culture* and elsewhere, derives cogency from Whitehead's notion of causal efficacy, the seeds of that notion in my thinking stem from the Modernist's insistence upon the continuity of the Christian Movement within Western experience.... I felt that Mathews' acknowledging the continuity of the legacy amidst changing forms and social circumstances had validity.... The rationale implicit in

---

Wieman put the issue is this stark form, and announced that he would abandon the unmanageable and pursue clarity of meaning.

[34] On the relation of process theology and the early Chicago School, see John Cobb, "The Origins of Process Theology," in Leroy S. Rouner, ed., *Meaning, Truth, and God* (Notre Dame: University of Notre Dame Press, 1982), pp. 91-111.

Whitehead's 'causal efficacy' seemed to provide an appropriate analogy for expressing the Modernist thesis."[35]

From the demise of the modernist period around the time of his graduation,[36] through the tenure of Wieman and later of Loomer and other process thinkers, who had the more ahistorical orientation toward theological ideas, Meland remained the sole embodiment of the socio-historical legacy at the Chicago School until his retirement in 1964. He was shocked to discover in Wieman's thinking and teaching his indifference to the developmental character of thought. Abstract study of an idea by the typological method common in philosophical thinking and the failure to see the nuances, transitions, reversals, and revisions of an idea in its social and historical context seemed arbitrary to Meland.

Meland's interest in the constructive interpretation of the "themes of faith" or the "legacy of faith" instead of the reformulation of systematic doctrines in contemporary terms is reminiscent of the modernist distinction between persisting convictions and theological doctrines. Meland's alternative to the notion of the evolution of social minds which suggest analogies for doctrine (Mathews) was his concept of "the ebb and flow of psychical currents of awareness and sensibility within the structure of experience" which evoke or restore to conscious awareness what is redemptive in a culture. His notion of a cultural legacy which focuses on redemption as a structure of experience and orbit of meaning was a sharp break with the modernists inquiry into doctrine.

IV. "BETWEEN MODERNISM AND THE NEW REALISM": 1929-1936

One morning in 1929 Mathews cabled Meland in Marburg with the message, "Have fine offer Central College Missouri Religion and Philosophy Urge you accept." He immediately wired back, "I accept."

---

[35] Personal letter to Larry Axel, 12 February 1981.
[36] In 1928 he completed his D.B. thesis, "The Development of Christocentric Theology in America," and was made a Fellow in Systematic Theology and elected President of the Theology Club. In March, 1929, he had his successful Ph.D. exam with Mathews, Eustace Haydon, Wieman, and A. C. McGiffert. His dissertation was on "A Critical Analysis of the Appeal to Christ in Present-Day Religious Interpretations."

Meland began his teaching career at Central College, a Southern Methodist school in Fayette, Missouri. His seven years there as Professor of Religion and Philosophy were both happy and stormy. Lacking pedagogical skills, he at least conveyed integrity as he gathered around him a group of young and loyal followers. Although he was regularly examined, discussed, or denounced by committees from the Board of Trustees or the Southern Methodist Conference of Missouri, he was reappointed year after year, even awarded tenure as (or because?) he was about to leave for southern California.

Oblivious to the powder keg on which he sat and the suspicious Southern Methodists around him, he imbibed a rich diet of reading and aesthetic stimulation. His reading and reflection induced a major shift in his thinking. It was a period of reorientation away from the methodologism and moralism of modernism toward more asethetic preoccupations. Partly as a reaction to the aesthetic impoverishment he felt with the empiricism and pragmatism of the Divinity School, partly from his experience in Europe which aroused new depths of aesthetic appreciation, partly because of his wife Margaret's background in art appreciation and interior decoration, the world of beauty, especially art and poetry, became a living reality to him as he dove into a wide range of literature on aesthetics and European and American letters. All of these influences constituted a "reorientation" in his thinking away from moralism toward aesthetic sensibilities.[37]

As he began his teaching at Central, he stood between the modernism of the Divinity School, with its combination of sociohistorical method and its ethical idealism, and the new realism, with its themes of objectivity and emergence. The fruits of his labor in Marburg and his own nascent naturalism and realism were published as *Modern Man's Worship*. This book expressed a new synthesis of feeling and reflection that had taken place as a result of his first encounter with two cultures of the West, historically related but so at odds in basic

---

[37] Meland continued his interest in ethics, but he thought about it more in the context of "human fulfillment" than of moralistic emphasis and interpreted the moral concern within the context of appreciative consciousness. See the work of John Spencer on Meland's aesthetic ethic: "Meland as a Resource for Political Ethics," in John B. Cobb, Jr. and W. Widick Schroeder, eds., *Process Philosophy and Social Thought* (Chicago: Center for the Scientific Study of Religion, 1981), pp. 153-170, and "Meland's Alternative in Ethics," *Process Studies* 6 (Fall, 1976): 165-180.

apprehensions, sensibilities, and styles of thinking. *Modern Man's Worship* expressed themes that were to become deeply structural and durable in his thought. The book was his initial effort at joining and developing the mystical naturalism of Smith and the new realism in religious sensibilities of Wieman.

The lure of the future as promising and dangerous (what he called "the perilous open") was vividly present in the opening pages of this book, and it recurred in many of his articles published during the thirties and early forties. His orientation was mystical in mood even as it was empirical in method (a Chicago empiricist responding to the *sensus numinous* of Otto and to his own mystical version of naturalism), not an easy blend for one trained in the socio-historical empiricism and pragmatism of the early Chicago School and Wieman's brand of empiricism.

Although Meland had enrolled in Wieman's first course at the Divinity School and audited others, his close association with Wieman began only while teaching at Central College. He was technically not a student of Wieman's at Chicago, for Wieman came to Chicago after Meland had completed his residency work. The relationship between the two was always a ambiguous and ambivalent one, in which Meland never could quite decide how much he sympathized with Wieman and how much he was critical of him. At the time he thought of himself as critical of Wieman, yet *Modern Man's Worship* shared the concern about objectivity (what he called "the objective mood") in worship with Wieman. The relationship began in earnest in the summer of 1934, when he and Wieman discovered while watching a tennis match between Alonzo Stagg and his son how they were working along the same lines in interpreting current philosophies of religion. The idea for *American Philosophies of Religion* was born in that conversation at the tennis court. Meland had audited Wieman's "Philosophy of Religion" and "Philosophy of Worship" courses in the summer of 1933, and did research in "Contemporary American Philosophies of Religion" at the University of Chicago with Wieman in the summer of 1934.[38] They

---

[38] Meland took the first course Wieman offered in the autumn of 1927, "Philosophy of Theism," for which he wrote a thirty page paper entitled, "An Analysis of Christian Thinking with Reference to Religious Objectives." Wieman wrote concerning the paper, "An intensely interesting paper. A+." In addition to *Modern Man's Worship* and *American Philosophies of Religion*, Meland

remained close friends throughout the thirties, although the close rapport began to dissipate as Wieman moved on to new concerns and Meland moved to the West coast.

V. "A TIME OF INCUBATION": 1936-1945

In the autumn of 1936 Meland joined the faculty of Pomona College in Claremont, California, teaching courses in the history and philosophy of religion. This was "a time of incubation" for his aspiration to be a constructive theologian. Although his field of study at the Divinity School had been Christian Theology and Ethics, his research and teaching at Pomona was the history and philosophy of religion. He gave much of his research time to the study of the major world religions. In addition, religion and culture joined myth as preoccupations in his work. His teaching in the philosophy of religion explored the aesthetic and cultural formulations of the religious outreach in Western culture, especially in specific creative people in art, music, literature, and science. This shift was personal, but it also reflected a shift in the field of theology itself, as systematic efforts gave way to the psychological and philosophical approach to religion.

Following *Modern Man's Worship*, his focal point of inquiry moved from mystical naturalism to a theory of religion, specifically, a theory of the nature of the religious response. Meland began to dig beneath the various definitions of religion in psychology, sociology, and ethics, and concluded that the basic nature of "the religious outreach" is a psychical energy and a creatural response. This investigation led him toward research in human origins and anthropology. What emerged from this prolonged concentration of study was an amplification of his understanding of religion as "aspirational outreach." The religious response is as elemental and basic as breathing or as any other organic response indispensable to the creature. This outreach is rooted in a psychical condition of the human organism which he designated "the attachment to life" or "the praise of life," something akin to Schweitzer's reverence for life. The religious response is the most elemental condition of appreciation and praise within the human psyche at the level of creatural existence.

---

published 27 articles as well as other reviews and mimeographed papers while at Central College.

At this stage in the development of his career, Bernard also began to acquire some sense of "the continuity of diverse interests" in his work. He began to find his own voice in distinction from Smith and Wieman, a discovery which unified several strands of his research. Specifically, his mystical naturalism and his interest in religion and culture provided the focal center of his work throughout the thirties. His concern with religious outreach in the study of worship and the history of religions, his conversation with modern poets as people speaking out of a distraught cultural situation, and his study of the American experience in terms of the cultural motifs and aspirations of a people cut loose from a tradition began to forge a conscious unity in his work.

From 1937-1939 he wrote a series of essays that continued to elaborate his mystical naturalism. These papers were the culmination of his exploration during the thirties of the literature of cultural anthropology, especially the literature on myth, and of aesthetics, especially modern poetry. These chapters, collected under the title, *In Praise and Life*, were praised by publishers but never published.[39] Although his work at the Divinity School after 1945 superseded his attention to mystical naturalism (he moved to faith instead of mystical naturalism as the key to religious knowledge), his empirical realism, which retained a strong theme of "the creatural stance," had marked affinity with his earlier mysticism. By the late 30s the stimulus of G. B. Smith's mysticism had been correlated with strands of Wieman's realistic empiricism to form Meland's own distinctive form of religious response, which he eventually called "the appreciative consciousness."

The Pomona incubation period also focused on educational issues, especially the philosophy of higher education. *Higher Education and the Human Spirit* gathers up his papers from this period concerning education. He felt the impact of Robert Maynard Hutchins's crusade at the University of Chicago, prompting his first article on education in 1936 as a reply to Hutchins. He shared the "search for the center" in education, as seemed to be a requirement of the time. He offered his

---

[39] Although there is evidence in the archives of the near-publication of this book, it never appeared in print. The reason is as yet impossible to determine. Nevertheless, the purpose of the book was clear. It was intended as a companion volume to *Modern Man's Worship*, a further development of his mystical naturalism throughout the late thirties. While at Pomona, he published *Write Your Own Ten Commandments* (Chicago: Willet Clark and Company, 1938), and published 32 articles plus several reviews and mimeographed essays.

notion of the cultivation of "the appreciative consciousness" as an antidote to the debilitating effects on the human spirit of much higher education in the thirties. A number of his essays stressed the study of religion in the liberal arts college as part of a unifying vision in the educational experience instead of a special lobbying interest at the edge of the campus. He saw the entire college curriculum as a potential resource for articulating and affirming the values of our culture as a spiritual outreach.

One of his most significant efforts at Pomona, and one of which he spoke with pride, was "the chapel experiment." Throughout the eight years he was on the faculty, chapel was used as a meditative and reflective period to nurture the feeling response as well as reflective thought. Chapel period was conceived more to nurture aspirations, affections, and sensibilities than to sponsor religious services. Because of the exceptional talent of the students and the cooperation of various department heads at Pomona, he was able to experiment with poetry, drama, symphony, choral music, and dance as religious expression. During the early years of the experiment, Robert Shaw, who later organized the Robert Shaw Chorale, was a student in his courses and president of the student body. One year Shaw conducted the chapel choir, which gives some indication of the kind of support Meland had for his project. The chapel periods varied from week to week from a simple period where prayers and verses were read to dramatic sketches and religious dramas.

It was at Pomona that Meland began to be "the repentant liberal." Emerging from the pragmatic atmosphere of Chicago in the late twenties, he began his theological career with little capacity to enter into the mood of crisis theology, and he had no taste for it. Even during his study in Germany in 1928, when this movement was gathering momentum, he felt no compulsion to seek out Barth, Brunner, or even Tillich. "I left Germany without having had the slightest stimulus toward understanding Barth or toward grappling with the issues which he had posed." To be sure, he was critical in his dissertation and first published essay of the christocentric liberalism of Herrmann, Harnack, and others, but that opposition was on grounds of their supernaturalism, not on the grounds which motivated Barth and the neoorthodox revolt.

He was "a fairly well insulated liberal" when he began teaching at Central. However, he was more susceptible to the mood of continental thought than he imagined, as he began to react thoroughly to the complacent scientism of his student days. Niebuhr had broken through his defenses in subtle ways which he had not yet recognized. But it was Niebuhr the social critic and realist about human nature, especially the Niebuhr of *Leaves from the Notebook of a Tamed Cynic*, who influenced him early on more than Niebuhr the dialectical theologian. Meland's two early essays in *Homiletic Review* revealed the early influence of Niebuhr. He used Niebuhr's *Moral Man and Immoral Society* in a social ethics class in 1931. This move, however, was only a half-way house toward Meland's own reconception of human nature. He had not yet met Niebuhr in his more radical dimension. Even through the early years at Pomona, Meland was primarily a liberal disgruntled with the pragmatic modernism of his 1925-29 student days at the Divinity School.

A major "turning point" toward his theological postliberalism was precipitated by two conferences he attended while teaching at Pomona. The importance of these events is evident both in personal correspondence around that time and in an article published in *Christendom* in 1937. The article reported some of the findings of the Pacific Area Conference of the World's Student Christian Federation at Mills College (Oakland) on August 23-September 2, 1936. "This was one of the most painful experiences of theological deliberation I have ever endured." Sharp lines were drawn between the liberal and dialectical theologians at this meeting. At the end of the ten day period of discussion, each member of the group was commissioned to write a statement of common faith. The discussion seemed profitless, but "because of my remarkable gift at double-talk," Meland's summary statement was selected as being most representative of a consensus of theological opinion. This statement was published as "Toward A Common Christian Faith" in *Christendom* during the opening week of the Oxford Conference in 1937.[40]

Meland had formulated a statement of faith to which Barthians could give assent and in which he could find his own affirmations as well. The avowed liberals voiced no complaints during its preparation.

---

40 In a letter to Charles Clayton Morrison, editor of *Christendom*, Meland says, "I am again submitting my article, TOWARD A COMMON FAITH, having revised the framework....As you will see, I have pointed the discussion toward the Oxford Conference, bringing in the exchange of thought at the Oakland conference as a sort of case study and pre-view of what might be hoped for in the cooperative deliberations at Oxford." 10 March 1937.

When the report was read in the conference, however, Henry Seaman vehemently denounced this lapse into creedalism (he did not know Meland had written the statement). Later when Meland informed him of the fact, Seamon's blood pressure was so aroused that he brushed aside Meland's remark as being just one more unbelievable irrationality. But Meland had discovered he had much in common with dialectical and continental theologians and little with West Coast liberals "who seemed to be mouthing the same cliches we had argued about in The Divinity School at Chicago a decade or more earlier."[41]

The impact of the Oxford Conference on him had been prepared for by this "baffling experience" at the World Student Christian Federation meeting in Oakland. Meland was an Associate Delegate to the World Conference on Church, Community and State on July 12-26, 1937 in Oxford, chaired by William Adams Brown.[42] The conference again was divided between various Christian groups. In that context, the American mind seemed suddenly to jell into a character distinctively its own. Henry Van Dusen was the spokesperson for the Americans, along with Georgia Harkness and Reinhold Niebuhr. Continental theologians led by W. A. Visser 't Hooft, however, dominated among the delegates. Meland thought he should be counted upon to bolster the ranks of the liberals. However, a strange reversal took place. He joined the group concerned with the problem of formulating a statement of faith. They battled for ten days. What distressed him was that he found himself repeatedly being more sympathetic toward what the Continentals said than toward the counter-attacks or constructive efforts of the liberals. The liberal remarks seemed dated, irrelevant, utterly unpenetrating. He

---

[41] In a letter to Loomer on Thanksgiving Day, 1944, he says, "At first I resented the rise of the neoorthodox emphasis because it seemed a costly interruption of theological labors that were yet unfinished; but I have really become reconciled to it as a phase of the present effort to deepen liberalism, as you put it. Certainly liberalism needed deepening. The simple linear lines of liberal theology, with its anti-metaphysical bias, could only make for a shallow substitute for the social gospel in the second generation of liberals. This has impressed me more and more as I have come to know some of them in Southern California who have remained untouched by reactionary or critical winds. Even theology falls out of their thinking. What remains is a kind of common sense religious education. You can hardly restrain the impulse to 'smack 'em down' with a bolt from Calvinism."

[42] He was also an invited "registered visitor" to the World Conference on Faith and Order at Edinburgh on August 3-18 following the Oxford Conference.

did not vocally desert the liberal stand in that encounter, "but something of a sobering nature was obviously happening to me."⁴³

Increasingly, Meland became "a repentant liberal" at Pomona. He acknowledged that for some time there had been "a marked shift in my thinking as I have tried to come to terms with conditions and influences which have been pressing hard upon our minds during recent years." A major influence on him, beyond his experience of the two conferences, was "the growing literature of theological reaction. One has not been through the fire and flood of theological reconstruction in our time until he has braved the onslaught of the dialectical theology." Neoorthodox literature expressed the anguish and dislocation which plagued the mind in the thirties. But "the story of my own relation to this movement of thought is not one that particularly enhances me as a contemporary theological thinker, for it reveals how fixed and complacent I was, along with other midwestern and far-western liberals, in the grooves of an unreconstructed liberalism long after the deluge of disillusionment had begun to envelop our thinking."

The break with the old liberalism became sharp in his writing during the forties. He began to speak of going "beyond liberalism," to criticize the paucity of imagination in liberalism and their ignorance of the tragic sense of life by reducing tragedy to a method. Increasingly, his language became the language of "indirection,"⁴⁴ and he emphasized even more the "new realism" in theology. The theme of human fulfillment had occupied his writings during the thirties and is a reflection of his confidence in the liberal doctrine of humanity throughout that decade. Although he did not abandon the liberal orientation, he had been sobered

---

43 Papers were circulated and discussion already begun by those participating in the section on "The Christian Understanding of Man" prior to the conference. In the 19 March 1937 letter to Morrison, Meland says, "I found myself more in agreement with Brunner's statement that most of the American and British critics. It gradually dawned on me that our neo-naturalism, growing out of organismic thought, moves toward the same sort of communal emphasis in theology that the continental thought comes to. Our motivation differs, but our results are strikingly similar." In the Loomer Thanksgiving Day letter, he continues, "I have often thought of Wieman and Barth as the two towering exponents of religious realism; not that their solutions were similar, but that their antipathies and concerns were akin. Thus the fact that Wieman has seemed to find more and more rapport with the Barthians has not been surprising."

44 Bernard Meland, "The Genius of Protestantism," *Journal of Religion* 27 (1947): 283ff.

and chastened by the new circumstances to such an extent that his earlier expectations seemed facile. For example, he spoke less of the social process as the bearer of future good, and argued that sheer process may be an ambiguous force bent upon evil rather than good. Furthermore, the concept of person or personality no longer held a spell over him as an assured good or criterion of value. The person may become an ambiguous value in need of clarification and transformation which requires a mysterious work of grace. In the forties, then, faith as a resource of judgment and grace began to supplant mystical experience in his writing. Liberals had not been prone to recognize the new realism in theology, both a theological realism about a grace beyond the human measure and a social realism about human nature.

Another major shift in his thinking occurred at this stage in his career. Confrontation with the fact of human evil or the ambiguity of human good marked this period. His thought shifted from progressive optimism to the tragic sense of life. The easiest course would have been to reverse his position and disown any of the hopes of his earlier days. But instead of reversing himself, which seemed to be a pathological adjustment, he opted for reconception, a reorientation of liberal mental habits and outlook in the light of new perceptions and resources. The shift involved a degree of repentance, even though he did not disown his history in this act of conversion. "I am aware that however much I press the demands of this new realism which has engulfed me regarding man's nature and his hopes, I must do so within the perspective of a reconstructed liberal. The road back is not available to me." Thus, while his liberal orientation was retained, it was reconceived.

Meland's reconception was influenced by his deeper encounter with two dialectical theologians, Niebuhr and Brunner. His confrontation with Niebuhr's radical criticism of the liberal mind came through persons who studied with Niebuhr or were strongly under his influence, like Theodore Carswell Hume[45] who was at the Claremont Church while Meland was on the faculty at Pomona. Meland's first significant personal encounter with Niebuhr occurred in the winter of 1945 when Niebuhr came to the west coast to deliver a series of lectures at Occidental College and the Claremont colleges. Meland was one of his hosts. He was also influenced on these issues by Wilhem Pauck, who in

---

[45] See Bernard Meland, "Theodore Carswell Hume: His Thought and Work," *Social Action* 9 (1943).

1945 had spent several weeks with him in Claremont. Pauck had convinced Meland that theological liberalism could achieve vitality and respect only as it joined in conversation with those who attacked its premises.[46] In addition, Meland had been reading Kierkegaard and Barth, along with Niebuhr.

The neoorthodox movement in theology influenced more his method than his specific theological ideas. Niebuhr set theological issues in a perspective which required the full play of the imagination. Niebuhr had cast off positivism and the whole legacy of rational analysis. He, instead, insisted that the human dimension was of such complexity and scope that rational attempts to interpret human nature and meaning were bound to be fragmentary and deceptive. By use of the imagery of transcendence, Niebuhr sought to re-examine humanity through the "method of indirection" instead of the linear method of scientific and logical analysis. Meland's philosophical predilections led him to reject Niebuhr's theological framework, but he appropriated Niebuhr's insights into the scope and subtlety of human nature and the importance of imagination in his own constructive theological understanding of human nature.

Meland also began to read Emil Brunner's work when his *Word and the World* appeared in English in 1931. He was more impressed with the prophetic ring to Brunner's early works than with his constructive efforts. Prior to the Oxford Conference of 1937, he read Brunner's papers on the Christian understanding of human nature, which also seemed to have some affinity with the emerging realistic theology taking form in America. Although Brunner's later books led Meland to a sharper sense of the divergence between them, he accepted much of Brunner's criticism of liberalism. The points at which he turned away from Brunner were those in which Brunner's thought is dictated by his particular philosophical framework. For example, he rejected Brunner's antipathy toward mysticism. Brunner thought mysticism presupposed the identification of human and divine consciousness, thereby blurring the distinction between God as person and the human as person. Meland never repudiated the witness of the mystic. Furthermore,

---

[46] In a letter to Wilhelm Pauck, 16 January 1945, Meland says, "I, personally, developed considerable enthusiasm for Niebuhr while he was here. I had never had occasion to talk with him before or to penetrate his thinking. It was an experience that affected me deeply, and I must say greatly helped and impressed my own thinking."

although Brunner's caution against subjectivism was sound, the conceptual ground for his analysis was his reconstructed neo-Kantian philosophy which heightened the antipathy to any natural human knowledge of God and impelled him to define the content of the divine-human encounter primarily in ethical terms.

Brunner's neo-Kantian version of Christian faith separated the realm of experience, which is susceptible to empirical analysis, from the realm of faith, which transcends such knowledge. Therefore, the Kantian dualism was there in Brunner, except more in the form of the Reformation appeal to faith than Kant's postulates of the mind, which he drew more from the Enlightenment. But the conceptual framework which informed Kant's critical rationalism continued to inform Brunner's appeal to faith. Insofar as Brunner, like Niebuhr, attempted to escape a rigid logic of positivism, he was contributing to the postliberal effort to achieve a language of indirection in which subtle meanings can be grasped. Meland was wholly sympathetic to this postliberal agenda, except he worked within a philosophy of radical empiricism, which took the human emergent seriously as both a limiting and informing condition, instead of a Kantian dualism.

The most important thing to note about Meland's relation to dialectical theology during the late thirties and early forties is that a rapport developed between forms of dialectical theology and forms of realistic theology that sought to go beyond liberalism. This rapport increased as conversations between the dialectical and realistic theologians developed, represented most explicitly in the work of Daniel Day Williams,[47] but conspicuous in the writings of Meland and Loomer.[48] Although there was little chance of them coalescing, since basic metaphysical differences divided them, they shared the postliberal awareness of "otherness" in theological inquiry.

Meland looked back upon the period between *Modern Man's Worship* and his joining the Divinity School faculty as "a time of incubation." During that season he wrote more articles dealing with

---

[47] This conversation is most evident in his *God's Grace and Man's Hope* (New York: Harper & Brothers, 1949), and his *What Present Day Theologians Are Thinking* (New York: Harper & Brothers, 1959). See, also, the occasional essays, chapters 12-20, in Daniel Day Williams, *Essays in Process Theology*, edited by Perry LeFevre (Chicago: Exploration Press, 1985).

[48] For Loomer's most explicit discussion, see his "Neo-naturalism and Neo-Orthodoxy," *Journal of Religion* 28 (April, 1948): 79-91.

religion and the nature of religion and culture than with theological themes as such. He taught courses in the history and philosophy of religion. This all made a permanent contribution to his mode of theologizing. It oriented his thinking toward issues of faith and culture. However, it was all preparation for his work as a theologian.

VI. "A CONSTRUCTIVE THEOLOGIAN": 1945-1964

Meland joined the Divinity School and the Federated Theological Faculty of the University of Chicago in 1945.[49] The autumn quarter of 1945 was a troublesome, even traumatic period throughout the University. The bombing of Hiroshima and Nagasaki had occurred within weeks of the opening of the quarter. The University's own participation in creating the bomb had evoked a searing sense of guilt and remorse, culminating in Hutchins's voicing the mood of the period by saying, "We have but five years to ponder the good news of damnation!" The Federated Theological Faculty was in its initial stage.[50] Problems of procedure and program were rife. Meland had come into a situation of agonizing perplexity.

World War II was a trauma to his thinking, as reports of death of students who had been in his classes at Pomona reached him, along with the overwhelming reports of the dropping of the atomic bombs and intimations of the holocaust. These settled "like an impenetrable mist of anguish and despair over the whole of our existence." As late as 1954 he wrote of the agony and hopelessness of the post-war years, even of the "psychical changes within the structure of experience of our Western culture." The need for forgiveness and judgment, and in that order, began to appear in his writing.

His primary agenda when he returned to Chicago was to be a constructive theologian.[51] His program, however, was determined by

---

[49] In a letter to Willard Sperry at Harvard, 8 January 1945, the week Niebuhr was at Oxidental and the Claremont colleges, Meland indicated that he had considered accepting the offer in 1944 to become President of Park College, but "I have decided not to pursue it. I shall hope to give myself to theology instead."

[50] The Federated Faculty was to last until 1960. For a history and commentary on the Federated Faculty, see Bernard Meland, "A Long Look at the Divinity School in Its Present Crisis," *Criterion* I (1962): 21-30.

[51] In what amounted to a 14 page letter of application addressed to Loomer dated 9 December 1944, he said he saw himself standing between Wieman and

his understanding of the direction American theological thought had taken since his and Wieman's *American Philosophies of Religion*. In the seven years since its publication, it had become increasingly clear that the immediate future belonged to "the supernaturalists," his term for the dialectical theologians who drew on the neo-Kantian strategy for theological thinking. This temporary triumph was not altogether mischievous insofar as it expressed an effort to provide a postliberal theological understanding of Christian faith. What remained unresolved in this preoccupation with traditional concepts and beliefs, however, was how to include the new knowledge in science and philosophy into Christian theology. "We have hardly begun to work seriously upon the task of giving theological interpretation to the new accumulations of insight which have been gathering momentum during the last two decades."[52] In referring to Whitehead, Wieman, and Hartshorne as philosophers who worked with the new physics, he said, "Yet, none of these men has concerned himself with the task of the systematic theologian." This effort at exploring the significance of the new theism for theology proper, then, became one of the primary tasks of the constructive theologian.[53]

One of the significant changes that occurred when he arrived at Chicago was his move from interpreting Christianity as an expression of universal religious sensibilities to the Christian faith as bearer of a special and decisive judgment upon human existence. This shift became most apparent in *Seeds of Redemption*,[54] lectures given at the Fourteenth Annual Pastor's Institute of the University of Chicago in the summer of 1945, and *Reawakening of Christian Faith*[55], the Clark

---

Pauck in his theological interests. "I see myself between these two emphases [Wieman and Whitehead, on the one hand, and the neoorthodox reform, on the other], somewhat in a liaison role; for I believe I have more of a theological interest than either you or Wieman, and more of a philosophical and metaphysical bent than Pauck," 2.

[52] Bernard Meland, "Some Unanswered Issues in Theology," *Journal of Religion* XXIV (October, 1944), 234.

[53] In a letter dated 20 February 1945 addressed "Dear Cush!" he says, "Having made this decision, however, I am really looking forward to being at Chicago, seriously at work in the role of a theologian. That's what I've wanted to do, and being able to feel that the mantle of G. B. Smith is somewhat upon me, I shall get a certain inexpressible lift in just being there."

[54] Bernard Meland, *Seeds of Redemption* (New York: Macmillan, 1947).

[55] Bernard Meland *Reawakening of Christian Faith* (New York: Macmillan, 1949).

Lectures at Pomona College in 1947. The move came in part from "the intimations of tragedy that began to gather in my own experience." Constructive theology came to be understood as the act of declaring his orientation of faith in the midst of this disorientation.

Although Meland never repudiated his earlier writings, he did see a hiatus between his writings published during the thirties and early forties and those published after 1945. *Reawakening of Christian Faith* was the watershed initiating a line of inquiry coming to fruition in *Faith and Culture* and *The Realities of Faith*.[56] Clear formulations of the shift appeared in *Seeds of Redemption*. In retrospect, however, one can detect in the realism of even his first book, *Modern Man's Worship*, the roots of the ethos of thought and feeling that informed his thought after 1945.

Another shift was detectable during this period. This new mood was "to persist as a chastening direction of my own theological reflections throughout the following decade and possibly throughout my theological career."[57] The center moved from humanity's "religious outreach" conceived in a general sense in his mystical naturalism in the thirties to a more immediate and concrete concern with human living and dying as these had come into focus in Christian symbols and metaphors during the war. The dropping of the bombs and the disclosures of the concentration camps reset human concerns in a new cultural context in ways that heightened the sense of judgment and guilt throughout the whole of Western experience.

His efforts at reconception pushed his method in two directions. He began to reformulate his earlier mystical naturalism as a sense of wonder, awareness, and appreciation of the depth of lived experience. And he began to employ process philosophy as an adventure of ideas

---

56 Meland's thought can be divided into three distinct periods with major emphases: 1) from *Modern Man's Worship* through *American Philosophies of Religion*, in which mysticism and naturalism are the major themes; 2) from *Seeds of Redemption* through *Higher Education and the Human Spirit*, in which faith and appreciative consciousness are the major themes; and 3) from *Realities of Faith* through *Fallible Forms and Symbols*, in which theology and culture are the major themes. None of these themes is abandoned or appears wholly new, yet each theme predominates and is given its major definition during one of these three major periods.

57 See his address to the Divinity School, "An Age in Between," *Divinity School News* 21 (1954):1-7. For further evidence of direct effect, see "Philosophy of Religion Following the War," *Journal of Bible and Religion* 15 (1947): 86-89.

which might provide an overview for interpreting this depth. The former pointed to the importance of myth and the poetic idiom of indirection in theological construction. The latter enabled the theologian to be attentive to the constructive implications of the philosophical imagination.

Reawakening of Christian Faith introduced resources that were to become explicit and basic to his theological program at Chicago, viz., the appeal to myth in theology. Faith is a deep psychical expression of the human spirit conveyed in myth that has to be understood and assessed in terms other than rational. He had no sure grasp yet of this mythical structure, only that what was important in response to the dimension of faith was more aesthetic than moral or logical.

These efforts all lead toward his "summit view." His first effort to advance his theological work beyond *Reawakening of Christian Faith* was *Faith and Culture*,[58] the first of the trilogy constituting his summit view and the book for which he is best known.[59] *Faith and Culture* resulted from a series of seminars at the Divinity School on the mythical structure of faith.[60] Although Wieman had decried the reappearance of myth in theology, it had now become a more accepted term, partly through the influence of Niebuhr. So Meland set out to state his own theory of the mythical response and the structure of meaning it conveyed. This led him to an awareness of the sharp difference between earlier liberal theories of religion and his own. Liberal theologians wanted to dissociate Christian faith from whatever dissipated ethical sensitivity, repudiating any imaginative or aesthetic formulation of Christian themes in liturgy or literature that employed evocative words.

---

[58] Bernard Meland, *Faith and Culture* (London: George Allen and Unwin, 1955).

[59] "I consider *Modern Man's Worship* and *Faith and Culture* as being in some sense related, though they are separated by more than twenty years. I think I have never departed from the appreciative response as being basic in the religious act." Letter dated 7 April 1956.

[60] *Faith and Culture* appeared somewhat by accident. "He had written up (in long-hand) a set of lectures and had presented them in a seminar at the Divinity School. One of the students, Carl Wennerstrom (Jeanne's husband), asked if he might have them so that some of the students might get together on their own to discuss them. Before Meland knew it, Wennerstrom—on his own initiative—was circulating the lectures in mimeographed form among a great many students and they were receiving a favorable response. Well, thought Meland, he might as well staple them together and send them in somewhere for publication. The result: *Faith and Culture*." Letter from Larry Axel, 15 June 1978.

Meland wanted to associate Christian faith with the aesthetic and mythical response.

His own empirical orientation by now had come to share some common sensibilities with Barth, Brunner, Niebuhr, and Tillich. Although their thought was shaped by a modified Kantianism, influenced by insights from Kierkegaard, Buber, and existentialist or phenomenological writers, his thought was shaped by the radical empirical process mode of thought. Nevertheless, he viewed their varying approaches "as being two different paths circling the same mountain." Each was a different way of countering liberal subjectivity in the interest of theological realism and of maintaining some disparity between ultimacy and immediacy.

He understood *Faith and Culture* as a way of stating his reconception of Christian faith which distinguished it from historical liberalism yet did not disavow liberal sensibilities as radically as did the neoorthodox theologians. He said, "This book is thus post-liberal only in the sense that it carries historic liberalism to a new stage of modern consciousness; and in doing so, corrects or reconceives some of its own limitations of vision." *Faith and Culture*, therefore, was a fundamental reassessment of the liberal legacy, his constructive proposals for reconstructing the liberal tradition. He described both *Faith and Culture* and *The Realities of Faith*, the second in the trilogy, as "within a postliberal perspective."

Amidst all of the shifts and turns that we have examined, however, there was one decisive shift within Meland's thought during this period. Although he never repudiated the liberal perspective, he did reorient his thought toward the theological task of appropriating the distinctly Christian faith and heritage. He became what his whole thought pushes toward: a constructive Christian theologian. He appropriated the persisting liberal witness in theology while sharing many of the criticisms of the liberal heritage made by "the neoorthodox revolution in theology." He anticipated the postliberal moves away from classical liberalism toward the postmodern world. The summit trilogy, including *Fallible Forms and Symbols*, is a postliberal constructive theology written by one who believes the orientation toward empirical realism can be reformed in a postliberal context.

During his years as Professor of Constructive Theology, Meland became one of several interpreters of Whitehead's philosophy at Chicago. Wieman retired within two years of Meland's appointment to the faculty. Under Dean Loomer the Whitehead of *Process and Reality* dominated the entire theology field. While he left technical Whiteheadian exegesis to Loomer and negotiation between Whiteheadian and neoorthodox thought to Williams, Meland used the Whiteheadian framework to give structure to his themes of elementalism, appreciative consciousness, emergence, depth, faith, myth, and culture. His interest in Whitehead went back to his graduate studies in the Divinity School when Wieman introduced Whitehead to graduate students. However, the significant impact of Whitehead on Meland's thought was not so much through Wieman as through the influence of Whitehead's thought on "the new vision of science" introduced by physicists and philosophers of science in the thirties and forties, such as J. E. Boodin, Max Planck, Arthur Eddington, and especially Jan Smuts, C. Lloyd Morgan, and Samuel Alexander.

His distinctive use of Whitehead, and his marginal participation in technical Whitehead scholarship during his nearly two decades at the Divinity School, was determined by the fact that when he returned to Chicago the interest in and use of Whitehead was shaped by the younger members of the faculty. This stimulus derived from interest in Charles Hartshorne and was organized and vigorously pursued by Loomer, the new Dean who had written his dissertation in 1942 on "The Theological Significance of the Method of Empirical Analysis in the Philosophy of Alfred North Whitehead." Meland shared their appreciation of Whitehead and participated in their discussions, including a sequence of courses begun in 1953 on "Christian Theology in Relation to Philosophy." However, since Loomer was examining *Process and Reality* page by page and Hartshorne was teaching courses on Whitehead, he addressed specific themes in Whitehead as they related to contributions by James and the emergence evolutionists, chiefly Alexander, Smuts, and Morgan.

But his own unique appropriation of Whitehead's thought was shaped not only by his need to carve out his own area of Whiteheadian scholarship among colleagues devoted to Whiteheadian exegesis and by the fact that he was offended by the "cultic" tone surrounding Whitehead's thought at the Divinity School. More decisive was the fact that what impressed him as a graduate student was Whitehead's philosophy of nature, not the metaphysics of *Process and Reality*. The Whitehead he was primarily interested in antedated *Process and Reality*, which had become the canon of the theology field in the forties and fifties. So his interest in Whitehead when he returned to Chicago was not so much to elaborate and apply the metaphysics to theology as to correlate this earlier strand of Whitehead's thought with the empirical and realistic strands of his own thinking. The probings into Whitehead and the new vision of science, as well as James' radical empiricism and Merleau-Ponty's phenomenology, resulted in his concept of "empirical realism." He tried to hold these various perspectives in juxtaposition as beams of light illuminating different aspects of experience as lived.

His work as a constructive theologian began in earnest in the late forties with his rediscovery of the meaning of creation and with his realization that redemption is the renewal of the creative act of God. This, in part, was based on his grasp of the elemental meanings of the myth through poetic perception. It was also influenced by his fresh appropriation of a metaphysics that provided cognitive understanding of what is given in poetic form. Meland was distinctive in his belief that poet and metaphysician could be brought together in a common witness to the basic good of existence that shapes every moment of life. His forty page poem "God in the Morning" was his monument to this discovery. He rediscovered the Bible and Whitehead at the same time and for the same reason.

Faith and myth and their relation to reason also became important in his thinking in the fifties. His refocusing on the theme of faith represented, as noted, one of the most important shifts in his thought, based in part on his increasing criticism of rationalistic formulations. The issue of the relation of faith and reason was one of the keys to his evaluation of the entire liberal movement in theology. Descartes and Bacon, different as they were in their modern rationalism and scientific empiricism, converged on the autonomous reason in separating the modern from historic resources of faith. What theology needed was to reverse the emptying of Christian concepts of their mythical character, as in Deism and the Enlightenment and Positivism. This process had led to a cultural loss that impoverished every phase of modern life where sensibilities, imagination, and feeling were involved. "How are we to go beyond liberalism in reconstructing our thought?" Depth and stature of thinking needed to be restored to theological inquiry.

Meland was appointed to give the Barrows Lectures in India in 1957-58, traveling from Kashmir to the southern most peak. During that trip he and his wife Margaret visited Istanbul, Beirut, Jerusalem, Delhi, Agra, Calcutta, Serampore, Bangalore, Rangoon, Hong Kong, Kyoto, and Tokyo, sailing on the SS President Hoover. The Barrows Lectures, offered under the general title of "Spirit, Man and Culture," were delivered in Bangalore on January 7-10, 1958, and in Rangoon on February 10-17, 1958. During this visit he was struck by the "dignity and degradation...gentle intelligence, a body that moves with grace, smoldering pride, complexity of character" of the Indian people. That experience confirmed his awareness of the degree to which people in a given culture move within "an orbit of meaning." This phrase originated from conversations with Hindu philosophers and historians. It included not only concepts but bodily feelings and sensibilities; it persists mostly as a reservoir of felt experiences. It exists within a "mythos" that is distinctive and expressive of the historical "structure of experience" of a people. The meaning of these terms lay in his study of cultural anthropology and history of religions, and began to appear in *Faith and Culture*. Here the notions were given explicit formulation as concepts for theological inquiry. They became increasingly important in his interpretation of the Christian legacy and his reconstruction of liberalism.

In 1964-65 Meland again was appointed by the Haskell and Barrows Lectureship Committee of the University of Chicago to return to India to give the Barrows Lectures the second time at University of Calcutta and University of Poona. The earlier visit had fixed in his mind the firm impression that secularization was proceeding at a rapid pace in India. The second Barrows Lectures, therefore, were on the theme of the secularization of modern cultures.[61]

VII. "FROM THE SUMMIT VIEW": 1964-1993

Faith and Culture and *The Realities of Faith* represented a temporary plateau from which he took a final, longer summit view of the constructive problems in theology during his final years of writing.[62]

---

[61] While teaching at Chicago, he wrote *Seeds of Redemption* (1947), *America's Spiritual Culture* (1948), *Reawakening of Christian Faith* (1949), *Faith and Culture* (1953), *Higher Education and the Human Spirit* (1949), and *Realities of Faith* (1962). In addition, he published 45 articles plus reviews and mimeographed essays.

[62] "Well, as you can see, it has been an uphill climb all the way, if I can presume to regard *Faith and Culture* and *The Realities of Faith* in any sense as being a summit view."

Following his official retirement from the Divinity School faculty in 1964, he continued to teach, lecture, and write, elaborating his empirical realism. During the final years of his teaching at the Divinity School and soon after his retirement, he explored affinities between empirical realism and phenomenology. As he indicated in his essay in *The Future of Empirical Theology*, the volume he edited from a conference on the one hundredth anniversary of the Divinity School in 1966, his realism was akin to Michael Polanyi's and Merleau-Ponty's insistence on the significance of personal knowledge and intentionality, both concepts indicating how much the past ordering of experience shapes and informs one's present formulation of ideas and beliefs.

Meland taught for the next four years in the Divinity School as Emeritus Professor, and then spent the 1968-69 academic year at Union Theological Seminary in New York as a Visiting Professor. At Union he offered, at Williams's suggestion, a first semester seminar on "Sources of Process Thought," followed by one on the odyssey of his own thought, "Faith and Culture." In the opening paper for the second seminar he described his thought as "one theological expression within that process mode of inquiry," and specifically his "empirical realism within the tradition of process thought." In speaking to the seminar, he said, "When I had written *Realities of Faith* I said to myself and to my colleagues in Chicago, 'That's it! I'm signing off on this problem of faith and culture as a constructive theological inquiry.'" In one sense he did, because his last book, *Fallible Forms and Symbols*, is in fact his final book on method. All of the major themes of the fifty years of religious inquiry appear there, but the major intent of the book was in retrospect to critique contemporary developments in process theology and to state as clearly as possible the theological method he had employed throughout the years.

In retirement he continued to lecture widely. For instance, in April and May, 1967, he lectured at United Theological Seminary of the Twin Cities, Syracuse University, the National Council of Churches, and the Western Division of the American Philosophical Association. A decade later he was still lecturing for two weeks at Williams College, Cornell University, and Christian Theological Seminary. His correspondence during this period is filled with letters to former students answering inquiries about the Chicago School and his own thought.

Meland intended in retirement to complete his multi-volume historical study of "A History of Liberalism in Religious Thought." That project was never completed. This was a great loss to the scholarly community for two reasons. First, no one knew better than he the history of modern liberal theology throughout its four major phases. Second, no one embodied the tensions and revisions of the last phase of liberalism more thoroughly than he did. Although this history of liberal theology remained incomplete, after his retirement he published *Secularization of Modern Cultures* (1966), *Fallible Forms and Symbols* (1976), and 30 articles and reviews; he also wrote other unpublished essays.

Bernard Meland was an extremely private, proud, alert, healthy person. He sustained all of these qualities until the very last days of his life. In the summer of 1987 he was diagnosed with giant cell arteritis or temporal arteritis. Unusually mentally alert in his last years, he developed some paranoia symptoms in 1989 and began to decline mentally in November of 1992. By that time he had moved into a nursing home on Oak Street between Dearborn and Clark near the Water Tower in downtown Chicago. On February 8, 1993 Bernard Meland died at the age of 94. Memorial services were held in Bond Chapel at the Divinity School of the University of Chicago. He is interred in Frankfort, Michigan.

2

Experience in the Radical Mode: Meland as an Epistemologist

It is commonplace to speak of contemporary theology as postEnlightenment, postmodern, and postliberal. The Cartesian quest for clarity and certainty has dissipated in the face of growing skepticism about our capacity to establish knowledge in secure foundations, whether those foundations be revelation of the word of God, or authority, or rationality, or particulars, or universals, or essences, or sense data, or atomic facts, or synthetic a priori propositions, or the givenness of experience. Two important contributions to the quest for a postliberal epistemology are offered by Gordon Kaufman in *An Essay on Theological Method*,[1] and by George Lindbeck in *The Nature of Doctrine: Religion and Theology in a Postliberal Age*.[2]

In Kaufman's view the predominant characteristic of liberal theology is that it begins reflection by an appeal to religious experience. Liberal theology claims a pre-conceptual base in experience, regardless of whether that is thought of as an experience of a special object (such as the holy or God) or as a special quality of experience (such as absolute dependence or oneness with the universe). Instead, he argues, tradition and language provide the actual basis of theology, for "the raw pre-conceptual and pre-linguistic ground of religious experience is simply not available to us for direct exploration, description, or interpretation,

---

[1] Gordon Kaufman, *An Essay in Theological Method* (Missoula, MT: Scholars Press, 1975).
[2] George Lindbeck, *The Nature of Doctrine: Religion and Theology in a Postliberal Age* (Philadelphia: Westminster Press, 1984).

and therefore it cannot provide us with a starting-point for theological work."³

The proper business of theology, then, is to take control of our construction of a world through which we can create more humane meaning and significance. The idea of God, Kaufman argues, is an imaginative construct which helps to unify the totality of experience. The criterion for theological epistemology is not truth as the correspondence of our concepts with our percepts, whether given in classical theology through objective descriptions of doctrine or in liberalism through our direct perceptual receptivity, but is rather coherence and the pragmatic usefulness of such concepts as world and God.⁴

George Lindbeck is even more pointed in his criticism of liberal epistemology. He describes liberal methodologies as "experiential-expressive," by which he means liberals understand theology as noninformative and nondiscursive symbols of inner feelings, attitudes, or existential orientations. His cultural-linguistic alternative locates religion in a cultural system. The function of theological doctrines is their usage as communally authoritative rules of discourse, attitude, and action.

Lindbeck does not deny there is a relation between experience and language, but the order of the inner and the outer in liberal religious theory is reversed. Language, the means of communication and expression, is a precondition, a culturally formed a priori for the possibility of experience, including religious experience. "We cannot identify, describe, or recognize experience qua experience without the use of signs and symbols. These are necessary even for what the depth psychologist speaks of as 'unconscious' or 'subconscious' experiences, or for what the phenomenologist describes as prereflective ones. In short, it is necessary to have the means for expressing an experience in order to have it."⁵ The effect of Lindbeck's proposal is to abandon the notion that the source of religious thought in any sense rests in experience prior to language and culture.

Neither of these postliberal proposals takes account of the alternative of radical empiricism, or what Bernard Meland sometimes calls "empirical realism," as a basis on which to explore the relation of experience, language, and culture. While Kaufman and Lindbeck are

---

3   Kaufman, *An Essay in Theological Method*, p. 7.
4   Ibid., pp. 71-72.
5   Lindbeck, *The Nature of Doctrine*, pp. 36-37.

deeply aware of the relativity of all human constructs, they do not seem to give serious consideration to any empirical account of experience rooted in post-Kantian American empiricism, pragmatism, and naturalism. "At issue, finally, is not simply the question of the relativity of worlds to words, a harmless assumption, generally granted, but the question of how far are we to take this assumption? Assuming a dialectical relation between experience and interpretation, the problem becomes one of critically incorporating both as a paired phenomenon in a theory that does not displace either by the other."[6] Meland's radical empirical epistemology and his empirical realism constitute an alternative to the impasse between liberal foundationalism, the search for a basis of beliefs in some item of knowledge that is self-evident or beyond doubt, and the implicit relativism of some recent antifoundationalism.

As an empiricist Meland claims all knowledge is justified by experience. His empiricism is in part "a recurrence to pre-Kantian modes of thought."[7] At the same time, he denies that experience is primarily sense experience, and offers an alternative to the abstract concept of experience advanced in the classical empiricism of John Locke and David Hume. It is important to remember that Whitehead's polemic was not against the substance philosophy of Aristotle or the classical theism of Aquinus or the skepticism of Hume but rather against Hume's concept of experience. Post-Kantian empiricism returns to Hume but constructs a radical revision of Hume's empiricism which makes it less abstract and less subject to Kaufman's and Lindbeck's criticisms.

Meland's post-Kantian revision of empiricism leads him to a subtle and complex account of the relation between experience, language, and culture. What results is an "objective relativism," a view which stands between a naive foundationalism, on the one hand, and a subjectivism which portrays experience as merely the product of language and culture, on the other. My thesis is that Meland's empirical realism constitutes a genuine postliberal theology through the way he conceives the relations between pure experience, history, language, and culture to be internal and of one piece. He proffers an alternative to the sundering of experience from language and culture found in the postliberal

---

[6] 6. Nancy Frankenberry, *Religion and Radical Empiricism* (Albany: SUNY, 1987), p. 67.

[7] Alfred North Whitehead, *Process and Reality* (New York: Macmillan Press, 1978), p. xi.

philosophy of religion of Wayne Proudfoot[8] and the postliberal theologies of Gordon Kaufman and George Lindbeck. The reason Meland's empirical realism is a successful alternative both to the liberal enclosed subject and to the postmodern autonomy of interpretation is that his radical empirical realism represents a different understanding of experience and of its relation to language and culture than either classical empiricism or postmodern philosophies of religion and theology.

I. FROM MYSTICAL NATURALISM TO APPRECIATIVE CONSCIOUSNESS

Meland's empirical method in theology does not appeal to religious experience, as do the methods of Frederick Schleiermacher and Rudolf Otto, or even to a religious dimension of experience, as does Paul Tillich's method, but to experience as such in its depth. The problem for the empirical theologian who appeals to common experience as the basis and justification of religious knowledge and not to a transcendental region or dimension of religious experience is that ordinary experience is conceived by classical empiricists to consist only of sense experience. Few religious empiricists have found in the impressions of the five senses, as understood by British empiricism, an adequate home for the depth and range of qualities which religion portrays.

Hume teaches that all of our ideas follow from and copy sense impressions. He enunciates three rules of empiricism.[9] First, all our simple ideas in their first appearance are derived from simple impressions. Second, experience consists of atomistic, solitary impressions, so different impressions are not only distinguishable but separable. Third, these separable impressions of sensations exhibit no necessary connection; their relations to entities in the external world become attached only by practice, custom, or habit. The result is that "all relations and dynamic continuities were supposed to be foreign to experience, mere by-products of dubious validity."[10]

Meland claims that Humean empiricism is not empirical enough. Religious knowledge is rooted in experience (empiricism), but experience

---

[8] Wayne Proudfoot, *Religious Experience* (Berkeley: University of California Press, 1987).
[9] Frankenberry, *Religion and Radical Empiricism*, pp. 38-45.
[10] Ibid., p. 44.

is wider and deeper than sense experience (radical empiricism). Drawing on James's notion of "the perceptual flux" and on organismic thought based on the new physics and emergent evolution, Meland claims that the most immediate empirical datum is not sense experience but the sheer act of existing. Lived experience as a bodily event is richer than sense experience. Empirical realism, like phenomenology, begins with "the primacy of perception."[11] But perception is deeper than consciousness and richer than conception. The perceptual field is the ongoing stream of occurrences in which we participate bodily. The idea of the perceptual flux "conveys the fullness of concrete ingredients, and it renders the internal access to meaning as knowledge by acquaintance infinitely richer than the knowledge about acquired through conceptualization."[12]

The range of qualities conveyed in empirical realism, however, is not "a penumbra of mystery that simply supervenes experience; it is a mystery and depth of the immediacies themselves."[13] Experience as lived conveys a contextual ground of relations which is part of every concrete experience and constitutes a holistic event which is more paramount than our conceptions. Relations are not imposed by the mind on reality. Relations are experienceable and experienced in a radical empirical view of the world.[14] They are felt as immediately as anything else and are "as real as the terms they relate."[15] When perception instead of sensation or conception is given priority, experience includes transitions, activity, the sense of beauty, a "more," aversion and attraction, and quality.[16] This contextual or relational ground of every event is seen to be a datum in its own right independent of language and thought.

In radical empiricism this contextuality of experience appears at "the fringe of consciousness." Deeper than all forms of conscious experience

---

[11] For a statement of the similarities between radical empiricism, phenomenology, and existentialism on the primacy of lived experience, see, Bernard Meland, "The Self and Its Communal Ground," *Religious Education* 59 (1964): 363-69, and "Can Empirical Theology Learn Something from Phenomenology?" *The Future of Empirical Theology*, ed. Bernard Meland (Chicago: University of Chicago Press, 1969), pp. 283-305.
[12] Meland, "Can Empirical Theology Learn from Phenomenology?" p. 296.
[13] Bernard Meland, *The Realities of Faith* (New York: Oxford University Press, 1962), p. 223.
[14] Bernard Meland, *Fallible Forms and Symbols* (Fortress Press, 1976), p. 55.
[15] Frankenberry, *Religion and Radical Empiricism*, p. 86.
[16] William Dean, *American Religious Empiricism* (New York: SUNY, 1986), p. 36.

are these happenings and configurations of events in which relationships and complexity of meaning provide a depth of context which defies ready observation or analysis.[17] Perceptual experience is "a richer event than conception can possibly be, providing every occurrence of awareness with a 'fringe,' implying a 'More,' much of which persistently evades conceptualization."[18]

This notion of the depth and complexity of lived experience has a nuanced history of development in Meland's thought. Throughout the 1930s he develops his notion of "mystical naturalism" to which he was introduced in the seminars and personal conversations with G. B. Smith. Burdette Backus, in his review of Meland's *Modern Man's Worship*,[19] notes that the book is about mysticism, but not in the "occult, misty sense."[20] It is mystical in the sense that it claims the roots of human life go into the universe itself, and that in all that we are—biological organism, mental attainments, and social institutions—we are true children of the earth.

Meland's phrase "mystical naturalism" is intended as a term to distinguish his own naturalism from religious humanism. Both perspectives see humanity as a child of the earth, a product of the natural order. They differ, however, in their response to their recognition that humanity is earthbound. The latter ends in an "anthro-inflation," an exaltation of humanity promoting a "man-centered order of existence." For all the humanists's anti-supernaturalism, they end up with a truncated supernaturalism, in which the top half of the dualistic scheme is eliminated, only to be replaced by an inflated humanity. The mystical naturalist, on the other hand, with a sense of belonging to a vast, cosmic neighborhood in which many forms of life seek fulfillment, turns to these natural sources of human life with new devotion and discovers what actually sustains and promotes humanity and its kinsmen of the wild.[21]

---

[17] Bernard Meland, *Faith and Culture* (London: George Allen and Unwin, 1953), p. 39; and *The Realities of Faith* (New York: Oxford University Press, 1964), p. 93.
[18] Meland, *Fallible Forms and Symbols*, p. 3.
[19] Bernard Meland, *Modern Man's Worship* (New York: Harpers, 1934).
[20] Burdette Backus, "Mystic Naturalism," *The New Humanist*, (January-February, 1935), 33.
[21] Bernard Meland, "Mystical Naturalism and Religious Humanism," *The New Humanist* (1935), 72-73.

Mystical naturalism is primarily a mood, an atmosphere, an orientation of the earth creature. Meland refers to it as "the worship mood." He asks rhetorically,

> Have you ever communed in the first person with this total wealth of living life about you? Have you ever stood with awe and wonder before the unbounded totality of all reality — this ongoing process we call the universe, feeling your own intimacy with all its life, thrilling with the realization of the magnitude of relationship, relating to all the world's life, past, present, and future? If you have, you have experienced first-hand religion.[22]

Mystical naturalism is an emotional orientation to the universe in which humanity acknowledges its intimate relations with the life of nature, recognizing that it is a child of the earth, born of its processes, nourished at its sources, sustained and eventually dissolved by its own movements.[23] Although Meland is somewhat fearful of describing this mood as an emotion or a feeling, because each conveys an excess of undirected and uncontrolled sentiment, he risks calling it such.

> Emotion, defined as the surplusage of feeling arising from sensibilities, appreciation, wonder, and concern, has a legitimate place in education, as it has in life itself. Intellect purged of emotion to the extent that it is unresponsive to these sensitivities is the faculty of a denatured human being, and it results in decisions and judgments that exclude the claims of these qualities of spirit. Life in the large is not a clear matter. Mystery and the sense of awe and wonder are genuine ingredients of the living consciousness.... For you simply do not comprehend the world or man if, in studying their features, no penumbra of unexplored and unexplorable data attends your consciousness.[24]

Emotion, then, refers more to an aesthetic sensitivity than to a psychological state. Mysticism as emotion has more to do with imaginative involvement with and total response of an organism to the complex environment than with sentimentality. It exhibits more a sense of awe and appreciative awareness than sheer sentiment.

In his review of Henri Bergson's *Two Sources of Morality and Religion*, Meland refers to Bergson as the kind of mystic "who breaks through the

---

[22] Bernard Meland, "The Worship Mood," *Religious Education* 26 (1931), 665.
[23] Bernard Meland, "Kinsman of the Wild," *The Sewanee Review* 41 (1933), 444.
[24] Bernard Meland, *America's Spiritual Culture* (New York: Macmillan, 1948), pp. 150-51.

matter-arrested level of the human species." However, Bergson is not naturalistic enough.

> My chief misgivings about Bergson's thesis arise at this point. Whether the method and findings of the traditional mystics may be transported unmodified into a world view that has been naturalistically determined, is, I think, seriously open to question, and the results confusing.[25]

What Meland attempts in his version of mystical naturalism, which Bergson never does, is to take traditional mysticism, with its dualistic, even supernaturalistic assumptions, and interpret the intuitions and sensibilities of the mystic into naturalistic terms.

Mystical naturalism is *naturalistic* "in the sense that I take the universe, described by the sciences, as the natural home of man, and the environment in which he must fulfill his life"; it is *mystical* "in the sense that I affirm the possibility of having religious relations with the *Cosmic Phase* of man's world."[26] Mystical naturalism is essentially an orientation of the creature to the natural world. The creature has a strong sense that she is a physical and psychical organic unity with the forces of nature. She knows she is a product and expression of earth forces. She is at home in the universe. She accepts her creaturehood. She knows she can be relaxed and sustained by the forces of nature in the way the swimmer is sustained by the sea.

This mood of at-homeness in the natural world persists throughout Meland's fifty years of religious inquiry. However, the phrase is not retained in his writings after the 1930s. The notion increasingly is referred to as "the creatural stance" and "elementalism."[27] These terms not only avoid the liabilities of the word mysticism, they also designate primary characteristics of this mood and underscore the naturalistic context of their meaning.

The theme changes in formulation, from "mystical naturalism" in *Modern Man's Worship* to "creatural stance" in *Fallible Forms and Symbols*.

---

[25] Bernard Meland, "The Mystical Adventure," *Christendom* 1 (1936), 197.
[26] Meland, *Modern Man's Worship*, p. xi.
[27] For a more elaborate discussion of this dimension of Meland's thought, see Larry Axel, "The Root and Form of Meland's Elementalism," in Michael Shermis, ed., *The Writings of Larry E. Axel (1946-1991): Studies in Liberal Religious Thought* (Lewiston: Edwin Mellen Press, 1992), pp. 81-103.

In *Seeds of Redemption*, he claims that "the basic religious experiences are elemental experiences."[28] As late as 1974, he writes,

> The stance I find necessary to assume in addressing any theological inquiry, but especially one that raises questions concerning horizons of sensitive awareness 'transcending,' exceeding, or transforming our human dimension as a natural structure, is singularly elemental; that is, one that probes initially this elusive area of creaturely awareness...namely, that in theological inquiry the sense of creaturehood precedes the more ambitious problem of creating a world view, or a systematic cosmology.[29]

In his final book he continues to identify himself as "an elementalist, meaning that *we live more profoundly than we can think*, not only when we are unable or unwilling to think profoundly, but even when we address ourselves in the profoundest way possible to issues of our existence."[30]

II. THE APPRECIATIVE CONSCIOUSNESS

The notion of elementalism reaches its zenith in Meland's notion of the appreciative consciousness.

---

[28] "Modern man needs to be pressed back to these elemental events in his life again and again by way of recovering some measure of cosmic expanse in his living and, more particularly, to retain a vivid sense of his own creatureliness and his dependence upon that which daily sustains him. This awareness of elemental experiences is the best antidote to the sophistication which atrophies our sense of reverence, and to the blight of mediocrity that settles over us when we cease being concerned about significant events of living." *Seeds of Redemption* (New York: Macmillan, 1947), p. 42. In *Secularization of Modern Cultures* (New York: Oxford University Press, 1966), he writes, "The context of human existence still presents to each of us a sense of something given, to which we are related in elemental ways. However far we develop and use our human powers, we do not slough off this elemental condition of being creatures of a Creative Passage that is not made by us, not really influenced or altered by us in anything that our sciences or philosophies undertake. It is given as a primordial fact of our existence. We can obscure this sense of creatureliness, block it from view, proceed with the business at hand without thought of it, and, in our sophistication, we can disavow it. But this changes nothing except our attitudes and states of mind. The realities of existence presented by this elemental fact of creaturehood persist as ineradicable circumstances of this living context," pp. 117-18.

[29] Bernard Meland, "Grace: A Dimension within Nature," *Journal of Religion* 54 (April, 1974), 120.

[30] Meland, *Fallible Forms and Symbols*, p. 82.

> Religious sensitivity has to do, first of all, with our attachments to life as creatures. This defines the most elemental condition of our existence. It concerns, next, those developing sensitivities and sensibilities through which we engage in the apprehension and enjoyment of the qualities of experience.[31]

The primary resource for the enrichment of his elementalism is radical empiricism. Creaturalism and conjunctive relations are merged in Meland's concept of appreciative consciousness. The mature formulation of this complex notion is developed throughout the 1950s.

Elementalism and empiricism are joined within the framework of James's radical empiricism. James's empiricism gave Meland a perspective on the richness of experience within a naturalistic framework.

> Radical empiricism consists first of a postulate, next of a statement of fact, and finally of a generalized conclusion. The postulate is that the only things that shall be debatable among philosophers shall be things definable in terms drawn from experience. The statement of fact is that the relations between things, conjunctive as well as disjunctive, are just as much matters of direct particular experience, neither more so nor less so, than the things themselves. The general conclusion is that therefore the parts of experience hold together from next to next by relations that are themselves parts of experience. The directly apprehended universe needs, in short, no extraneous trans-empirical connective support, but possesses in its own right a concatenated or continuous structure.[32]

Through James's notions of the fringe, the edges, the more, and the perceptual flux, Meland finds an empirical way to understand experience which includes transitions, processes, tendencies, conjunctive relations, and a sense of lived experience which the mystic knows but is unable to express and formulate within the framework of classical empiricism. Meland now has a way to interpret mysticism within a strictly naturalistic framework. He is able to get beyond an impasse created by Otto and Bergson. They try to operate out of a naturalistic orientation, but they can maintain the insights of mysticism only through

---

[31] Bernard Meland, *Higher Education and the Human Spirit* (Chicago: University of Chicago Press, 1953), pp. 156-57.
[32] William James, *The Meaning of Truth* (New York: Longmans, Green, and Co., 1909), pp. xii-xiii.

a supernaturalistic language of numinous and intuition, both of which supervene nature.

Radical empiricism is occupied with the phenomenal field of "lived experience" (concreteness). Its concern is with the full meaning of experience as concrete event. In this view the self is not a transcendental ego but is a subjective existence intimately and organically related to the objective world. Human beings have immediate access to what opens out into the world as "lived experience." Thus the self and the world are configurations that allow no dualism. Furthermore, the "perceptual flux" of experience conveys in experience as lived much more than can be readily conceptualized. This *More* in experience as lived is a primary empirical datum.

The formative influence behind the concept of appreciative consciousness is James's description of conscious experience and its implications for perception and conception. Kant proposes the transcendental ego with its a priori categories as the organizing agent of conscious experience. This effort, however, James claims, is one-sided and artificial because it concentrates on rational need at the expense of the empirical circumstances of mind and consciousness. Conscious experience and mind are deeper than the focusing of mind in rational consciousness. The empirical alternative to the transcendental ego, with its mentalism which results in the inevitable split between body and mind and finally between subject and object, is attention to the feeling of relations within the fuller context of conscious experience. This empirical orientation means, for James and for Meland, a reconception of mind and its relation to conscious experience.

James does not think of the mind as some one thing among many within the organism which can be located in the brain or in some portion of the brain. Neither does he set the mind above the organism as a supervening activity. Mind and body interpenetrate. Mind, indeed, is of a piece with the biological organism, partaking of its moods and drives as well as its peculiar organization of impulses. Mind is, as it were, the "luminous center" of the living organism.[33]

What James means is that the body and the mind are two different dimensions of the same organism. Consciousness can become so acute in attentiveness to a particular need that the organism will seem to be operating as an intellect. At other times the mental powers are so

---

[33] Meland, *Higher Education and the Human Spirit*, pp. 51, 37.

dormant that intellect seems to be absorbed into bodily senses. Thus, the predominance of conscious attention or sensory absorption by the organism depends on the varying kinds of stimulation of the organism. However, conscious attention always reaches subliminal depths beyond the moment of immediate attention. In part these depths are neurological. The organism bears within its sensitive nerve endings the memory of the sensitized organism in the past, therefore making available past feelings and responses. The organism carries along this past as subliminal depth until aroused in the nervous system.

James maintains that a radical empirical view of experience and mind, which takes account of the concrete occurrence, reveals a "fringe of experience" or a "fringe of consciousness" attending all forms of focused consciousness.[34] Through his doctrine of "the fringe" James tries to preserve the rich fullness of the stream of thought. The fringe contains not only an outer range of stimuli but also "the feeling of tendency," which Meland takes to mean that within the fringe of experience relations are experienced. Meland means that in all experience we have an intuitive sense or feeling of the internal relatedness of ourselves and our environment, even if not immediately conceived.

This fringe accompanies *all* experience, aesthetic and scientific as well as individual and communal. When the organism is in a state of conscious awareness, the fringe imposes a certain vagueness on thought. When clarity is sought, the fringe must be canceled out or ignored. This canceling of the fringe of consciousness because of its vagueness and unmanageability for the sake of precision and clarity means that the mind has to be abstracted from the full range of experience. This abstraction has led to the body-mind dualism, and to the subject-object problem in philosophy. For Meland this notion of the fringe of consciousness offers the definitive justification for the role of sensitive awareness in thought. Inside all descriptive analysis and logical exposition is this rich texture of feelings and relations which extend the meanings achieved by rational thought.

The actual resources of meaning, then, are the deepest reaches of bodily feeling and the widest range of perceptual awareness. Perceptual experience, however, is not simply a vague, inferior, or preconscious level of conscious thought. The perceptual field is the more deeply involved orientation of the human psyche in which the report from

---

[34] Ibid., pp. 53-54, 58-60.

experience is full and concrete. The perceptual field is awareness of a depth of which conscious experience as an attentive act can never attain. Conception is a conscious mode of attention, namely, a selection; perception is the deeper orientation of the organism to the full range and depth of experience.

To summarize, Meland's attempt to designate the interpenetration of the *More* of the fringe of consciousness and the perceptual field with thought is embraced in his phrase "appreciative consciousness." The phrase aims at the opening of oneself to the full impact of the concrete datum. The basis for all knowledge is experience, but experience includes more than sensation and conscious awareness. The fundamental claim that lies behind all of his reflection on epistemology is that perception is deeper than conception. Human beings are cradled in a context of relationships deeper than conscious awareness and more ultimate than the human structure.

The epistemological problem, from his point of view, is not how to establish certainty or total clarity of thought, but how to be attentive and responsive to the fullness of reality while achieving intelligibility. Knowledge involves not only conceptual clarity and certainty but intimation of and attentiveness to the full range of actuality conveyed in experience. Meland proposes an analogy of the role of reflective thought from within the appreciative framework.

> It is very much like allowing one's visual powers to accommodate themselves to the enveloping darkness until, in their more receptive response to the shrouded shapes and forms concealed by the darkness, one begins to see into the darkness and to detect in it the subtleties of relationship and tendencies that have eluded one, but which now yield a visual field.[35]

III. COGNITION WITHIN THE APPRECIATIVE CONSCIOUSNESS

This analogy is suggestive, but it needs to be clarified. What does *cognition* mean within the appreciative consciousness? Cognition is not identical to experience, nor is it simply openness to the fringe of experience. Although the basis for knowledge is experience, cognition is a reciprocity between experience and language. Receptivity toward the

---

[35] Meland, "Can Empirical Theology Learn from Phenomenology?" p. 292.

full range of the data is one element in cognition; interpretation within frames of meaning is the other.

The way Meland holds together experience in the radical mode and interpretation of meaning can be discerned by noting that for him there are at least three possible organizing principles in experience and thought.[36] One is the rational, beginning with Aristotle, in which a mathematical conception of the world order is determinative. The second is the moral emphasis of Kant. Here the premise of universal order is continued, but it is not reducible to rational understanding. The moral consciousness provides the basis on which to know the more ultimate character of the world. Both of these views are based on the premise of a given, static universal order.

In the recent past, however, an emphasis has appeared in Western thought which seeks to come to terms religiously and philosophically with the dynamic character of the world. The cognitive correlate of this creative view of the world is located more in the "appreciative consciousness." The appreciative consciousness is an aesthetic mode of receptivity and attention within experience which relates the depths of experience to cognitive inquiry.

There are two ways of trying to recover qualitative meanings in cognition. One is to reserve a place for the appreciative functions of life by citing two sides of life (mechanism and spirit, as in idealism), or two rhythms of life (fertility and utility), or two realms of being (the world of action and the world of contemplation). The outcome of this procedure is to drive a wedge between appreciative and active interests. The other alternative, and the one offered by the radical empirical perspective, is to acknowledge the "appreciative consciousness as a constant and indispensable companion and resource for critical thought."[37] That is, the appreciative consciousness can be recognized as "a regulative principle in thought."[38]

Specifically, cognition within the appreciative consciousness includes three distinct stages. The first stage in the epistemological correlate of experience and interpretation is maximum receptivity,[39] which Meland

---

[36] Meland, *Higher Education and the Human Spirit*, p. 48, and *Faith and Culture*, pp. 25-36.
[37] Ibid., p. 63.
[38] Ibid.
[39] Meland, *Realities of Faith*, pp. 193, 196.

also designates as *open awareness*.⁴⁰ He advances as the first stage of knowledge not a priori categories or clear and distinct ideas but receptiveness to the full datum of experience. Open receptiveness is not a full achievement, however. Living creatures, individual or organized, in order to survive through dependable and repeatable procedures, tend to channel and even fix their routines of thought as well as their behavior. Every creature must live in terms of a structure, and the structure, by wresting order from novelty, is in itself delimiting. Nevertheless, open awareness is a condition to be sought, because the full datum is not available in interpretation.

Open awareness is to be sought for two reasons.⁴¹ One reason relates to the creative character of the world. Nowhere is there a static order to which an object or event can be readily referred. Patterns, categories, and criteria, useful as they are for pursuing definitive meanings, are approximate, tentative, and subject to revision as the creative passage continues. The other reason relates to the mystery or fullness of objects or events which burst every definitive category. "A sense of the-more-than-the-mind-can-grasp as well as a sense of expectancy concerning every event, knowing that creativity is occurring, that time is real, attends every act of cognition where the appreciative consciousness is operative."⁴²

The second stage of cognition within the appreciative consciousness, in which the object is appropriated in its concrete fullness, is the act of *identification*. This is the stage in which the object is related to the conscious ego. The conscious ego creates the meaning of the object within the limited frame or structure of the perceiving mind. Specifically, the meaning of the object is cognitively appropriated within a given frame of symbolization.

We can better understand this aspect of identification if we contrast Meland with Kant on this point. Kant holds, in his theory of the forms and categories of the mind, that while knowledge arises in sense experience, it is formed by the imposition of the a priori categories of the mind on the stuff of experience. These categories are invariable forms implicit in the conscious ego through which reason impresses itself upon experience.

---

⁴⁰ Meland, *Higher Education and the Human Spirit*, p. 63, and *Faith and Culture*, pp. 161-162.
⁴¹ Ibid., p. 64.
⁴² Ibid.

Meland insists that there is a bias of personal idealism at work here, elevating human consciousness to absolute status. He seeks a more empirical understanding of the forms and categories. What Kant arbitrarily formulates as the innate categories of the mind can be empirically equated, "in part at least," with structures of meaning which arise within every individual consciousness in the act of symbolization whereby the growing consciousness is individuated. That is, the act of symbolic construction replaces a priori categories of the mind. "What happens in every act of cognition is that the fullness of meaning attending any datum is funnelled into some conscious experience and made part of the internal stream of thought which has been structured in a given way through a process of symbolization by which every conscious mind internalized its objects."[43] This process of symbolization, then, is the source of individuated consciousness.

But if these are not a priori symbols, what is their source? The source is cultural. Symbols are "consciously assigned meanings" whereby the emerging conscious ego is formed by its social context. "Cognitively speaking, every individual is contained within a given sequence of assigned meanings which define his structure of personality."[44] At the level of communicable symbols, in terms of which rational discourse takes place, each knower knows experience only within this partial perspective which her or his living experience itself forms throughout the succession of moments of awareness and activity defining conscious life.

Thus, to a considerable degree the act of cognition always implies the fragmentation of meaning, i.e., the appropriation of the rich fullness of experience within the restricted range of a partial perspective. This applies not only to the simple form of symbolization in private experience but also the more disciplined forms of cognition as in scientific inquiry or logical research. Identification through symbolization is always a partial fragmentation of the rich fullness of experience.

Identification, however, implies more than the cognitive appropriation of the object through symbolization. Identification also participates to some degree in the "feeling-context." This is a more undifferentiated aspect of the second stage of cognition. Meland refers to

---

[43] Meland, *Higher Education and the Human Spirit*, p. 65.
[44] Ibid, p. 66.

it as "the wisdom of the body."[45] This phrase refers both to the subjective act of feeling into the event and to "a penetration of the realm of internal relations where the *me* and the *it* find their common ground."[46] Although the body is less individuated by the assertive consciousness than the mind, it nevertheless provides a more durable and dependable context of appropriation as a threshold to the deeper stratum of organic being.

Meland is not proposing that the wisdom of the body is an alternative to the conscious mind in cognition. The mind is more focused, more specialized. However, its symbolization is precarious and unreliable unless related to the activity of the body which operates below the level of consciousness. "The vital energy that rises to psychic heights in creative effort, moral courage, and rational discourse has its source in the intricate workings of this body-life."[47] The act of feeling into a situation or object, the full meaning of which cannot be grasped, is an important aspect of cognition itself.

The third stage of cognition is *discrimination*, the analytical stage in the appreciative consciousness in which examination of the structure of the object and description of the relation of the object to its context is made. This stage is analytical in the sense of "noting the vivifying contrasts which differentiate the datum and which set it apart as a distinct event."[48] However, even the analytical element in cognition cannot be identified with precision. First, and most basic, the act of analysis does not involve extricating the datum from its context. An event is never known or even analyzed properly apart from its context, for the relations are as real a part of its meaning as an internalized core. Thus, analysis within the appreciative consciousness must take the form of examining the parts with a full sense of their relational aspects. This kind of analysis, or discrimination, can never be precise.

Meland does not argue that mathematics or logical thought do not and cannot produce knowledge. Nor does he argue that the kind of analysis wherein the data are extricated from a context and then dissected into multiple parts is not knowledge. He argues, however, that

---

[45] Ibid., pp. 55-57, 66.
[46] Ibid., p. 65. Meland is drawing here not only on the work of Bergson and James but also on Dorothy Emmet, *The Nature of Metaphysical Thinking* (New York: Macmillan, 1960) and Susan Langer, *Philosophy in a New Key* (New York: Mentor Books, 1951). See, for example, Meland, *Faith and Culture*, pp. 88-92.
[47] Ibid., p. 69.
[48] Ibid.

those kinds of analyses do not constitute full or adequate knowledge of an event, for knowledge of any event includes discrimination of its relations. To identify knowledge with analysis that takes no account of relations is an abstraction. The analysis of precision is but one, and an abstract, element in knowledge of *any* object or event. The qualitative features of any datum are mutually qualifying. "Any attempt to understand the one apart from the other falsifies the meaning of the datum."[49]

Another reason for not identifying cognition and precision relates to the doctrine of emergence. There are some levels of emergence in which relations and creative possibilities form the essential stuff of meaning, such as human aesthetic and spiritual activity. This does not deny the relevance of abstract knowledge in these higher levels of knowing. However, discrimination becomes the very essence of cognition in these levels, for "the fact of structural evolution by which a new degree of complexity and of creative organization of parts occurs within the psychophysical organism, giving more range and subtlety to its operations, compels a differentiation in methods of inquiry for exploring meanings in these various levels."[50]

In summary, the key feature of Meland's epistemological reflection so far is his claim that in every cognitive act, perception has precedence over precision. His intent is to keep appreciative awareness and critical inquiry in alternation,[51] and to insist that we have in every cognitive act partial knowledge and partial mystery.[52] Perceptiveness is not indifference to structure or the absence of a sense of structure. Rather, perceptiveness is awareness of structure seen in new organic imagery, hence structure attended by a qualitative dimension hidden or barely perceptible. This means that for Meland the most we can locate in the cognitive act is a "margin of intelligibility." All attempts at structure and order in the cognitive act are tentative and partial.

---

[49] Ibid.
[50] Ibid., p. 70.
[51] Meland, *Faith and Culture*, p. 120.
[52] Meland, *America's Spiritual Culture*, pp. 152-153.

IV. FRAMES OF MEANING AND FUNDAMENTAL NOTIONS

If there are no a priori forms of sensibility or categories of the mind, enabling the mind to impose structure on the flux of experience,[53] how is discrimination, the analytical stage of cognition within the appreciative consciousness, possible? This question is answered, from Meland's radical empirical perspective, by seeing how the mind, as a specialized function of the organism, receives the forms by which to know. While maintaining that the self feels as well as thinks with its body, Meland has no intention of reducing cognition to the level of sensuous feeling or of dissipating it into mysticism, the threat James and especially Wieman fear when attention is given to the fringe of consciousness as cognitively relevant.[54] Cognition is a focused form of consciousness going beyond the feeling and immediacy of the organism by way of memory, discrimination, and imagination.

The main point of this emphasis on the interdependence of mind and cognition and the body and feeling is that all dimensions of knowing, i.e., all cognitive acts which can be said to issue in statements that are

---

[53] One can sympathize with Meland's attempt to extend the scope of relevant data and to qualify the reductionistic implications of the common usage of precision and clarity but still wonder how thoroughly he succeeds in accomplishing his goal. Two questions appear at this stage of our analysis. (1) Even if knowledge cannot be identified with "precision," can the "imprecise" element be designated only as a "surplusage" or as a vague intuition of relationships? Does that element or dimension not have to be at least somewhat more precise than that? Yet Meland, even in his later usage of metaphysics, does not seek to establish greater precision than these designations. (2) Has Meland answered Kant's problem, proposed an alternative, or ignored Kant's problem? One can understand the reluctance, from a radical empiricist's point of view, to accept a priori categories of the mind. However, that reluctance is not necessarily justified because of a commitment to empiricism, even broadly defined. Can an empiricist establish how knowing (conception and judgment) is possible by appealing exclusively to the conventions of cultural conditioning? Meland seems to wonder himself in terms of his own qualification, "in part at least," but we never find out what that other part is if it is not a priori categories of the mind. This problem, which has already arisen at this point, is not answered but compounded by what follows in Meland's thought.

[54] On James, see, Meland, "What Can Empirical Theology Learn from Phenomenology?" pp. 285-286, and *Higher Education and the Human Spirit*, pp. 44-45, 54-61. On Wieman, see Meland, "What Can Empirical Theology Can Learn from Phenomenology?" pp. 30-40, *The Reawakening of Christian Faith* (New York: Macmillan, 1949), pp. 41-47, *Higher Education and the Human Spirit*, pp. 57-61, and "The Root and Form of Wieman's Thought" in *The Empirical Theology of Henry Nelson Wieman*, ed. Robert Bretall (New York: Macmillan, 1963), pp. 44-68.

meaningful and true by satisfying specific canons by which a person presumes to know a thing to be true,[55] have a dimension of imprecision which is cognitively relevant. Further, there are some levels of thinking and knowing (namely, those beyond survival, communication, and analysis involving constructive understanding, imaginative interpretation, and metaphysics) which must place precision at a minimum and open awareness and appreciative response at a maximum, even though intelligibility instead of precision is the cognitive correlate of that form of thinking and knowing.

For Meland the cognitive function of the mind is to achieve "intelligibility," appropriately defined and delimited. At times and for certain purposes, such as in scientific endeavors, intelligibility drives at precision, with the feeling dimension ignored, thereby distorting full knowledge of the object or event but nevertheless useful for certain purposes. At other times, as in the humanistic disciplines, the full context of the event is sought and so only a margin of intelligibility is possible.

The epistemological question that follows is this: How is intelligibility, however defined in its appropriate context and function, possible? If the forms of perception and of conception are not a priori, how is cognition as a specialized function of the organism possible? The answer, for Meland, is that the mind assumes "frames of meaning" from the culture through a process of "symbolization." Since the perceptual and conceptual powers of the organism functioning as mind do not possess innate content in the sense of a priori forms, these powers are dependent on the shaping of the culture. We must be clear about what Meland does not argue here. His argument is not, as in Kant's epistemology, that sense impressions are needed to activate a priori forms. Rather, Meland holds the mind-organism is immersed in experience, broadly defined, and that conceptualization depends on the symbolization learned from the language of the culture in which the organism is cradled.

The facilities for symbolization, language, are an emergent quality of the human organism in a culture.[56] The self is the result of conscious awareness (not transcendental universals or forms) interacting with concrete symbols and signs that designate the reality awaiting recognition. Two sources determine the nature of the growth of this

---

[55] Meland, *Faith and Culture*, pp. 113-114.
[56] Ibid., pp. 184-185.

individuated event within the context of events. One is the mechanism of the organic structure, the creatural grounds for symbolization, namely, the genes, the endocrine glands, and the cortical mechanism which determine the range and degree of sensitivity of the organism. The other is the resources of meaning of a culture which are, in time, internalized through the facilities of these mechanisms. The process through which this takes place he calls "symbolization." [57]

Human distinctiveness arises from its capacity to engage in symbolization ranging from elemental conversations to problem solving, to daydreaming, to analysis, or to abstruse discourse on higher mathematics. A person can participate in this cognitive process to the degree that the facilities of symbolization permit interaction with cultural meanings. This interaction is compared by Meland to the digestive process.

> The perceptual and cognitive powers of the person draw into the individuated experience the stuff of culture in much the same way that the person eating imbibes food. Musing and reflection are like mastication. The stuff of cultural meanings is literally chewed over and absorbed by the reflective mind in ways peculiar to the particular mind and imagination at work.[58]

Here is the place where Meland simultaneously agrees with and departs from Kant's resolution. He agrees that in our habits of perception and apprehension, the forms of sensibility and the categories of the mind are determinative. However, in Meland's view, Kant made too much of their subjective character and therefore drew the wrong conclusions. The categories are not "unvariable forms implicit in the conscious ego," but are "frames of meaning" that have become an organic part of the conscious life of the person through individuation, and individuation, as we have noted, is an interaction between cultural and individual processes. Perception is simultaneously a bodily event and a valuing event, "coterminous with the act of individuation by which what is encountered is felt, grasped, apprehended, valued, and finally interpreted within a frame of meaning that is organic to the conscious life of a person."[59]

---

[57] Ibid., p. 133; see, also, *Higher Education and the Human Spirit*, p. 65.
[58] Ibid., p. 134.
[59] Meland, *Realities of Faith*, p. 173.

By "frames of meaning" Meland refers to *forms of perception* that have become a part of the conscious self through interaction with the culture. Frames of meaning are internalized forms of linguistic meaning. They bring to bear on the individual the accumulated meanings of a culture. They set bits of experience in a context and determine their interpretation. Thus frames of meaning determine the content of such fundamental categories as space, time, substances, and so forth, as well as, for example, how a Native American will respond to a steaming locomotive when first encountering it.

Frames of meaning are fashioned from "fundamental notions," through which perceptual experience is apprehended and interpreted.[60] Fundamental notions are usually provided by a few seminal minds, such as the fundamental notion of order provided by Newton, or of creativity provided by Whitehead. At their worst, fundamental notions and new frames of meaning exert a highly contemporary influence. At their best, however, "they exercise a critical judgment upon all previous frames of meaning by disclosing what has been left uncalculated in their surveys of experience."[61]

The source of the fundamental notions which shape the frames of meaning is the language of a culture. This source must be understood dynamically, and, Meland notes, it must not ignore the imaginative capacity of individuals to formulate new frames of meaning and fundamental notions. The creation of meaning is organic to the living situation of a period and place, to the experience available within that environment. This living situation includes frames of meaning within a structure of experience which persists from previous periods. Furthermore, there are strands of meaning that persist as undercurrents of protest and nonconformity to the dominant imagery. The dominant imagery of a period, however, arises out of new, innovative experience of a people.

Regardless of how universally shared and binding the frames of meaning and fundamental notions of a cultural epoch are, the thinking

---

[60] Ibid., pp. 174, 76; *Reawakening of Christian Faith*, pp. 37, 86, 87, 91; *Seeds of Redemption*, pp. 119 ff. "The structuring of the mind and of the bodily feelings is a deeply cultural process in which formative ideas, however adequately or inadequately acknowledged, have their way." Bernard Meland, "Interpreting the Christian Faith within a Philosophical Framework," *Journal of Religion*, XXXIII (April, 1953), 88.

[61] Meland, *Realities of Faith*, p. 175.

and knowing made possible by them can only be described as tentative, fragmentary, partial, limited, and relative. The basic reason, above all else, is that experience and environment are dynamic, changing, and therefore ever new. Consequently, thought and knowledge, which are bound inseparably to experience and context, can never be static or full.

This basic premise expresses itself in several ways. Every frame of meaning is sensible up to the point of what has been left uncalculated by some previous conceptual framework. Further, neither one of them, nor all of them together, can take fully adequate account of what is left uncalculated in perception or cognition. Therefore, precision is an illusion, partly because of limitations inherent in the structure of an organism and partly because of limitations inherent in the linguistic meaning available within a culture. Finally, frames of meaning are at best tentative ways of attaining a synoptic view of experience and of gathering the fragments of experience into an ordered and disciplined discourse. All of this leads to the conclusion that knowing is limited, and that it is limited in part because of cultural factors. In a basic sense, then, Meland's epistemology includes a strong element of cultural relativism in it, which we will analyze at the end of chapters three and four.

V. LANGUAGE AND REALITY

There is one great difference between symbolism and direct knowledge. Direct experience is infallible. What you have experienced, you have experienced. But symbolism is very fallible, in the sense that it may induce actions, feelings, emotions, and beliefs about things which are mere notions without that exemplification in the world which the symbolism leads us to presuppose. I shall develop the thesis that symbolism is an essential factor in the way we function as the result of our direct knowledge. Successful high-grade organisms are only possible, on the condition that their symbolic functionings are usually justified so far as important issues are concerned. But the errors of mankind equally spring from symbolism. It is the task of reason to understand and purge the symbols on which humanity depends.[62]

Bernard Meland is an empiricist in Whitehead's sense of the term. Knowledge is grounded in immediate lived experience. However, his empiricism is not subject to the criticism of liberalism promoted by some

---

[62] Alfred North Whitehead, *Symbolism: Its Meaning and Effect* (New York: Capricorn, 1927), pp. 6-7.

postliberal critics. He is not an empirical foundationalist in the sense that experience provides a infallible foundation for the search for direct, objective, and certain knowledge of the world. Experience is not a ground of certainty; it is a medium of disclosure. Experience is not an intermediary "thing" that stands between us and the world; it is the medium of the disclosure of a world or an environment to the knower. Perhaps it is better to speak of experiencing instead of experience when talking about the relation of the world and a knower as Meland conceives it.

Furthermore, although Meland might be interpreted in some passages as an expressivist who understands language only as illuminating and informing primary experience, a more adequate way to understand him is to see his epistemology as a theory about the reciprocity between experience and language. Meland never holds a view in which individuals have some kind of unmediated pure experience of reality and then search for some more or less adequate way to express that experience. Experience and language are equally primal and configure each other in mutual formation. His distinctive contribution to the contemporary discussion is his view of the reciprocity between experience and language.

Meland's empiricism does not retain the liberal assumption that there is an unmediated, self-authenticating truth contained in pure experience prior to language for which we endlessly seek a conclusive or adequate linguistic formulation or expression. Furthermore, his new realism enables liberalism to break free from the mentalism that shapes liberal thought since Kant. His contextualism contains a richly-textured otherness of which human beings are intuitively aware in experience and to which they are intrinsically related through experience. This otherness, though, is not either an objective world outside the subjective knower or an absolute nounema mediated through pure experience. "Otherness" is a social, cultural, linguistic, historical, and natural context which not only bears up but constitutes the knowing subject. Thus, his view of the interpenetration of context and experience moves him beyond classical liberal epistemologies toward the postliberal emphasis on the importance of language and culture in religious knowledge. What is distinctive about his contribution to the postliberal discussion is his refusal to see experience as merely a function of language. Experience is a relational event in which the reciprocity between an experiencer and a culture constitutes a knower as an historical creature.

There are clearly places in Meland's later writings where he appears to maintain the older liberal distinction between pure experience and language. He appears to advance a concept of pure experience prior to and independent of language. Thus, when speaking of reality in terms of the primacy of lived experience and of the richness of the lived experience, he speaks of the "distance,"[63] the "primal disparity,"[64] the "stark contrast," and even the "dualism,"[65] between language and reality. On occasion he says that "words follow" experience,[66] and speaks of words "expressing" experience.[67] Such terms imply a disjunction if not a bifurcation of experience and language, and seem to locate Meland as epistemologist in the older liberal camp which appeals to pure experience prior to language as the foundation of knowledge. He seems in these locations to be an old-fashioned foundationalist seeking religious knowledge in pure experience prior to the misrepresentation or inadequate representation of language.[68]

These formulations lead Nancy Frankenberry to speak of the problem of "the linguistic gap" in Meland's epistemology. He maintains, she argues, a gap between extralinguistic meaning and its linguistic expression, and between lived experience and the capacity of linguistic expression.

> The never fully resolved difficulty of Meland's empirical realism, as it is also of James's psychology and Wieman's contextualism, is to reconcile the prereflective flow of the dynamic felt qualities of lived experience with the structures of reflective and linguistic expression.... This emphasis may be the inevitable outcome of Meland's understanding of the nature of language and linguistic meaning as secondary processes of instrumental-expressive value only, apparently playing no constitutive role in the very having of human experience.[69]

---

[63] Meland, *Fallible Forms and Symbols*, p. 130.
[64] Ibid., p. 23.
[65] Meland, "What Can Empirical Theology Learn from Phenomenology?" p. 304.
[66] Ibid., p. 303.
[67] Meland, *Fallible Forms and Symbols*, pp. 24, 28.
[68] This interpretation of Meland is offered by Gordon Kaufman, "Empirical Realism in Theology: An Examination of Some Themes in Meland and Loomer," in *New Essays in Religious Naturalism*, Highlands Institute Series II, ed. Creighton Peden (Macon, GA: Mercer University Press, 1993), pp. 136–160.
[69] Frankenberry, *Religion and Radical Empiricism*, pp. 141-42.

She charges him with moving from the truism that reality exceeds thought to the more controversial corollary that experience exceeds language. In her view, language "codetermines the very possibility of any experience at all," and radical empiricism should recognize a reciprocal and even codeterminate relation between experience and language.[70]

Meland's thought, though, is more subtle than a single answer to the question of whether language distills and distorts experience or experience is a function of language. There is a sense in which Meland maintains the older liberal view on this question by arguing from his earliest to his latest essays that there is a surplusage of meaning in any linguistic system. He maintains the view that not only reality but experience is deeper and richer in meaning than any language scheme. Language does not produce experience; experience is independent of and has dimensions of meaning (a surplusage of relations) beyond language games. To claim there is a surplusage of meaning, however, is not to claim that experience exists prior to and independent of language, and that language is merely expressive and not constitutive of meaning. All things considered, there is no final "gap" in Meland's thought between language and experience in the sense that experience has meaning apart from language. There is always a reciprocity between language and experience.

Why, then, does Meland use terms like distance, disparity, contrast, and even dualism in his late writings when talking about the relation of experience and language? I offer two reasons here. First, the terms are used in the context of his highly polemical argument in *Fallible Forms and Symbols* against the direction rationalistic process philosophy, with its lust of clarity, certainty, and coherence, had taken in recent years.[71] In order to counter claims for the adequacy, or even precision, of language, he speaks of the disparity and contrast between language and its rich environment. Second, he usually uses such terms while discussing the relation of language and reality, not language and experience, maintaining only that experience, insofar as it conveys the richer depths of reality, is richer than language. Meland wants to insist on not

---

[70] Ibid., p. 143.
[71] He even speaks of the "dementia" of some forms of process philosophy in the search for clarity and certainty. *Fallible Forms and Symbols*, p. 24.

confusing language and reality,[72] or coalescing language and reality.[73] The emphasis on disparity is meant to counter "the tendency to confuse reality with language about reality."[74] Any epistemology which believes that the word is the thing, whether it be rationalism, or postliberal cultural-linguistic regulative schemes, or neo-Kantian constructivism, is to be resisted by stressing the distinction between language and reality in its full richness and by claiming that there is no linguistic adequacy in representing the fullness of reality. We live more deeply than we think, so there can be no verbal adequacy. There is a context, a penumbra, a richness the body knows in an environment. This richer range of relations known in experience can revise or even veto language and stands as a constant denial of the adequacy of language to picture reality fully.

There is no doubt, then, that Meland is not a postliberal theologian in the sense that language is reality or all reality or even experience is reduced to language. There is a theme of a surplusage to experience beyond language that runs throughout all of his writing. However, to claim that language does not constitute reality or does not exhaust reality is not to claim either that the meaning of experience or even experience as such is independent of language. Some postliberal epistemology seems to reduce experience and even reality to language. Meland's postliberal empirical realism, however, moves beyond this kind of "naive linguisticism" to a theory of how experience and language actually do interpenetrate.

For Meland, there is a reciprocity and even codeterminate relation between language and experience. "Now what all this technical talk comes to is that affinities between reality and modes of expressing reality are acknowledged, but in a way in which language and reality, while related, *do not coalesce. Yet, neither are they dissociated.*"[75] (italics added) Reality is deeper than thought, but there is no "unbiased" or "unmediated" experience or any "pure" knowledge or basis for "direct" knowledge which is prior to and independent of the language of the knower. The experience to which he refers is not "pure experience"

---

[72] Meland, *Fallible Forms and Symbols*, p. 31.
[73] Meland, "Grace: A Dimension of Nature," 122.
[74] Meland, *Fallible Forms and Symbols*, p. 31.
[75] Ibid., p. 22.

independent of the knower and "untainted" by language and culture,[76] but is the "rich," "lived" experience conveyed in the body of the knower through the environment and various contexts in which the knower lives. These contexts are individual (organism), cultural (linguistic), cultic, and cosmic.

There is, for Meland, no "pure experience" prior to or apart from culture. Experience is an *event* or a *structure* which is constituted through the interaction of bodily response and cultural symbolization. Experience has meaning only as a "structure of experience" which bears the form and content of a cultural context (see chapter three).

> While the realities of faith with which we are concerned in living are energies within experiences that are now immediately upon us, it is nevertheless true that awareness of this inherent efficacy within the structure of experience among any people rests back upon, or in some subtle way issues from, a cultic or cultural legacy of long-standing which may best be expressed in terms of themes or motifs of faith.[77]

The term "realism" in Meland's "empirical realism," therefore, is decisive in his understanding of experience. He is an empiricist in the sense in which Whitehead speaks in the quotation at the head of this section. But he is not a "simple" empiricist, if that means an appeal to uninterpreted pure experience or to the absence of any theory, including a theory of experience. The term "realism" is a particular interpretation of experience, a construction of experience, if you will, and that construction is as much a part of what he meant by empiricism as any appeal to "pure experience."

In a response to Frankenberry's criticism, Meland says of his "empirical realism" that "in this correlation of terms I mean to project a perspective of realism as an overview, providing provisional glimpses, or even sustained rational perspective, upon these lived experiences."[78] His realism is an "overview." Experience in the perspective of an empirical realist is a concept shaped by Whitehead's philosophy of

---

[76] For an interpretation of radical empiricism as advocating this kind of pure experience and direct knowledge, see J. Wesley Robbins, "Neopragmatism and the Radical Empiricist Metaphysics of Pure Experience," *American Journal of Theology & Philosophy* 14 (January, 1993): 19-34. See, also, Gordon Kaufman, "Empirical Realism in Theology: An Examination of Some Themes in Meland and Loomer."

[77] Meland, *Fallible Forms and Symbols*, p. 31. See, also, *Realities of Faith*, p. 77.

[78] Bernard Meland, "In Response of Frankenberry," *American Journal of Theology & Philosophy*, 5 (May & September, 1984), 134-35.

organism, a construction which interprets experience from a certain perspective. Linguistic construction is as much a part of what he means by his notion of "empirical realism" as is an appeal to experience. "Whitehead's overview of realism in my mode of empirical realism presumes to provide facilities for at least insinuating conceptualizations enlarging upon James' 'sense of the More'."[79] In responding to Frankenberry's critique of the disparity between language and reality, he says, "it would seem clear that her continuous interpretation of my empirical realism as being shorn of any connotation of realism, thus impelling her to deal with my conceptualizations as being solely empirical, must result in ignoring such adjustments in conceptualization as I have sought to effect and employ."[80]

One of the most important issues for the future of empirical theology is how to understand the relationship of experience and language. In contemporary theological discussion, language is the focus of much of the discussion, while experience is played down or even interpreted as little more than a function of language. In this context, empirical theologians are dismissed as foundationalists, theologians in search of a pure experience as the pre-linguistic grounds for clear and certain knowledge untainted or unprejudiced by language. The apparent alternative is a kind of relativism in which reality *is* language or reality is linguistic *all the way down*. Since earlier empiricists, who were in search of certain knowledge based on the foundations of experience, did not follow this reductionistic path, empiricism seems to be anachronistic in the contemporary discussion.

My claim, however, is that Bernard Meland offers the most comprehensive and nuanced postliberal understanding of experience among the contemporary empirical theologians. He offers a middle way between foundationalism and relativism. His entire project is an effort to understand the complex and subtle relation between experience, language, culture, and history, thereby revising and enriching liberalism while maintaining an empirical orientation in theology.

Contemporary empiricists who have been influenced by Meland's form of empirical realism are neither foundationalists or relativists. John Cobb, Nancy Frankenberry, William Dean, Marjorie Suchocki, and Jerome Stone, for example, all speak of a "reciprocity" between language

---

[79] Ibid., p. 136.
[80] Ibid., p. 135.

and experience. They claim that in the contemporary arguments over deconstruction, historicism, neo-pragmatism, postliberalism, and other forms of linguistic relativism, an empirical approach demands an understanding of the reciprocity between language and experience. What John Cobb says about Whitehead also describes Meland.

> For the Whiteheadian there is a vast and incomprehensibly rich field of events in which human events constitute a very small part. Language enables human beings to orient themselves in this larger field far more creatively than can creatures who do not speak. On the other hand, language also simplifies and even falsifies the context of events in ways that can be disastrous.... There is a pre-linguistic element in human experience as well.... Physical feeling remains prior and primary. It is not constituted by language, and it remains as an ultimate judge of the adequacy and appropriateness of language.[81]

Meland's epistemology offers a view of the reciprocity between language and experience. To ask which comes first is like asking the question about the chicken and the egg. There is, for him, a back and forth, mutually constitutive interplay between language and experience. Experience is a social, not a subjective, concept. It is, as Jerome Stone argues,[82] essentially "a transactional concept." Stone suggests there are three ways one might conceive of experience as a transactional concept: as a reciprocity between self and world, between organism and environment, or between language and lived feelings. Meland's empirical realism understands experience in the latter sense.

---

[81] John Cobb, "Two Types of Postmodernism: Deconstruction and Process," *Theology Today* XLVII (July, 1990), 156. See, also, John Cobb, "In Defense of Realism," in Sheila Greeve Devaney, ed., *Theology at the End of Modernity* (Philadelphia: Trinity Press International, 1991), pp. 179-199. Nancy Frankenberry also speaks of the reciprocal, even codeterminate relation between language and experience in *Religion and Radical Empiricism*, pp. 136-144. In a similar vein, Marjorie Suchocki says, "My thesis is that language is indeed inescapably human, but that humans are inescapably a part of nature, and that therefore language is not alien to nature. Rather, language gives expression to nature as well as to history, disclosing interconnectedness as an essential element throughout all existence. Language, for all its opacity, is fundamentally connective, and therefore reflective of reality as a whole rather than human culture alone." "Deconstructing Deconstruction: Language, Process, and a Theology of Nature," *American Journal of Theology & Philosophy* 11 (May, 1990), 135. See, also, William Dean, *American Religious Empiricism*, chapters 2 & 4.

[82] Jerome Stone, *A Minimalist View of Transcendence* (Albany: SUNY, 1992), pp. 127-135.

Stone argues, on the one hand, there is little or no pure experience, and if there is such, it is of passing interest and little meaning. On the other hand, we are not out of touch with our world. Experience is not language all the way down. Through language we are in transaction with our world, not adrift in a linguistic sea. There are no anchors or sure foundations, but we do have fallible but helpful feelers, clues, and hints of a world. Therefore, Stone argues, experience is a transaction in which language and feelings are constituents of the transaction. There is no basic priority given to either one or the other.

Meland's view of experience is transactional in the sense that experience is a reciprocal interaction between the felt relations of lived experience and the frames of meaning and fundamental notions that route and interpret lived experience. There is a nonlinguistic dimension of experience, viz., the persistent feeling context, bodily acquaintance with extra linguistic realities and sensibilities. But language, especially through its frames of meaning and fundamental notions, which we have analyzed in this chapter, and culture, through its structure of experience, which we will analyze in the next chapter, are formative of experience. Knowledge is a transaction between lived experience and symbolization.

Indeed, of the large group of process theologians who employ Whitehead's understanding of the relation of experience and symbolization, Meland is the one who insists most persistently on the relational, transactional nature of lived experience and language, and develops the most sustained and elaborate interpretation of the interpenetration of experience and language. His empirical realism offers to the contemporary discussion a way to understand this codeterminate relation, and a middle way between the extremes of empirical foundationalism and linguistic relativism.

3

Experience and Culture: Meland as a Theologian of Culture

The dualism that characterizes most modern philosophy still reigns in much postmodern thought. The Cartesian separation of mind and matter, self and world, and the Kantian isolation of the numenal and phenomenal worlds, have developed into a linguistic dualism. These various dualisms all assume that self and world, history and nature, language and reality are isolatable from each other. The philosophical problem is how to get these two spheres together. These linguistic dualisms have challenged the Humean ideal that all knowledge is derived from experience. They, instead, have taken the Kantian line that perception of reality is impossible apart from conception. Much postmodern thought might even be called a kind of linguistic Kantianism. Linguistic Kantianism, to be sure, locates the organizing imagination in the structures of language instead of the structures of the mind, but it nevertheless assumes there can be no nonlinguistic perception of reality. In its extreme form, any world beyond the self and language becomes so vague or inaccessible that the dualism almost becomes a monism of language.

Likewise, liberal theology is dominated by the distinction between an objective and value-free world out there known by the senses, and a subjective and value-laden world in here known through speculation or feeling. A kind of Kantian linguistic dualism also continues to shape the assumptions and developments of several forms of postliberal theology. In postliberal theologies as diverse as those of Gordon Kaufman and George Lindbeck, there can be no direct apprehension or experience of God. God is a human construct either of the theological imagination or the linguistic conventions of the community. Both Kaufman and

Lindbeck are influenced by the neo-Kantian tendency to identify what is thought to be real with the way people construct it, so that both history and culture are simply a chain of linguistic worlds or interpretations, thereby collapsing natural history into human history.

Bernard Meland formulates a theology which moves beyond the objective/subjective split and any form of dualism between an isolatable self and world. He offers what William Dean calls "a third option, a value-laden historicism, beyond objectivism and subjectivism."[1] Meland sees the subject as internally related to the object. He develops what we might call a "naturalistic historicism," or what during his fifty years of religious inquiry he calls a theology of culture within a naturalistic framework. The human mind and spirit as well as the body must be understood as products of the processes of nature. Unlike some modern philosophies of culture and theologies, Meland does not presuppose a supernatural realm, be it Being, Mind, Noumena, or Spirit, which is fundamentally discontinuous with the natural order and supervenes, intervenes, or otherwise impresses itself upon the natural world. His theology of culture is rooted in "the realization that man is a child of the earth, a genuine product of the natural order, and therefore intimately akin to its life."[2]

I. NATURALISM AND EMERGENCE

Meland, however, is as severe a critic of philosophical materialism as of theological supernaturalism. He refuses to reduce nature to a deterministic mechanism. Nature includes depths and mysteries which are too readily excluded, or at least ignored, by earlier forms of naturalism. He seeks a "new naturalism," a "more discerning religious

---

[1] William Dean, *History Making History: The New Historicism in American Religious Thought* (Albany: SUNY, 1988), p. 45.

[2] Bernard Meland, "Mystical Naturalism and Religious Humanism," *The New Humanist* VIII (April-May, 1935), 72. For a broader discussion of naturalism, see John Herman Randall, Jr., "The Nature of Naturalism," ed. Yervant Krikorianin, *Naturalism and the Human Spirit* (New York: Columbia University Press, 1944), pp. 354-382, and Arthur Danto, "Naturalism," in *The Encyclopedia of Philosophy* V, ed. Paul Edwards (New York: Collier Macmillan, 1967), pp. 448-450, and Vergilius Ferm, "Varieties of Naturalism," in *A History of Philosophical Systems*, ed. Vergilius Ferm (Paterson, New Jersey: Littlefield, Adams, 1961), pp. 429-441. For a discussion of the relation of naturalism and religion, see Sterling Lamprecht, "Naturalism and Religion," in *Naturalism and the Human Spirit*, pp. 17-39.

naturalism."³ The goal that underlies Meland's philosophy of culture is to understand nature in such a way that spirit and culture embody a depth within the natural world instead of an intrusion of a supernatural world into the natural world.

His new naturalism hinges on shifts he detects in late nineteenth and early twentieth-century science which point to a revised concept of nature. The ideas of emergence in post-Darwinian evolution and of relativity in post-Newtonian physics suggest a conception of nature in which depth and mystery are acknowledged. Although the human being is fully a child of nature, nature is conceived to be richer and more complex than nineteenth-century materialism and mechanistic philosophies thought.

Charles Darwin is the chief representative of nineteenth century science. This particular form of science begins in the early seventeenth century with Francis Bacon and continues to develop during the eighteenth century through the influence of Isaac Newton. Meland describes this science as "environmentalism" or "functionalism." Nature is envisioned as a vast, mechanistic world order. As we investigate the immediate data at hand, we gain mastery over nature through measurement and prediction. In its Darwinian application, the human being is understood exclusively in terms of its functional adaptation to the changing environment. Mechanism and materialism are the fundamental characteristics of nature in this kind of science. Summarizing the Darwinian concept of nature and human beings, Meland says,

> The compulsion to attain controlled conditions conducive to precise measurement and prediction, carried the day, and thereby kept biology within the traditional scientific imagery of the seventeenth and eighteenth century physics. Thus the evolutionary theory formulated by Darwin presupposed the mechanical orderliness of nature, and adhered to a reading of the organism's external behavior of functional adaptation to environment.⁴

---

3 Bernard Meland, *The Realities of Faith* (New York: Oxford University Press, 1962), p. 130, and Bernard Meland, *The Reawakening of Christian Faith* (New York: Macmillan Company, 1949), p. 34. For a systematic formulation of the new naturalism in theology, see Bernard Loomer, "Neo-naturalism and Neo-orthodoxy," *Journal of Religion* XXVII (April, 1948): 79-91.

4 Meland, *Realities of Faith*, pp. 144-145.

An alternative interpretation of nature and the relation of human beings to nature appears in the late nineteenth and early twentieth centuries in the emergent theories of evolution. Emergent theory replaces mechanistic materialism with an organic view of evolution. While nature is the only realm of being there is, and is largely continuous, i.e., orderly and predictable, there is also an element of discontinuity in nature. Variations in nature are no mere chance response to a condition in the environment, as if unrelated parts were going their own way, conditioned only by incidental or accidental factors in the environment. Nature is "a whole-making activity." It produces new levels of reality resulting from novelty and differentiated structures. Nature is creative and produces patterns which cannot be derived in a mechanistic way from previous structures as a necessary and predictable result. "Emergence with structure" implies structural change and qualitative innovations which, as it were, set the one apart from the other, even as their continuity in nature is acknowledged.[5]

In addition, the new physics, which creates a whole new ethos of thought, challenges the Newtonian concept of orderliness which leads to mechanism. As the result of several new discoveries in physics, concepts such as complexity, depth, relatedness, unclarity, and indeterminacy begin to affect the concept of nature. In 1895 Roentgen discovers the X-ray, followed in the next year by the discovery of radioactive elements by Becquerel and the Curies. Soon thereafter Rutherford discovers the proton. The seemingly irreducible atom, instead of being a single entity, is actually a tiny planetary system, a merry-go-round in miniature. This is the beginning of a shift from an atomistic conception of reality to the ontological notion of the individual in community.

This shift in basic imagery in physics introduces at least three reconceptions into the new science. First, matter, or physical reality, is not multiple, tiny, autonomous pellets but a field of force. This means relationships loom as basic in the nature of reality. Relationships and organic unity are characteristics of reality. Second, relativity theory eliminates absolute space. The loss of a fixed base of reference with its replacement by a space-time continuum introduces the note of complexity into nature. "This loss of a fixed base of reference, and the recognition that there are many frames of reference from which

---

[5] Ibid., p. 130. See, also, Bernard Meland, *Higher Education and the Human Spirit* (Chicago: University of Chicago Press, 1953), p. 168.

phenomena or movements are observable, is what has contributed to a sense of disorder, if not chaos, in one's thinking as one contemplates this change."[6] Third, orderliness gives way to chance in quantum-theory and to the principle of indeterminacy. Science no longer pictures reality. It is no longer a discipline of absolute certainty. Physics becomes the science of statistical measurement applied to large masses, not individual phenomena or events. The whole Newtonian vision of order and causality shifts. In the new science, probability replaces the picturing of precise description.

The implication of this shift in scientific thought for the concept of nature is radical. The vision of order as such, even of ultimate order, as a venture of faith, is not challenged.[7] Rather, the concept of order is reconceived to include complexity and ambiguity, thereby qualifying the mechanization of nature which follows from the Newtonian version of order. In the new imagery nature is seen more as the "primal context" of humanity, including dimensions of reality characterized by a depth and a mystery not of our own making.[8]

Meland never abandons his assumption that nature is all there is. Rather, he claims that this reconception of nature sets humanity in a richer and more mysterious context. The Newtonian vision shrinks the concept of nature to a point at which humans must disavow any deeper realities if these are not subject to the clarity and precision of Newtonian imagery. There is a discrepancy between what the Newtonian world of thought can clearly perceive and analyze and the reality which underlies us but persistently evades our observation. The deeper realities are experienced in our feelings and emotions. Since these deeper dimensions

---

[6] Meland, *Realities of Faith*, p. 148.

[7] Ibid., pp. 150-155. See, also, Bernard Meland, *Secularization of Modern Cultures* (New York: Oxford University Press, 1966), p. 149.

[8] The phrase "primal context," one of Meland's frequently used diffuse neologisms, refers to the human intuition of nature in its deeper dimensions. "The context of human existence still presents to each of us a sense of something given, to which we are related in elemental ways. However far we develop and use our human powers, we do not slough off this elemental condition of being creatures of a Creative Process that is not made by us, not really influenced or altered by us in anything that our sciences or philosophies undertake. It is given as a primordial fact of our existence." Meland, *Secularization of Modern Cultures*, p. 117. See, also, Bernard Meland , *Faith and Culture* (London: George Allen & Unwin, 1953), p. 135, and Bernard Meland, "Alternative to Absolutes," *Religion in Life*, XXXIV (Summer, 1965), 345-347.

are not something outside of nature, they are present to scientific inquiry when it is open to the depth of nature and our relation to it through emotion. Meland's anthropology, then, depends primarily on the idea of emergence and on the idea of a "primal context" pointed to by shifts in imagery in modern science, especially biology and physics.

We also exist, however, within a specific context, namely, the human structure, which is the particular dimension or level at which creaturely existence occurs. Another way to state this is to say that human existence is one characteristic structure of life. This means that it, like all other structures, is unique among natural structures. "This fact, that we are in a sequence of evolving structures, and that we constitute one characteristic structure of life at a specific level of differentiation, implies both the range of our possibilities and the limitations under which we exist."[9] This emphasis leads Meland to stress the bodily basis of human life and its continuity with other previous levels of emergence. In the last analysis the psychophysical organism is the bearer of life and the basis of continuity with other life. The limitations of the human structure depend on its literal continuity or solidarity with antecedent forms of life: a bone structure, internal organs, a blood stream and vascular system, and so forth. This body life of humans is a miniature repository of much else that antedates the animal structure. The character of this bodily substructure determines the limits to which the human emergence may flower. Meland's favorite way of stating the continuity and creatural limitations of man is to say, "the sea water flows in our veins."[10]

The human dimension, however, is "an emergent with a visible structure of its own." One of the distinctive contributions of Meland's anthropology is his attempt to delineate this unique structure. This is especially important in a naturalistic anthropology which disavows any disjunction between humanity and nature. He achieves this by showing that the human organism is not only a repository of substances derived from antecedent forms; it is also dynamic, i.e., volatile and eruptive with psychic disturbances. The human, specifically, is the psychophysical organism which possesses unique sensory equipment that enables the emergence of higher levels of consciousness. It is the creature in which the "psychical thrust" is advanced to the degree that the organism

---

[9] Meland, *Secularization of Modern Cultures*, p. 119.
[10] Meland, *Faith and Culture*, p. 133.

releases an abundance of surplus stimuli.[11] The mechanism chiefly responsible for this advance is the cerebral cortex. The abundance of stimuli beyond the adaptive demands of the organism gives rise to levels of consciousness which enable us (1) to expand our moments of awareness into the past and the future, (2) to develop special capacities of relation to the environment, immediate and primal, and (3) to engage in imaginative expression. We are, in short, capable of diversified levels of consciousness.

The first level of consciousness is designated by Meland as "waking consciousness," the awareness of oneself and the world.[12] On the basis of surplus stimuli, we are able to transcend our routine habits of survival thinking. This capacity gives rise to reflection, the utilization of stored meanings in the understanding of perceived events. So equipped, we possess powers of observation which may be further refined, disciplined, and stimulated to achieve greater capacity for understanding and responding.

II. THE IDEA OF SPIRIT

Meland initially finds it difficult to appropriate the idea of spirit in his anthropology. One reason is that he consistently resists idealism, the major philosophical movement in nineteenth- and early twentieth-century European and American thought which attempts to rescue human dignity from the older naturalism and materialism by opposing nature and spirit. Meland refuses to set the human over against nature. He also refuses to see subjective experience and mental events as the primary characteristics of reality.[13] Supernaturalists and dualists think of spirit as a supermundane order of existence, and some social sciences reduce spirit either to an illusion, or to an idealization, as, for example, Durkheim, who says spirit is an emotion acting as a mass force to rout the control of reason.[14] Only as spirit is interpreted as a novel event within nature, and not as a special order of reality discontinuous with nature, is Meland prepared to talk about spirit at all.

---

11   Bernard Meland, *America's Spiritual Culture* (New York: Harper & Row, 1948), p. 81.
12   Bernard Meland, *Seeds of Redemption* (New York: Macmillan, 1947), p. 72.
13   Meland, *Realities of Faith*, pp. 86-87, 97, 127-129, 132, 197.
14   Meland, *Seeds of Redemption*, pp. 35-36, and *America's Spiritual Culture*, pp. 77-79.

Spirit is, first of all, an emergent within nature.[15] Whatever is distinctive about spirit depends upon and grows out of the creative processes of nature. To reinforce the emergent character of spirit, Meland suggests an analogy. Spirit has the same unique but dependent status as psychical activity has when it emerges from the physical, or as organic tendencies have when they break through the inorganic. This, however, does not imply reductionism. Spirit as an emergent, therefore, can be interpreted in terms of the lower structures only to a degree. It is an emergent in so far as it evolves as a distinctive quality of the psychical function of the natural processes.

The emergent quality of spirit becomes evident when we recognize that there are qualities of human being which appear to be features of human consciousness yet are not altogether characteristic responses of the human structure. These novel features are crucial in Meland's anthropology and set his concept of spirit apart from all idealistic and humanistic concepts of spirit. He considers rational and moral consciousness to be the representative features of human consciousness.

However, these do not exhaust the meaning of spirit and the spiritual nature of human beings. There are other responses of the organism which are not altogether representative of the human structure. These are responses which are human but are related to a "good not our own," to a resource or context beyond our own mental and moral consciousness. "Man moving toward spirit is the ethical and rational man awakened to *more subtle sensibilities* such that his very moral and intellectual concerns may be transformed into a more perceptive and discerning wisdom."[16]

Spirit points to our capacity to create a surplusage of meaning and to direct it toward reflective ends. It highlights our capacity to give qualitative meaning, which is, for Meland, the capacity to give sensitivity to force. Spirit is "the qualitative advance" in the human structure in which the data of experience are handled in a sensitive and imaginative way, namely, with an "overtone" and "surplusage" of meaning not available in other organisms. Spirit is, first, a fruition of the organism, and second, our fruition in terms of an overtone of sensitivity created by our distinctive capacities.

---

[15] Meland, *Faith and Culture*, p. 173, and *Higher Education and the Human Spirit*, p. 142.

[16] Meland, *Higher Education and the Human Spirit*, p. 125. See, also, *Faith and Culture*, pp. 160-175, and *Realities of Faith*, pp. 231-242.

This "surplusage" is available, above all, in moments of reflection and sensitive awareness. We participate in spirit when we respond to the surplusage attending the clearly given event. Although we share with lower organisms the ability for functional thought, for example, for survival thinking, humans distinctively are capable of imaginative response based on our awareness of the complexity of the relationships in our world. Our appreciative consciousness is our awareness that we are part of a much deeper context, the *more* of experience, and our sensitive response to the *more* of this context. The highest form of human consciousness, for Meland, then, is not rational or moral but *appreciative consciousness*. This is the quality of the human response that is creative of spirit.

The key to Meland's idea of spirit is his claim that the appreciative consciousness includes more than a quality of the human response. "The emergence in man of capacities to create and to respond to meanings at the level of spirit is not to be interpreted, necessarily, as an indication that spirit is synonymous with the fruition of man's nature."[17] Spirit includes a depth of relationship within the natural world not of our own making. This means that spirit has a double reference, one distinctively human and the other more inclusive of the context of the human dimension. These responses are among the more incalculable forces in human nature. They are not consciously created or forced. This fundamental point is what separates Meland's naturalism from humanism. Spirit as a quality of human response participates in spirit as a "depth of sensitivity" beyond the human structure.

Spirit, then, entails a dimension of sensitive relations beyond the human equation. It includes the "communal ground of being" or the "social matrix." These two phrases imply the social nature of reality from the perspective of a doctrine of internal relations. In his later writings Meland stresses spirit as the communal ground of all living. It is the realm of sensitivities, a "kind of womb or matrix out of which the waking life of individual persons emerges and in which individuals participate."[18] This emphasis, we must note, is of a piece with the realistic emphasis in his writings. Humans encounter in appreciative awareness, or simply in the act of living, the reality of spirit; we do not create spirit by sensitive awareness. Spirit is a "structure of sensitivity or

---

[17] Ibid., p. 124.
[18] Meland, *Realities of Faith*, p. 233.

a matrix of sensitivity which we have only limited powers as human beings to apprehend."[19] Nevertheless, we live by reason of it; we participate in it; we are concretions of this communal ground. The emphasis here is upon spirit as a gift of grace, a good not our own, a goodness that comes into the human structure and situation, rather than upon value humanly derived and conceived.

This depth of sensitivity in which a life is cast is only partially apprehended in intermittent moments of experienced relationships when the self and the not-self are brought into vital rapport. The limited human structure and response cannot fully apprehend, let alone comprehend, this dimension of sensitive relations designated by the word spirit. Spirit is a social reality not as much known as lived in. It is apprehended in moments of sensitive awareness, such as joy and sorrow, in acts of repentance and forgiveness, in freedom and in community, and especially in moments of wonder.[20] It is an operation of goodness which spontaneously and intermittently erupts into human relations and into the human character. Noticing these instances of spirit is more a matter of pointing, of appreciating, and of enjoying than of articulating.

Spirit enters our horizon when the appreciative dimension comes into play, that is, when in an act of perception our imaginative capacity is set loose. One grasps the working of spirit when the perceptive powers of a person elicit a deeper quality of meaning from within a group, or when a person's intellectual powers fix on some understanding of human nature and destiny, or when creative imagination and accomplishment are exemplified.[21] Above all, however, spirit is expressed and discerned in situations of extremity, in "fugitive instances within human behavior."[22] Meland refers here, specifically, to situations which bring us to a vivid awareness of the limits of selfhood, either through a sense of defeat, depletion, or despair, requiring the healing of forgiveness and a redemptive good; or through a heightening experience of appreciative awareness in which that which is not-self can be apprehended as in the I-Thou relationship.

---

[19] Ibid., p. 225.
[20] Meland, *Faith and Culture*, pp. 167-173.
[21] Meland, *Higher Education and the Human Spirit*, pp. 5-6. Other descriptions can be found in Meland *America's Spiritual Culture*, pp. 79-80, and *Higher Education and the Human Spirit*, pp. 126-129.
[22] Meland, *Faith and Culture*, p. 171.

Spirit, then, is in us and beyond us as human structures. Although Meland eschews any sort of dualism, his realism does envision a duality within human experience.

> It is this subtle distinction between responses in the human structure which are characteristically expressive of the human level of personal spirit and the qualities of spirit that appear in human relationships, intimating a good not its own, which suggests the duality of human nature. In effect it is a genuine discontinuity that is being observed here, laying bare the limits of the human consciousness as a creatural boundary, and at the same time, disclosing a horizon of mystery attending these human transactions.[23]

This duality of spirit is thoroughly naturalistic rather than idealistic. Kant and Hegel, Meland maintains, retain some elements of a faculty psychology which views the spiritual dimension as a range of meaning supervening upon the sensory organism. This is the basis in idealism for conceiving of the human spirit as preeminently the transcendental ego and for stressing the work of the mind in its conceptual form as our distinctive spiritual activity. In contrast, Meland, along with Bergson, James, and other radical empiricists, sees human spirit as "living, pulsating thought, partaking of sensory experience and participating in practical pursuits." Body and mind are not disparate; they interpenetrate, each deeply involved in the other. Indeed, for Meland, mind is the psychical level of activity of the body, or is "the body in its luminous, attentive, and cognitive moments."[24]

Decisive in Meland's idea of spirit is his emergent theory of evolution which stands in contrast to the Darwinian-Newtonian imagery. He insists that idealistic images of humanity depend upon the mechanism of Newtonian science. Since nature, so conceived, leaves no room for freedom and spirit, a realm of spirit as a supervening reality separated from nature is dictated, and an "ontology of freedom" as a quality of human being superseding the mechanistic determination of nature is required. In idealistic images events involving freedom and decision must be set over against the deterministic processes of nature. Freedom becomes the antithesis of determinism, the latter referring to the ontic structure of nature and the former referring to the distinctive ontic structure of human being.

---

[23] Ibid., p. 131.
[24] Meland, *Higher Education and the Human Spirit*, p. 37.

For Meland the notion of dimensions or levels of nature represented in emergent theory presents a view of nature in which human freedom and natural structure exist simultaneously. Freedom is possible in emergent thinking because mechanism and fixity are reduced to a minimum, while freedom and flexibility exist within a field or structure of relationship. Meland does not need an ontology of freedom which poses freedom as a distinctive ontic structure or quality above nature. "I am convinced that, apart from an ontology of freedom with its particular concept of transcendent mystery, or an ontology of spirit made possible through emergent theory of creativity, there is no way to seize upon this insight [of spirit] except as one resorts to supernaturalism."[25] Meland's metaphysics of spirit interprets freedom within a thoroughly naturalistic framework.

III. EXPERIENCE AND CULTURE

Although culture plays a predominant role in Meland's thinking, he devotes almost no effort to a formal definition of culture. The social scientific understanding of this term shapes Meland's thinking from his earliest days as a student in the Divinity School. It is clear, however, that his concept of culture is derived from his anthropology. The key to his anthropology is his view that the human being is simultaneously an individuated self and a participant in contexts of relationships. The minimum characterization of a person is that she is an event, that is, a concretion or actualization of meaning. To emerge in the world is to take on instantaneously relations with every other event. "The full implication of the doctrine of prehension is that community is a constituent of the individual.... Man is an event in a context of events."[26] Although Meland never plays down the importance of individuation in his anthropology, it is the human involvement in the "social nexus" that dominates his thinking.

As noted above, spirit refers a particular flowering of the individuated self and to the "social nexus" or the relational ground of all being in which we participate. There are, however, three *degrees* or *aspects* of human involvement in spirit. These are (1) experience, (2) culture, and (3) faith. The concept of culture, therefore, must be understood as one aspect of our participation in spirit. This section and the one which

---

[25] Meland, *Realities of Faith*, pp. 289-290, 295.
[26] Meland, *Faith and Culture*, pp. 127-128.

follows will explicate how Meland understands these three aspects of our participation in spirit.

Culture and faith must be subsumed under experience because experience is the primary means of participation in spirit. Experience is the primal source of all awareness.[27] Experience is the beginning of and the sole basis for any awareness and knowledge of ourselves and our world. This is what Meland primarily means when he says that his philosophy and theology are "empirical," in contrast to historical or ontological.[28] It is the facts of experience that are basic. But the *facts* of experience depend on a *concept* of experience.

What, then, does Meland mean by experience? A hint can be taken from his emergent and process framework. Experience does not refer to a particular kind of experience, as, for example, in classical liberalism, where experience refers to conscious experience.[29] Experience refers to the immediately given. But in Meland's view, following Bergson and James, the immediately given includes depths and relationships not recognized by earlier empiricists. Experience, therefore, includes our awareness of happenings and configurations of events that are deeper than conscious awareness.[30] The "perpetual flux" conveys much in experience *as lived* that cannot be readily conceptualized.[31] This sense of the *More* in experience that is lived, in contrast to restrictive portions of experience that are conceived, gives Meland the empirical ground for his idea of spirit.[32]

---

[27] Meland, *Realities of Faith*, p. 208.
[28] See Bernard Meland, "Introduction: The Empirical Tradition in Theology at Chicago," *The Future of Empirical Theology*, ed. Bernard Meland (Chicago: University of Chicago Press, 1969), pp. 6-13.
[29] Meland, *Faith and Culture*, p. 38. See Richard B. Brandt, "Empirical Theology," *Encyclopedia of Religion* (Paterson, N.J.: Littlefield, Adams and Company, 1964), pp. 248-249.
[30] Ibid., pp. 38ff. There is a shift in Meland's thought here away from his earlier view of experience which was dominated by Wieman's narrower identification of experience with what scientific method could clearly articulate. See, for example, *Reawakening of Christian Faith*, pp. vii ff. Also "The Root and Form of Wieman's Thought," in *The Empirical Theology of Henry Nelson Wieman*, ed. Robert Bretall (New York: Macmillan Company, 1963), pp. 44-63.
[31] Bernard Meland, "Can Empirical Theology Learn Something from Phenomenology?" in *The Future of Empirical Theology*, ed. Bernard Meland (Chicago: University of Chicago Press, 1969), pp. 285-286.
[32] This unusual use of the word "more" occurs frequently in Meland's later work. When italicized and/or capitalized, Meland intends to use it as a shorthand way to

For Meland conscious experience is not the key to the empirical orientation. Humans are aware of reality at a deeper and more contextual level. Experience is "not so much an interplay of explicit sensory responses as a bodily event which conveys to the living organism, in a holistic way, its rapport and participation in a nexus of relationships which constitutes its existence."[33] Experience is not immediately conscious, and much of it never becomes so. Much, if not most, remains below the surface of consciousness as bodily feeling or "duration," providing a substratum of organic acquaintance from which moments of conscious experience intermittently arise. Meland, like James, is sympathetic to mysticism as an effort to describe experience in this more primal sense. But he resists its dissipation into mysticism in favor of efforts to conceptualize experience at this level within appropriate limits.[34] The importance of this broader concept of experience, for Meland, is that it gives us an immediate and intimate, although not clarified, contact with the depth of relationships which he calls spirit. Conscious awareness and critical intelligence may introduce a margin of intelligibility. Further, the interplay of duration and critical intelligence may lift experience to a creative level where novelty and accumulative meaning become mutually qualifying. But moments of attention are rare and they partially distort.

Experience, however, is not merely duration. It is not only a sensory event at the level of bodily feeling. It is also a *structured* event. It is an ordering of responses within individual life. This "inner channeling" of events in individual memories, sensibilities, and bodily characteristics makes up the individual psyche. Experience, however, is not only a subjective event within the individual psyche. Experience is a happening in relationships and so also assumes a corporate character. This "outer channeling" of experience occurs in the form of social custom, precedent, legislation, moral and religious taboo and sanction, all of which are expressed through institutions, ceremonies, and public practices. Thus for Meland the social character of experience refers to all relationships,

---

refer to the depth of relationships in experience that are felt but not conceived without distortion or truncation. This word carries mystical overtones but cannot be equated with mystical experience because of his insistence that its reference has to do with everyday experience. Even though his usage must be criticized as dubious from the point of view of normal usage, Meland's intent and reference can be identified.

[33] Meland, *Realities of Faith*, p. 208.
[34] Meland, "Can Empirical Theology Learn Something from Phenomenology?" pp. 286, 296-297.

not only our relations to the primal context but also to culture. Experience includes the cultural shaping of experience.

It is important to note here, however, that Meland has more in mind than the conditioning of the individual psyche in the behaviorist's sense of that word when he refers to the "outer channeling" of experience. He means that the experiences and accumulated meanings of an entire group of people are structured and become an organic part of the experience of every individual psyche. "These inner and outer dimensions of accumulated valuations and meanings, together with the physical qualities that give them actuality and limited form, comprise the *structure of experience* that is operative in any period of time or generation within a given society."[35] This idea of the "structure of experience" occurs throughout Meland's writings and is the foundation of his concepts of humanity and culture and his view of the relations of religion and culture. The phrase has much of the overtone of the Jungian notion of the collective unconscious, although Meland is too much influenced by the process framework to adopt either the language or imagery of the Jungian perspective.

The structure of experience becomes a part of every psyche in so far as the individuated self participates in the accumulated meanings conveyed in the institutions and symbolization of a culture. Nevertheless, Meland again is referring to something more than conscious events. It is the "feeling-response formed into structural depths which give character to the conscious level of personality and culture."[36] The structure of experience is the persisting valuations of a culture which carry the net result of the feelings and valuations of the past into the present. It is the "enduring structural residue of the cultural history within its particular orbit of meaning."[37]

He finds the clues to elaborate this idea in both cultural anthropology, with its understanding of the importance of formative factors for the emergence of the cultural character of a people, and in the Whiteheadian notion of causal efficacy, wherein the past is seen to persist as a formative influence in the present.[38] His recurring example is the family; he contrasts the difference between a family history contained

---

[35] Ibid.
[36] Meland, *Faith and Culture*, p. 41.
[37] Meland, *Higher Education and the Human Spirit*, p. 12.
[38] Meland, *Faith and Culture* , p. 42. Also Meland, *Reawakening of Christian Faith*, pp. 72-73.

in letters, albums, and journals, with the family character possessed more hiddenly, born in the feelings, sufferings and joys of the family and living on in the character and disposition of the children. Similarly, every community and every culture carries in its structure of experience resources that can neither be easily explicated and described, nor extricated and destroyed.

The key to Meland's philosophy of culture, as it deepens, and therefore differs from, the contemporary discussion which identifies culture primarily with language, is that he thinks of culture as not only an objective structure of the life of a people but as a stream of life which bears certain valuations and sensibilities that are formative powers in the lives of participants.[39] This concept of culture explains why culture must be defined within the context of Meland's concept of experience. It is also the basis, as we shall see, for making culture a resource for faith instead of the antithesis of faith.

The immediate problem, however, is that by defining experience in such a comprehensive and relational way, the term culture seems to be indistinguishable from experience. In part this is acceptable to Meland because culture should never be seen as a mysterious entity existing apart from human experience. Experience is deeper and more inclusive of relations than sense experience reveals; it is broader, inclusive of more valuations than individuated subjective experience. To put it differently, experience is structured in such a way as to include not only individual patterning (inner channeling) but also that which is inherited from other living persons (external channeling or the structure of experience).

Nevertheless, culture can be distinguished from experience. Culture is a particularized fruition of humanity. Specifically, culture is a human fruition manifested in the ordered way of life of a group. Although this statement is not a definition of culture, it summarizes the major characteristics of Meland's concept of culture. (1) Culture is, first of all, an expression of the human spirit. Fruition includes all of the psychical and mental responses, individual and corporate alike, as being expressive of the human spirit. (2) Culture is manifested in an ordered way of life. Culture is expressed in the imaginative activities and creations of a people. It is embodied in their arts and crafts, their architecture, furniture and furnishings, their customs and designs, their

---

[39] This way of stating the concept has been suggested by Daniel Day Williams, "The Theology of Bernard Meland," *Criterion*, III (Summer, 1964), 4.

literature, their public and private ceremonies. It is expressed in their formative ideas, their habits of eating, their modes of livelihood. (3) Culture is the ordered way of life of individuals in community. It is composed of human creativity, decisions, and judgments which form a group consciousness. It is manifest in the corporate, qualitative manifestations of the human psyche expressed through a community.

The point is that for Meland culture includes group consciousness and distinguishable communities as well as creative expression. Specifically, culture is the total complex of human growth that has occurred within "a clearly defined orbit of human association."[40] It is a society perceived in terms of its total human expression wherein the accumulative qualities of lived history and experience are made vivid and distinctive. Meland admits the lines of demarcation between these societies are not fixed and enduring. Nevertheless, there is sufficient durability of large and small blocks of society throughout history to enable one to say that there have existed "clearly defined orbits of human association" in which distinctive and pervading qualities of experience have developed.

Meland makes a distinction between culture and civilization. Civilization is a particular stage of any culture. Thus culture exists even though the stage of history designated as civilization has not been reached. Civilization describes societies which "partake of something like a large generality of understanding."[41] This implies the access of individuals to reflection on the social process and a critical sense in matters of judgment. This freedom leads to a concern for human well-being. Civilization also implies some normative idea about the "fulfillment" of cultures. Fulfillment is defined as the creation of institutions, techniques, and social processes which channel stimuli into a rich variety of spiritual expressions, promote an abundance of psychic growth, and aid the culture in creating an organic unity of spirit.

A "spiritual culture" is the qualitative life and aspiration rising out of a people who seek to bring their common life to a fulfillment which has significance and enduring worth.[42] Although the character of the psychic response, and its degree of sensitivity, varies from culture to culture,

---

[40] Bernard Meland, "How Is Culture a Source for Theology?" *Criterion*, III (Summer, 1964), 13.
[41] Meland shares this concept with Alfred North Whitehead. See Alfred North Whitehead, *Modes of Thought* (New York: Free Press, 1966), chap. vi.
[42] Meland, *America's Spiritual Culture*, p. 90.

and, thus, no culture deserves to be neglected in its outreach of the human spirit, some cultures may deserve more attention than others when we focus on the fullness of the divine working in the human structure.[43] Meland's introduction of evaluative criteria raises the issue of the relativity of cultures, a question we will examine in detail below.

IV. FAITH AND MYTH

Faith is the third aspect of the human participation in spirit. Daniel Day Williams calls Meland's emphasis on faith after he returned to the Divinity School in 1945 the "one significant and decisive break" in Meland's thought.[44] In his earlier writings Meland represents a cosmic mysticism, or, as he calls it, a "mystical naturalism." What humans seek in religion is a sense of "at-homeness in the universe,"[45] or a "sense of belonging to a vast, cosmic neighborhood in which many forms of life seek fulfillment."[46] Although there is a sense in which this mystical theme persists throughout all of his writings in one form or another, from *The Seeds of Redemption* onward the emphasis shifts toward faith as a distinctive resource and as a distinctive mode of appropriation within the mystical response. The concept of faith carries more of a sense of the novelty of judgment and grace within lived experience, something more of the distinctive character of faith as a resource and response, than his earlier mystical naturalism conveys. The emergence of this theme is evident in the titles of three of his late books, *The Reawakening of Christian Faith, Faith and Culture,* and *The Realities of Faith*.

We may better understand Meland's idea of faith and its relation to culture if we review the possible alternative views he sees. Faith may be understood in a way that identifies it with the whole evolving structure of experience and its cultural expression. It may also be defined as a thing apart, a magnetic pull from a transcendent source, altering life and directing it toward higher fulfillment than either experience or culture can provide. Or, it may be seen to convey both immanent and

---

[43] Meland, *Faith and Culture*, pp. 84-85.
[44] Williams, "The Theology of Bernard E. Meland," p. 5.
[45] Bernard Meland, *Modern Man's Worship: A Search for Reality in Religion* (New York: Harper and Brothers, 1934), p. 141. See, also, "At Home in the Universe," ed. Thomas Kepler, *Contemporary Religious Thought* (Nashville: Abingdon Press, 1941), pp. 284-289.
[46] Meland, "Mystical Naturalism," p. 73.

transcendent characteristics. Meland chooses the latter, although it must be noted that even here transcendence is conceived within an immanent framework, not in terms of a Kierkegaardian supernaturalisim or total discontinuity.

Faith is, first of all, in its immanent aspect, a primordial, psychic energy related to the life process. It is a condition of trust which comes to dominate the psychical experience of a person and a people. In its minimum and most innocent form, faith is simply the will or capacity to live; in its barest manifestation it is wonder and expectancy. "This is not even a conscious intent. It is deeply organic, pervading the whole organism."[47] This sense of wonder is not just a vacuous outreach toward an empty Nothingness, but an expectation and somewhat apprehensive openness to what is envisaged in the relational ground. Trust, connoting a psychical resolution of the issues raised by wonder and expectancy, is a more settled form of faith.[48] In this elemental sense of trust, faith is given as a component of the creation. No life is possible without this condition. At this point, though, faith has no content. It is a preconscious orientation of the psyche, the "psychical pitch of the organism."[49] It is our initial intimation of context and participation in the relational ground, the reality of spirit.

The threat to this primordial condition, however, is constant. Apart from the disturbances of self-consciousness, faith might persist in the sheer act of existing apart from conscious appreciation. However, self-consciousness and individuation, marks of spirituality, are the disruption and falling away from this elemental condition. Individuation is, in humans, the heeding of the demands of the senses, appetites, and concerns, "the heeding of varying degrees of assertiveness and egocentricity."[50] Therefore, our spiritual emergence is also the disruption of the primordial trust given in existence within the communal ground. Meland identifies this with original sin, which, like birth and death, is part of the life span of every creature.[51] The nature of the human drama is tragedy. Original sin announces the tragic flaw in human life at the same time it affirms the good in human life. Self-emergence is inevitable and is sinful because of the fact that all selves exist in a nexus of

---

[47] Meland, *Realities of Faith*, p. 215, *Faith and Culture*, p. 65.
[48] Meland, *Faith and Culture*, p. 22.
[49] Meland, *Higher Education and the Human Spirit*, p. 175.
[50] Meland, *Realities of Faith*, p. 216.
[51] Meland, *Faith and Culture*, p. 142.

relationships, relationships with humans and other creatures, and relationships with the creative ground which is in God. There is the hazard in self-awareness of becoming oblivious to the communal ground, or even alienated from it.[52]

The second "dimension" or "level" of faith Meland designates as transcendent. Faith is also a gift of grace. It is a resource which reclaims human beings from the alienations of self-emergence. It is *an energy moving out of the creative and communal ground to restore us to an awareness of and responsiveness to "the good which is not our own."* Faith is the power of the New Creation to prompt a conscious commitment to the creative ground which claims us.

Meland refers to reclaiming faith as "faith in its mature state." [53] The depth of the primordial trust is reclaimed. The faith that is a gift of grace is the transcendent aspect of primordial faith. By transcendence Meland means that faith "supervenes our human structure."[54] He does not mean that faith supervenes nature as our creative and communal ground. He means simply that the limits of our human structure would be impotent to partake of the higher sensitivities of spirit within the communal ground were there not given to us as an act of grace a freedom and power to partake "of the creative ground and the redemptive life working simultaneously to impart to us a new freedom."[55] Faith as transcendent comes into our human structure as a renewed condition of trust and openness to the sensitive order of spirit.

---

[52] Meland, *Realities of Faith*, p. 216. This reference from *The Realities of Faith* seems to be contradictory from the preceding one from *Faith and Culture* in that the former speaks of the actualization of sin in every self-conscious person while the latter speaks only of the "hazard" of sin. Meland's intent is similar to Reinhold Niebuhr's and Paul Tillich's when Niebuhr speaks of the inevitability but not (ontological) necessity of sin. See Reinhold Niebuhr, *The Nature and Destiny of Man* (New York: Charles Scribner's Sons, 1941) I, pp. 251-260. Tillich speaks similarly in his systematic theology, although there appears to be more ontological necessity than Niebuhr wants to accept. For a discussion of the relation of freedom and ontological necessity in this interpretation of the meaning of original sin, see the discussion between Niebuhr and Tillich on this issue in Reinhold Niebuhr, "Biblical Thought and Ontological Speculation in Tillich's Theology," pp. 216-229, and Tillich's reply, pp. 342-345, both in Charles Kegley and Robert Bretall, eds., *The Theology of Paul Tillich* (New York: Macmillan, 1952).
[53] Meland, *Realities of Faith*, p. 217.
[54] Ibid., p. 182; see, also, *Faith and Culture*, p. 45.
[55] Ibid., p. 228.

However, transcendent faith is a dimension of primordial faith. It is ontologically continuous with creation. Thus, although Meland employs the idea of transcendence, its meaning is determined by a revised doctrine of immanence.[56] Immanence is determinative for both aspects of faith, not vice versa as it is in neoorthodox theology. However, immanence has to be reconceived by postliberal theology in the light of twentieth-century experience and thought. It can no longer be seen in a wholly rational and orderly way, as in the Hegelian doctrine of internal relations, or in a wholly continuous way, as in the older liberalism. Instead, "immanence simply presupposed that there are structures within the reach and recognition of man which disclose God's working in some form and to some degree."[57] Meland's postliberal immanence acknowledges discontinuities within the continuities of experience. The term transcendence designates that discontinuity. The "break," however, is *within* nature, not from outside of nature into it. The discontinuity is within the continuities of a communal ground and internally related world. Thus, the notion of ontological continuity, whether in the strong doctrine of internal relations, as in absolute idealism, or in the weaker doctrine, as in Meland's naturalistic emergence, is decisive for his concept of faith.

Faith is also a cultural energy, or, more precisely, it is a psychical energy released into the cultural stream. The relation of faith and culture, however, is more intimate than this statement indicates. Meland sees faith, as we said, as a gift of grace. As such it is a dimension of spirit which transcends culture. It issues forth out of the matrix of sensitivity that is the life of God expressing itself through the communal ground. However, the emphasis of the later writings is also upon the interpenetration of faith and culture. Culture is impossible without faith in so far as the most meager assertion of creative experience, out of which culture arises, depends upon the elemental condition of trust in the human psyche. Faith is the "formative ground" of all valuations,

---

[56] The shift in Meland's thought was away from generalized religious experience to the theme of the transcendence of the Christian faith. The motif of the former does not change, however, in that the relation to transcendence is one participated in by way of internal relations to all the concrete aspects of life around us. The idea of transcendence, therefore, is not one of separation between God and the world, but is the transcendence, as Clark Williamson says, "of a communal ground of being over all individuated existence which arises from it." Clark Williamson, "The Road to Realism," *Criterion* III (Summer, 1964), 23.

[57] Meland, *Faith and Culture*, pp. 37-38.

individual and corporate. In this sense it is a social and cultural energy. Likewise, faith is inseparable from culture in the sense that primordial faith needs formation and expression in order to be an available human resource beyond elemental vitalities. Without symbolic shaping by language, faith would persist only as an elemental vitality.

Faith and culture are further inseparable because the psychical energy of faith is released into the communal stream. The resources of faith, *both* in their primordial and redemptive aspects, become a part of the very structure of experience of a particular people.[58] The energy of faith issues in certain repeated valuations and responses of Western culture, such as responsibility, forgiveness, reconciliation, and love. These valuations and responses are not only individual but become communal in the sense that they are shared by the people in their life together and are transmitted as an inheritance from one generation to another. Culture, then, in its structure of experience, not only witnesses to but bears the realities of faith in both its immanent and its transcendent dimensions as much as religious institutions do. Faith persists among a people as a protoplasm. The sensibilities created by the response of faith are as much a part of the experience of the culture as a whole as they are of a particular religious institution. Faith, therefore, is both a primal response and a product. Its psychical energy and its cultural sensibilities are both part of the response of the individual.

The distinctive sensibilities of a culture born within its structure of experience form the *ethos* of a culture. Ethos refers to the character, sentiments, and disposition of a community. Drawing upon the insights of cultural anthropology and philosophy, Meland maintains that the people of any particular culture participate in these valuations and sentiments of the culture through the *mythos* of the culture.[59] Myth, contrary to the assumption and project of older liberalism, should not be — indeed, cannot be — disavowed because it uniquely reflects dimensions of the deepest life of a culture which can be neither expressed nor participated in in any other way. Although he distinguishes between *mythos* and myth, on the one hand, and

---

[58] Meland, "How Is Culture a Source for Theology?" 12.

[59] For example, the *mythos* of the covenant and of the cross persist in our culture as bearers of such deeply laid sensibilities as responsibility and as forgiveness and reconciliation. These are embodied not only in specific religious institutions to be shared by people of the cultus, but are embodied also in cultural forms of art, literature, song, and shared by the entire culture.

mythologies, on the other, the latter being expendable, Meland maintains consistently that myth is necessary to the healthy functioning of any culture.[60] He considers the recovery of myth to be one of his significant revisions of liberalism and contributions of a postliberal theology.

Myth is a universal human response providing the deeper orientation and bearing the ultimate insight of a people. It is the patterning of meaning and valuations imaginatively projected through drama and metaphor. Its function is to express the perceptive truths of the historic experiences and sensibilities of a people. Because these truths lie deeper than consciousness and are susceptible to only a margin of intelligibility or rationalization, myth is the only way they can be borne. Thus the deepest function of myth is to convey to conscious experience something of the depth of awareness in the experience of a people which would otherwise lie only at the level of bodily feeling. Even when definitive meanings can be given to myth, its significance is broader, for it bears the feeling and living force of the sensibilities of a people.[61] However transitory and expendable specific mythologies may be, the shaping of the human psyche by the *mythos* or myth is more enduring. As the persisting expression of the primal responses of a culture, not only in terms of language but also of sensibilities of thought and psychical orientation and expectation, myth is not expendable.[62]

Although the mythic response is a universal human response, the content of myths varies from culture to culture because the psychical responses vary from culture to culture. The human psyche, being formed by the valuational responses arising from the structure of experience, takes on the characteristic responses of the experience of a particular culture. Psychic life, like vegetable life, partakes of a "regional character" that can never be completely obscured or canceled out.

The Christian *ethos* and *mythos* have been the formative influences in shaping the sensibilities of Western culture. The "mode of existence, the bent of mind, the direction of human outreach in Western society, hence

---

[60] Bernard Meland, "Analogy and Myth in Postliberal Theology," *Perkins School of Theology Journal* XV (Winter, 1962), in eds. Delwin Brown, Ralph James, and Gene Reeves, *Process Philosophy and Christian Thought* (Indianapolis: Bobbs Merrill, 1971). For example, the New Testament can be deliteralized to correspond to our world view, but not demythologized in the sense of doing away with the crucial symbols of the cross, resurrection, etc.

[61] Meland, *Reawakening of Christian Faith*, p. 69.

[62] Meland, "Analogy and Myth in Postliberal Theology," p. 125, and *Secularization of Modern Cultures*, p. 125.

the motifs in art forms as well as his fundamental notions in thought,"[63] have been shaped by the Christian myth. The primal document is the Bible. The primary intuitions and perceptions that have gone into shaping the human psyche in the West first appeared there. What is crucial is not the mythologies or poetry or metaphors but the motifs or primal notions, the seminal perceptions conveyed there. The "root metaphor" of this *mythos* is the covenant relationship, a relation of faithfulness and freedom. In a similar way such motifs or metaphors as redemption, forgiveness, cross, resurrection, and love have shaped the Western view of the nature and destiny of humanity and the world.

The thrust of much of Meland's analysis of the relation of faith and culture is the argument that a culture cannot extricate itself from its myth, and that attempts to do so both betray how deeply laid the influence is and result in a great loss to the vitality and stature of the culture. He is concerned, especially in his later writings, to point out the impact and significance of the deeply laid, historical shaping of the sensibilities each culture, and to suggest that the ethos and mythos persists long after individuals within a culture have consciously disavowed it, or sought to counter its shaping within that culture.

Secularization is the attempt to disregard this deeper context of a culture, to "rout all reference to generative sources in feeling or awareness, out of which the symbols of a culture arise."[64] However, the psychical dimension of faith persists within the structure of experience from age to age, affecting people's elemental responses and giving direction to what is basically valued and affirmed. In that sense we cannot speak of a postChristian era or culture in the West.

> My method, I am inclined to believe, rests precariously upon the assumption that our culture cannot extricate itself from the Judaic-Christian *mythos*, any more than any existent event can relinquish its past as it lives on in the shaping of its present structure and dynamics; or, to speak of human events, as one lives on in the present shaping of one's individual psyche and structure of experience.[65]

---

[63] More specific and detailed content of this *mythos* is spelled out in *Reawakening of Christian Faith*, p. 79.

[64] Bernard Meland, "Alternative to Absolutes," *Religion in Life*, XXXIV (Summer, 1965), 351. Also, *Realities of Faith*, p. 63, and *Secularization of Modern Cultures*, especially chaps. i, iv, and v.

[65] Meland, "How Is Culture a Source for Theology?" 18.

The task of the postliberal theologian is to reappropriate the mythos from sheer mythology, not by literalizing it or by rationalizing it (that is, translating it into literal philosophical categories or psychologizing its meaning, as some earlier and some recent liberal theologians have done) but by giving it a meaning consonant with the depth of insight conveyed therein using the available imagery of our era. The theological task is to recover or to "restore of stature" the Christian witness which has been lost to the church and society through cultural accommodation, sentimentalization, and the attrition that comes through secularization. The theologian does this by attempting to interpret the Christian myth in light of the best imagery available today, namely, for Meland, through the insights of cultural anthropology, depth psychology, emergent evolution, and the new metaphysics. Instead of reappropriating (he called it "reawakening" in one of his books) Christian doctrine, however, his concern was to reappropriate the deeper themes of the Christian faith which are conveyed in an ethos and mythos which persists not only in the churches and in individuals but also in the culture.

Culture, therefore, is a "source" for theology in the sense that it is "a vortex of witness," along with the church (cult) and individual experience. More properly, it is a "medium" for the primary resource for theology which is the dimension of ultimacy within the Christian *mythos*. The source (i.e., the primary datum, perceived in culture, cult, or individual experience) is the set of realities of faith which speak through these data. "Each of these vortices points beyond itself to the living Christ as the continuing work of the New Creation, revealing the Infinite Structure of grace and judgment in each generation of history."[66] Therefore, if the phrase "source of theology" is applicable to any datum, it applies substantively to "the dimension of ultimacy within history and within present immediacies," and formally to "this revelatory event" of Christ. The object of theology is the dimension of ultimacy within culture, cult, and individual experience. Gerhard Spiegler points out that in this sense one cannot speak of Meland as a cultural theologian.[67]

Nevertheless, there is a sense in which culture is a "source" for Meland's theology. He maintains that "ultimacy and immediacy traffic together." This implies that culture not only shapes our encounter with ultimacy through its symbolic language, or even creates our sense of

---

[66] Meland, *Fallible Forms and Symbols*, p. 158.
[67] Gerhard Spiegler, "Ground--Task--End of Theology in the Thought of Bernard E. Meland," *Criterion*, III (Summer, 1964), 35.

encounter with ultimacy through its reservoir of language, as some postliberal theologians emphasize, but also bears ultimacy within its vitalities and forms. Grace is an energy *within* the structure of experience, not simply outside of it to be inserted into culture through the medium of linguistic rules. "What I should like to do is to argue that the culture makes a concrete contribution to theological understanding and thus, in a way, to tantalize you with the suggestion that the culture may be more substantive as a source for theology than I have acknowledged."[68]

V. RELATIVITY AND RELATIVISM

In his late writings Meland responds explicitly to the problem of historicism and relativism. He does this by showing how ultimacy and relativity can be reconceived together within a naturalistic framework, which finally relocates the idea of relativity beyond cultural relativism. For Meland the idea of relativity refers to two distinctive ideas simultaneously, namely, the limitation of all natural structures, and the depth and complexity of relationships within nature.

Meland notes the progressive modesty about ultimate claims that has overcome historicists and relativists. One example of this is the abandonment in contemporary science of "picture models," which correspond to an ultimate orderliness of reality, in favor of "disclosure models," which frequently dispel the mystery of reality through their disclosures of an order within ultimate mystery. This, however, is only one example of the "principle of limitation" which is applicable to every natural structure. Every human response and every field of inquiry is subject to the principle of limitation. Among humans this means we are limited in vision and understanding to what is available to the human structure, under conditions that influence and shape that structured experience.

This limitation includes, first of all, the limitations of finitude or creatureliness. There is a structure, physical and psychical, within which all human responses, perceptions, and conceptions take place. Limitation includes, also, the limitation of the cultural orbit of meaning which prepares the mind and the psyche within a given area of human association to receive and react to occurrences in specific and characteristic ways. This relative perspective that conditions scientific

---

[68] Meland, "How Is Culture a Source for Theology?" 16.

inquiry and understanding affects and conditions all religious responses and understanding as well. In reviewing Schubert Ogden's study of Rudolf Bultmann, Meland says of their claim that philosophy can understand and interpret the New Testament in universal, culturally unlimited concepts, "Does this not overlook the fact that all thought occurs in a cultural matrix?"[69] The fact of cultural history in every religion looms large, not only in the description of its history but also in the assessment of its witness of faith. Meland, then, agrees with historicists and relativists about the limitation of perspective and the conditioning character of that perspective on every group and every individual. The concrete religions, in so far as they are creatural and cultural responses, partake of this cultural relativity.

The problem of relativity, however, is deeper than the acknowledgement of creatural and cultural limitations. The issue is the nature of relativity itself. What does the "stance of multi-relationships," that is, the notion of depth and complexity in experience itself and the insight of recent relativity theory in physics, contribute to the problem of relativity and ultimacy? Meland is convinced that many relativists have not faced the thoroughgoing implications of their relativism because their Kantian orientation, through the dissociation of humanity from nature by way of an ontology of freedom, provides a "hiding-place" from the deeper truth of relativity. The concept of cultural relativity has been helpful for them in showing the relativity of religious institutions, values, and beliefs, and has been fruitful for purposes of social and theological criticism. But cultural relativism has never been a thoroughgoing relativity, for in its theological expressions it projects an abstraction of pure Christian faith— in a decision in faith—which makes faith devoid of cultural dependence and so vetoes the historicist implications of cultural relativity. Through an ontology of freedom and a leap of faith, they think they are able to exempt something from the thoroughgoing implications of relativity.

> This illusion stems from an inadequate grasp of the implications of relativity itself, and from a persistence of Absolutism that has not really come to terms with the current judgment of relativity theory upon the Kantian a priori and the mathematical assumption underlying it.[70]

---

[69] Meland, "Analogy and Myth in Postliberal Theology," p. 125.
[70] Meland, *Realities of Faith*, p. 166.

In Meland's view two recent movements deepen the implications of relativity and so eliminate all hiding places. One is the Jamesian and Whiteheadian notions of the concrete or contextual nature of all reality; the other is the notion of the field of force in modern relativity theory in physics. Both of these perspectives eliminate an absolute standing place and an absolute point beyond a relative context. However, at the same time both offer a deeper concept of the relative context and a means of conceiving ultimacy within a relative context without reverting to the transcendental ego or faith as a way to escape the relativity of history.

In radical empiricism depth and complexity replace clear and distinct ideas or the absolute standpoint of the transcendental ego. Our frames of meaning account for only part of the reality we feel or experience in more organic ways. The facts of experience reach beyond our mental creations to include the concrete context in which all thinking and living are cast. For Meland, "concrete" does not mean a fragmentary disclosure of the universal, but a unique and decisive disclosing of reality in all its fullness and glory as an event. Thus experience conveys the plural and relative character of all reality. "Existing, as a succession of lived experiences, participates in a context that may have far more to commend it as an ultimate stream of passing events than our forms can convey."[71] Relativity experienced and understood as reality in its concrete occasions of interrelationship, as the contextual configuration of events, deepens the notion of relativism. There is no dissociation of humanity from nature, and nature reveals in human experience the contextual (relative) character of all reality.

The deeper implications of relativism, both in its critical and constructive dimensions, are also found in the modern theory of relativity in physics. Relativity theory implies there is no fixed base of reference anywhere within spatial-temporal existence. Kant's transcendental a priori, upon which the dissociation of the human mind from nature rests, presupposes the ultimacy and absoluteness of Euclidean geometry, namely, a fixed point. Modern physics, however, recognizes that alternative geometries and perspectives are possible and in fact underlie relativity theory.

> More and more one is made aware within this perspective that the transcendental escape into an ideal moral subjectivity, immune from involvement in cultural relativity, is not an available option to the relativist

---

[71] Meland, "Alternative to Absolutes," 347.

who clearly understands its implications. For one can sustain this option only as one insists upon making absolute the geometrical perspective in the way that the Kantian a priori does. Any effort to insulate theological or moral thinking from the ambiguities of its own involvement in culture and in the physical universe must be doomed to failure. And any purist effort toward this end must be seen to be illusory.[72]

However, the contextual character of reality, described by radical empiricists as the *more* or "depth in duration," implying a notion of relativity as interrelatedness, is supported by modern physics in its idea of reality as a field of force. Mutual inherence, so to speak, goes all the way down. Although there is no absolute standing point and no Absolute supervening reality, there is a dimension of ultimacy *within* the context and the field of force that permits Meland to be a more thoroughgoing relativists than the Kantian relativists who exempt the transcendental ego or faith and who exempt the Absolute from relativity. At the same time he retains an "ultimacy" that "transcends" the materialistic and reductionistic readings of all contexts.

How, then, does Meland resolve the problem of ultimacy and relativity? With respect to religion and culture, he insists that the fact that one acknowledges the cultural conditioning of any religious faith does not argue that the religion is simply a product of the culture, i.e., a pious echo of cultural mores. Although to a large degree the religions are just that, every religious faith also speaks out of the depths of ultimacy within the interplay of cultural activities. Thus, in the historical religions, "ultimacy and immediacy traffic together."[73] To accept relativity, even the "metaphysical relativity" implied in physics as well as the cultural sciences, is not to forego ultimacy. We participate, "as creatures, in the ultimacy of the Creative Passage that underlies and carries forward all our humanity, and, in our several ways, we bear witness to this

---

[72] Meland, *Realities of Faith*, 167.
[73] Meland, *Secularization of Modern Cultures*, p. 151. The words Absoluteness and ultimacy both appear in Meland's writings, the former to be rejected, the latter to be appropriated. Although he never defines either word, by the former he refers to a realm of reality which is unconditioned by (unrelated to) the natural world. This realm could exist in this world or outside of it. But it is unaffected by the conditionedness implied in both cultural and metaphysical relativity. The word ultimacy, however, refers to a dimension or quality of the natural world. It has the connotation of givenness and of finality, but it is not something that exists as or in an unconditioned realm.

primordial Ground of our being."⁷⁴ The relative context itself, not the moment of escape from the relative context or the invasion from outside into relative context, bears a witness to ultimacy, to an ultimate measure and an ultimate goodness not our own. Relativity implies a disavowal of ultimacy only on the assumption of a fixed order of things and an absolute standpoint.⁷⁵ Relativity, instead, means that every concrete situation bears witness to a dimension of ultimacy peculiar to the interplay of circumstances and limitations that attend any concrete event. There is no immediacy in history or experience without its ultimate depth and reference. This is a point which the theory of relativity in physics makes clear, whereas cultural relativism does not. Relative means "contextual" and "limited"; it also means "decisive," in the sense that in this time and place reality in its rich fullness has "spoken." The depth of reality is present in every concrete event. It cannot be separated or clarified, but it persists as a lure and as a measure.

Meland, then, is not skeptical about the possibility of transcending one's own culture in the sense that one can participate in and witness to realities of faith that are deeper than conditioned cultural events. The Creative Passage is a given and a transcending depth of all reality. Although there is no absolute or unconditioned standpoint or reference, creativity within the human structure and awareness of a more ultimate level of sensitivity in experience and culture enable humans to transcend the limitations of their culture. Meland retains no notion of "the Absolute" or "the Unconditioned," because ultimacy is a dimension within nature, not a dimension or reality which touches finitude like a line touches a circle yet is beyond it. In that sense transcendence has no reference to any reality or quality of reality beyond finitude and history.

Cultural interpretations and assessments of experience are limited and thus fallible, just as the human structure is limited and thus fallible. Yet within these limitations and fallibilities, cultural creativities are subject to "a more ultimate level of sensitivity," and are therefore subject to a critical response. We participate in limited cultural forms, but we participate also in an ultimate dimension of depth and context that underlies and carries forward our humanity. "In this we are made more than victims of our illusions, or pawns of our cultural circumstances, for we have access to a perspective upon experience which compels self-

---

⁷⁴ Ibid., p. 162.
⁷⁵ Meland, *Realities of Faith*, p. 163.

criticism and stimulates our encounter with those whose experience differs from our own."[76] This ultimate oneness in our humanity, and this common indebtedness to the source of our being are the bases for transcending the limitations of the religions, and together they form the base for an encounter between the religions.

The question that remains at the conclusion of this analysis of Meland's philosophy of culture as it contributes to the solution of the problem of cultural relativism is whether he escapes a relativist position in the end? This issue is never dealt with explicitly by Meland. It is unclear throughout his constructive theology what is his final view about historicism and relativism. In so far as Meland explores this problem, he comes close to a position which can only be described as a cultural relativism of his own. Although he is a critic of thoroughgoing relativism, he implies that the final criteria for theological judgment are indeed cultural.

In a non-trivial sense one can say that his final criterion is experience. In this sense he is an "empirical theologian" who attempts to transcend a thoroughgoing historicist and relativist perceptive. Yet in a thoroughly postmodern sense, experience, culture, and faith are so interrelated in his thought that experience and faith are inseparable from culture in their very meaning. He is much closer to a postliberal view of experience, culture, and history than to a classical liberal view. In an essay written for the conference celebrating his retirement from the Divinity School of the University of Chicago, he is more explicit about the relativistic perspective as a determining element in his theological criteria than ever before. He is clear that the *mythos* of his particular culture is the decisive criterion in his own theological method. The *mythos*, to be sure, witnesses to the dimension of ultimacy—the object of theology—in human experience. But when the question of criteria of theological judgments is raised, the Christian *ethos* and *mythos* is decisive *because* it is the dominant *mythos* of our particular culture.

Meland recognizes that in Western culture the Christian myth (covenant) and the Platonic myth (logos) are both available. But he explicitly chooses the Christian *mythos* as the final point of reference instead of the Platonic for his theological method. Why? On what basis or according to what criterion does he select the Christian over the Platonic myth? The reason is not the appeal to biblical authority or

---

[76] Ibid, p. 162.

norms, or to the rational necessity of the Christian *ethos*, or even an appeal to experience. He chooses "not on philosophical grounds" but on "hints from cultural anthropology."[77] In Western culture the Christian drama with its metaphors and symbols has been the predominant factor in our structure of experience shaping our valuations and sensibilities. Although a general notion of experience is appealed to, and experience is the medium of the final object of theology (the good not our own), the Christian myth as the witness within our culture to that object is advanced as the criterion of selection and judgment.

The relativistic overtones of this methodological criterion become clear when it is contrasted to other alternatives. One could appeal to the authority of faith, faith here being defined in relation to biblical norms or ecclesiastical dogma. Meland, however, neither defines faith in this way nor accepts this procedure as legitimate in theological method. One could appeal to philosophical norms which transcend the particular cultures and religions (i.e., argue a particular philosophical view as true and then show how the Christian *mythos* expresses this abstract truth and its universal criterion). But, as we shall see in the next chapter, Meland rejects this method also, or at least modifies the cognitive status of metaphysics to such an extent that the *mythos* is determinative of metaphysics, not vice versa, thereby compromising the authority of the ontological approach.

He has, instead, gone beyond liberalism by appealing to the persistence, unique meaning, and necessity of myth, thereby interpreting the meaning of the Christian faith in terms of myth and what is witnessed to therein, instead of in terms of a fully rationalized theology. Given his stated criterion and his actual practice, then, it is difficult to understand his method apart from advancing a strong relativism. His method depends on the affirmation of and explication of the enduring *mythos* of the Judeo-Christian tradition in our structure of experience. The criterion for judgment of the meaning and truth of that *mythos* depends neither on faith biblically or ecclesiastically defined nor on metaphysics. Religion and faith are appraised within the cultural *mythos*.

The argument here is not that Meland is "merely" an historicist or absolute cultural relativist. His views of human experience and the transcultural and transcendent character of the "good not our own," which he takes to be commonly present and experienced, preclude that

---

[77] Meland, "How Is Culture a Source for Theology?" 12.

extreme conclusion. In addition, his views of process metaphysics, limited as it is with respect to its normative status in Christian theology, also prevent that conclusion. Rather, the point is that by making culture, by way of its dominant religious myth, so decisive in his theological method, he leaves open the possibility of interpreting his criterion as culturally determined, not simply conditioned. We shall pursue this question further at the end of the next chapter when we examine Meland's understanding of the nature and authority of metaphysics and its relation to theological method and cultural *mythos*.

4

Meland as a Process Theologian

I. THREE TYPES OF PROCESS THEOLOGY

On February 23-25, 1989 the Iliff School of Theology and the Center for Process Studies sponsored a conference at Iliff on "Methodological Alternatives in Process Theology." The sponsors identified these methodologies as rational, speculative, and empirical. The purpose of the discussion was to clarify the differences and commonalities between the three methods and to evaluate them.

The meeting was in effect an exploration of a distinction made by Bernard Lee in 1984.[1] Lee claims that there are two Whiteheads, and consequently two process theologies. Whitehead's philosophy is both doggedly empirical and insistently rational. It is empirical in the sense that it is tied to the generalized and imaginative description of immediate lived experience which is dim, massive, rich, penumbral, adumbrative, and only partially able to be tamed by sense data and clear consciousness. It is speculative and rationalistic in the sense that the metaphysical categories are trusted as elucidators of experience so long as they meet the rational criteria of coherence and necessity. Those theologians who read Whitehead with Hartshorne standing over their shoulder are more apt to have a fascination with the rational elements of Whitehead's metaphysical construction and a concern for coherence and necessity. Those who read Whitehead with James standing over their

---

[1] Bernard Lee, "The Two Process Theologies," *Theological Studies* 45 (1984): 307–319. See, also, William Dean, *American Religious Empiricism* (New York: SUNY, 1986), chapter 1, esp. pp. 34f. For a critique of Lee's analysis, see Joseph Bracken, "The Two Process Theologies: A Reappraisal," *Theological Studies* 46 (1985): 115-128.

shoulder are likely to be fascinated by his empirical method and his experiential concern for adequacy and applicability.

The speculative school, including William Beardslee, Delwin Brown, John Cobb, Philip Devenish, Lewis Ford, David Griffin, Schubert Ogden, and Norman Pittenger, has a passion for the possibility of conceptualizing the ontological structure of things, for clarity, for perfection, for the process of becoming, for seeing things as a whole, and for the ultimate character of things. The empirical school, including Henry Nelson Wieman, Daniel Day Williams, Bernard Loomer, William Dean, Nancy Frankenberry, Jerome Stone, and Bernard Meland, is preoccupied with meticulous fidelity to the deliverances of experience. Nothing is allowed at the level of abstraction that is not justified at some point by concrete experience. There is among the empiricists a keen sense of the limitations both of reason and language, less focus on the sure and the certain and more on the probable and the ambiguous, an affinity for the temporal, even the temporary, focus on the processes of resistance, a suspicion of abstraction, more interest in the increase in stature than in perfection, and more focus on relationality than on becoming. Lee concludes his analysis by saying "it is probably 'moods' and 'modes' that account for differences between rational and empirical theologians, rather than crystal-clear methodological and presuppositional distinctions. But the differences are real, and they are significant."[2]

The planners of the Iliff conference proposed a further distinction between the rationalistic and speculative components of process metaphysics. Much of the three day discussion focused on the baffling problem of the relation between the ideas of the universal and the concrete. The dispute was not about the presence, inevitability, and usefulness, but about the status of general ideas within the process perspective.

The emphasis of those who stressed the empirical underpinnings of process theology (represented by William Dean) was on the concrete particular and the condition of struggle for meaning. The empiricists wanted to stay close to the description of concrete experience, to an awareness of the non-conscious depths of experience, and were content with a smaller margin of intelligibility. Adequacy was measured by faithfulness to the full range of experience, and general propositions were viewed as hypotheses of interconnections.

---

[2] Ibid., 316.

The rational empiricists (represented by Philip Devenish) were occupied with metaphysics as transcendental analysis and the question whether there are logically necessary propositions in the sense that such propositions would be necessary truths if they are true at all. Their appeal was not so much to certainty of knowledge as to propositions which have the character of necessity. Adequacy was defined more in terms of the principle of non-contradiction.

The participants who were catalogued in the speculative camp (represented by David Griffin) were not as much interested in metaphysics per se as with universal common sense ideas, with cosmology, and with a speculative world view in which all the relevant facts fit together. They were committed more to propositions as speculative hypotheses than necessarily true ideas, so that adequacy was correspondence to all the facts and coherence of vision.

Two conclusions, essentially in agreement with Lee, emerged from the discussions. First, it is clear that there are affinities between all three of these methodologies in process theology. All take experience to be inherently valuational. Further, there is no evaluation of experience apart from a hermeneutic of experience. Finally, any adequate hermeneutic of experience includes the horizon not only of sense experience or of the self and others, but of self, others, and some vision of an encompassing whole. The three designations are not mutually exclusive methodologies; all three themes are present in each process "school." The differences are, rather, different ways of understanding the role of philosophy within a process perspective.

Second, although all three perspectives employ an appeal to concrete experience and to general propositions, there are basic differences between these branches of the process tree. One of these is a difference concerning both the character and status (though not the presence or usefulness) of ontology. Although all employ ontological ideas, radical empiricists view these more as hypothetical universals to be tested aesthetically and pragmatically than as universals that are necessarily true if true at all. There is also a difference in valuational theory. For the rational empiricist the most general features of value are to be sought, and they provide us with what is reassuring within the context of the encompassing whole. For the radical empiricist value is located in the concrete itself, namely, in the ambiguity, creativity, and struggle within concrete actuality. There is also a difference concerning the degree of intelligibility available to theology as such. The empirical branch in particular wanted to begin and return to the concrete particular, emphasizing the relativity and partiality of all rational and speculative thought.

The most fundamental issue of the conference, though, was the proper measure of adequacy for any theology. Although the rational and speculative emphases within contemporary process theology are not rationalistic in the pejorative sense of the term (deductions about the world from universal and indisputable ideas), the logical method in neoclassical metaphysics tends to overshadow the phenomenological method to the point that concrete reality becomes a vehicle for illustrating the viewpoint, thus seriously deprecating the depth of concrete structures. When philosophy is defined this way, and when theology proper is dependent on such transcendental analysis, radical empiricism tends to be dismissed as vague or relativistic, or even as not theology proper, because it does not and thinks it cannot locate transcendentals in the neoclassical sense.

Although these differences cannot be reduced to temperament, such variations are clearly present. Concerns such as what one takes most deeply to be important, the height of one's "boggle point" (David Griffin's term), and what is the most proper measure of adequacy for theological statements shape the orientations within a process perspective. For example, a radical empiricist like Meland does not assume that the discovery of necessary or general ideas is the most valuable and reassuring feature of the world. The thick richness of the Creative Passage within which we are born, live, and die is sufficient and secure enough for thinking, living, and living well.

All process thinkers, it was concluded, employ all three methods in their theological reflection. They differ on how these methods are understood and employed. Meland's predominant theme is that process theologians who employ rationality and speculation must not abandon the empirical richness, depth, and complexity of the encompassing whole and awareness of the difference between our ideas and the fullness of that reality. It is noteworthy that the figure to whom the advocates of the empirical branch at the Iliff conference consistently referred was neither Henry Nelson Wieman (and his quest for empirical certainty) nor (the early work of) Bernard Loomer, but Bernard Meland. Insofar as the empirical branch of the process tree is alive and well among contemporary process theologians, the advocates of this orientation have been influenced more by the radical empiricism of Meland than by these other process thinkers. Meland is the thinker who has done more than any other to keep process theology close to the empirical concrete in its richness, complexity, and ambiguity.

II. MELAND'S ORIENTATION TOWARD THE PROCESS VISION

Since the mid-twentieth century there have been two major alternatives to the neoorthodox response to the collapse of the older liberalism. One is the thought of Paul Tillich, whose theological thought is shaped by the mid-century infatuation with existentialism. Although Tillich, along with Barth, is perhaps the most influential Protestant theologian in the twentieth century, his theological orientation never develops into a school of theological thought. Paralleling Tillich's work and outlasting it in terms of breadth and length of influence is "an approach that has developed into a prominent school of thought,"[3] process theology.

There are some suggestive though not conclusive ways in which it is appropriate to identify Meland with the process school of theology.[4]

---

[3] Stanley Grenz and Roger Olson, *20th Century Theology: God and & the World in a Transitional Age* (Downers Grove, IL: InterVarsity Press, 1992), p. 130.

[4] A comment should be made about what the phrase "process theology" refers to in this chapter. It refers to all three of the designations John Cobb highlights in *Process Theology as Political Theology* (Philadelphia: Westminster Press, 1982), pp. 19-21, namely, a theology that emphasizes becoming over against substance, that systematically employs the philosophical conceptuality of Whitehead and Hartshorne, and that developed at the Divinity School of the University of Chicago during the thirties. In its most basic meaning here, though, it refers to that group of theologians who, for the last two generations, have appealed to the thought of Whitehead, and the interpreters of Whitehead, as the most adequate conceptual framework in which to explain or defend the Christian faith. This includes that group for which Whitehead's thought is the major, and in most cases the definitive, framework for their theological work (such as Cobb, Ogden, Ford, Griffin), and also that increasingly large group for which major concepts of the Whiteheadian framework are crucial for their work as theologians (such as Williams, Pittenger, Williamson). Excluded from this discussion is that process theology informed by Teilhard de Chardin. As far as I know there is no direct influence of Teilhard on Meland. There are also fundamental differences between the two, such as confidence in ultimate coherence and ultimate hope, to name but two. Affinities can be noted, to be sure, such as the importance of emergence, the mystical vision, and, in comparison to some process theologians, a christological focus. Nevertheless, the reference to process theologians here is primarily to that group of contemporary theologians who make Whitehead primary if not decisive in their work as theologians. A good

First, his doctoral work in The Divinity School occurs at the time of transition from the socio-historical focus in empirical method to the more philosophical focus represented by the arrival of Henry Nelson Wieman. That fact in itself, of course, does not make Meland a process theologian. It is noteworthy, however, that Meland, on occasion, notes his excitement about the coming of Wieman and the shifts that it occasioned in the Divinity School and in his own thought.

Second, he is one of the major historians of the Chicago School. That claim, also, does not make him a process theologian. But Meland is not simply an historian of the ideas and methods of the Divinity School. He embodies the sensibilities as well as the ideas and methods of the school as a theologian. As is stated in "The Citation" for the Alumni of the Year Award in 1970, he is "a personal summary of the work of the school."[5]

Third, he himself acknowledges the importance of process thinkers in the formation of his own thought. In this list he includes Bergson, James, the emergent evolutionists, and Whitehead, as well as Wieman and other colleagues. That the list of thinkers he designates as important for his thought is predominantly from a list of process thinkers is significant in determining where to "locate" Meland on the map of contemporary theologians. He is very early in his career identified with Wieman (which is only partially true) and has continued to be listed among the representatives of the Chicago School of process theologians to this day.

It is possible, of course, for all of these facts to be true but inconsequential for his constructive work. Our purpose here is to examine in more detail the implications suggested by this prima facie evidence. The argument of this chapter and the next is that Meland is both a process theologian and a rebel among the process theologians.

In what way and to what degree is process philosophy the resource and guide for his work as a constructive theologian? How do the Whiteheadian vision and the categorical scheme, discovered in the last year of his graduate study through Wieman, and encountered again through Loomer upon his return to the faculty of the Divinity School in 1945, function in his theology?

---

discussion of the larger field of influence on process theologians, which has direct relevance to Meland's thought, can be found in Randolf Crump Miller, *The American Spirit in Theology* (Philadelphia: Pilgrim Press, 1974).

[5] *Alumni*, November, 1970, 4.

The basic answer I propose is that Meland is a process theologian in the sense that he accepts and employs the process vision and scheme as a backdrop of his thinking, but that he is selective in his use of the scheme and distinctive among most process theologians in his relativist understanding of the cognitive status of the vision. It is appropriate to designate Meland a process theologian in a broad sense because of the important role the process orientation, vision, and terminology play in his thought. But even in this sense, and quite apart from his substantial critique of the Whiteheadian and Hartshornian school to be elaborated in the next chapter, he cannot be identified too closely with the process "school" of theology. His relativistic perception of the nature and role of process metaphysics precludes too facile an identification of him as a process theologian, especially in light of turns in scholastic directions which the movement has taken in the last thirty years.

In his first three books Meland clearly acknowledges the metaphysical questions as they relate to faith. But he plays them down in favor of his interest in faith in its appreciative dimensions and religion as the means of adjustment to the vaster resources of the natural order. This period, predominantly under the influence of Smith's mystical naturalism and Wieman's brand of empiricism, is more shaped by Whitehead's *The Concept of Nature* and *Religion in the Making* than by Whitehead's metaphysical speculations in *Process and Reality*.

No one should be surprised by this fact, since it is Wieman's introduction and exposition of *Religion in the Making* that introduces Meland to Whitehead's thought and shapes Meland's understanding of Whitehead. Furthermore, we should not ignore the impact of Whitehead's organismic thinking on Meland during the early period, for it is real and is acknowledged by Meland. What is noteworthy, though, is that Meland does not early on, and never does, confine organismic thinking to Whitehead or identify it with him. Throughout his career other organismic thinkers, especially Bergson, James, and the emergent evolutionists, play as much a role in his fundamental convictions about the organismic character of the world as does Whitehead. Indeed, after rereading all of Meland's books and articles within a two month period, I was struck with how little there is of direct appeal or even reference to Whitehead, and especially Whitehead in isolation from other organismic thinkers, in the early Meland corpus.

Immediately upon his return to Chicago, however, he begins to engage in a more direct discussion of the new metaphysics of Whitehead.

This middle period, from *Seeds of Redemption* through *Higher Education and the Human Spirit*, in which faith and the appreciative consciousness dominate Meland's interest, shows a more explicit appropriation of the Whiteheadian vision and scheme.[6] He identifies himself with Whitehead's vision, and elements of the scheme are employed, but not because it can establish its metaphysical truth over against older or alternative conceptual schemes. Rather, he finds in Whitehead's vision an acknowledgement of the feeling and sensitivity inherent in the natural order and a conceptual pattern which accounts for meaning in the creative process. "The distinctive turn of the new metaphysics lies in the fact that it has distinguished between that which is brute force in creativity and that which gives to creation meaning and character, a gentle working that is the redemptive influence upon force."[7]

In *Reawakening of Christian Faith* the same significance is given to the Whiteheadian vision. It designates those features of the life process in which creativity is given sensitivity and so ultimate character. "The problem of achieving greater sensibility in discerning the dimension of thought and feeling which extends beyond clear observation, without abandoning intellectual rigor in the pursuit of observable meanings, is the very real problem to which inquiry in the new metaphysics is addressed."[8] Whitehead's vision, which integrates the subject and object in an act of perception and so includes living emotion as well as apprehension of an object, resolves his dilemma. Relation, feeling, sensitivity, and meaning have significance in the understanding of the world as well as in the appreciative response to the world in Whitehead's metaphysics.

---

[6] Meland's work can be divided into three distinct periods with major emphases: 1) from *Modern Man's Worship* through *American Philosophies of Religion*, in which mysticism and naturalism are the major themes; 2) from *Seeds of Redemption* through *Higher Education and the Human Spirit*, in which faith and appreciative consciousness are the major themes; 3) from *Realities of Faith* through *Fallible Forms and Symbols*, in which theology and culture are the major themes. None of these is abandoned or appears wholly new, yet each theme predominates and is given its major definition during one of the major periods.

[7] Bernard Meland, *Seeds of Redemption* (New York: Macmillan, 1947), p. 57.

[8] See Bernard Meland, *The Reawakening of Christian Faith* (New York: Macmillan, 1949), p. 92.

III. MELAND AND PROCESS METAPHYSICS

A. The Basis of Metaphysics

Metaphysics, for Meland, is a way of knowing which can be justified only to the degree that its primal perceptions can be said to have a basis in experience or in history.[9] Although one may go beyond empirical lines of inquiry to offer a comprehensive vision of reality, the beginning point for all metaphysical thinking must be experience. The immediacy of lived experience, the depth and mystery of experience, is the substructure. He is highly critical of any understanding of metaphysics which sees it primarily as a mode of thought which begins with a priori categories or clear and distinct ideas and attempts to argue the rational necessity of a metaphysical scheme. One begins "not with a categorical scheme as if one were repeating the classical procedure of rationalism employing literal notions of space and time, but by emphatically acknowledging the primacy of perception as being the cardinal doctrine of process thought."[10] A metaphysics that is purely the work of the mind, however valid internally as an exercise of logic, is for him a "floating vision" having only the value of wishful thinking or of a reverie as an aesthetic creation.[11]

Metaphysics, however, deals with ideas, not primarily with intuition of the complexity of experience. Nevertheless, it is dependent on the fundamental notions and images that arise in each age to give intelligibility to experience as perceived, such as order or creativity. Indeed, metaphysics is a unique way of applying a level of generality to these fundamental notions that are dominant and persuasive. Concretely, for Meland, the metaphysics he follows depends on the fundamental notions of the sciences as they have come to embody the depth of experience in their notions of relativity, field theory, quantum, emergence, organicism, energy, and so forth. The appeal, it must be noted, is not to the authority of science per se, but to the unique achievement of science in embodying the fullness and mystery of experience in its imagery.

---

[9] Bernard Meland, "How Is Culture a Source for Theology?" *Criterion* 3 (1964), 11.
[10] Bernard Meland, "Can Empirical Theology Learn Something from Phenomenology?" in Bernard Meland, ed., *The Future of Empirical Theology* (Chicago: University of Chicago Press, 1969), p. 290.
[11] Meland, "How Is Culture a Source for Theology?" 11.

B. The Nature of Metaphysics

Metaphysics, however, is not a branch of the psychology of conscious perception. It is a unique cognitive use of experience and of the fundamental notions used to interpret experience. Metaphysics is the attempt to provide further intelligibility about reality by imaginatively projecting the fundamental notions employed in experience and the sciences into a broad scheme of generality. At times Meland seems almost to identify metaphysics with fundamental notions,[12] those notions that have "become organic to one's structured experience" and serve as "windows of the mind or, better still, disciplines of perception and awareness with which one encounters any event and in terms of which the imagination and interpretive powers are quickened."[13] At other times he speaks of metaphysics as based on these fundamental notions. The difference, apparently, is that in the former he is indicating how metaphysical ideas functioned in his own thinking, whereas in the latter he is describing the beginning point in imaginative projection and the higher degrees of generality sought in any vision.

The goal of metaphysics is to establish greater intelligibility by generalizing the fundamental notions that have become persuasive in experience into a vision of the whole of reality.[14] Metaphysical thinking seeks greater clarity about experience and actuality in terms of an imaginative vision of the rational structure of the world as a whole. A rational structure is not a goal in itself, however. Metaphysics seeks to "confirm" what is given in empirical observation and historical witness

---

[12] Bernard Meland, *Higher Education and the Human Spirit* (Chicago: University of Chicago Press, 1953), p. 24, and "Interpreting the Christian Faith in a Philosophical Framework," *Journal of Religion*, Volume 33 (1953), pp. 96ff. To the degree that Meland understood metaphysics as the discovery and use of the "fundamental notions" of our age he agrees with Collingwood that metaphysics is an historical discipline. R. G. Collingwood, *An Essay on Metaphysics* (Oxford: At the Clarendon Press, 1940).

[13] Ibid., p. 94. See, also, p. 24, where certain "fundamental notions" are enumerated, such as "things exist in relations," and "relations are dynamic," etc. Here, again, the aforementioned ambiguity arises. Meland is not clear whether these are proposed and defended as metaphysical principles or as ideas derived from experience and the reflection upon experience and the world by the sciences to be used as true ideas for metaphysical speculation.

[14] It is important to point out here that by "persuasive" Meland does not mean rationally necessary but rather accepted by thinking persons as the most accurate description of experience.

by rendering intelligible what is given more concretely in present experience and historical witness.[15] Such a scheme, though, is an imaginative vision and not a literal description because the rational structure of the world in its ultimate form, through which intelligibility is established and experience "confirmed," is not given in immediate experience or in other acts of analysis. It is a vision which is made possible by enlarging on the empirical given through a set of categories and principles which can project the larger context and thereby give rational order. It says, in effect,

> this is how it could be, given certain presuppositions which we are presently committed to assuming. It thus becomes a bold, though usually a highly disciplined projection of the lines of continuity, extending out from initial premises, controlled by forms and categories along with conceptual rules designed to guide its long-range reflection.[16]

Meland insists that ultimate rationality is "a venture in understanding" the long-range outcome of existence which is not a clearly given fact of existence in its concrete flux. By calling metaphysics a venture in understanding, he does not mean to imply that metaphysics is purely arbitrary and has no cognitive significance. It is not arbitrary because the vision and the categories are derived from experience in its most persuasive and compelling characteristics. It is cognition in the sense that it is the mind's attempt to wrest some larger intelligibility out of the empirically given data of lived experience.

The method of metaphysics, then, is "imaginative projection" or generalization of the fundamental insights and notions of the sciences.[17] Reason is the tool employed. A degree of rationality is assured because events do have structure. But events also have adumbrations as well which constitute their full reality. Metaphysics must take account of these as much as any other cognitive discipline. "If idealism was ready to universalize reason as a category and pragmatism could assume rationality or the appeal to reasonableness to be a nominative factor, the new metaphysical context in which we believe liberalism has promise

---

[15] Bernard Meland, *Faith and Culture* (London: George Allen & Unwin, 1953), p. 195, and "Interpreting the Christian Faith within a Philosophical Framework," 97.
[16] Bernard Meland, "The Structure of Christian Faith," *Religion in Life* XXXVII (Winter, 1968), 558.
[17] Meland, "Interpreting the Christian Faith," 90, and *Faith and Culture*, p. 18.

accepts both rationality and what is non-rational as twin facets of all events in existence."[18]

The rational method of metaphysics, therefore, is analogical rather than literal. Analogy takes account of the continuity and discontinuity between thought and reality. It does not offer a literal description of reality or an identity between mind and reality, as does rationalism. In metaphysical thinking the crucial methodological question is: "How do you employ such a tool of intelligibility as analogy in such a way that preserves the tension between what is manageable and unmanageable in the deeper experiences of creaturely existence?"[19] Metaphysics takes this understanding of experience and by analogy projects it into a vision of the character of all reality.

A concrete example of the basis and method of metaphysics is Meland's understanding of "the new metaphysics," or the process metaphysics which informs his thought. Process metaphysics, as a form of "rational empiricism," takes "the relativity of the event with utmost seriousness, yet sees that there is a generality of meaning issuing from each concrete occurrence that can be formulated as a true vision of experience. Such a vision is a venture in imagining first principles which will adequately express the world in its essence."[20] The basis for this vision, or at least the cue, is taken from organismic thinking in biology at the turn of the century. The crucial insight, however, derives from the fundamental notions of emergence, relativity, and field theory in the new physics.[21] The fashioning of these fundamental notions into a metaphysical vision occurs when "creativity within structure" is taken to be the basic characteristic of all reality and a set of categories to render this insight intelligible is developed by Whitehead.[22]

As to the metaphoric character of this vision, Meland appeals to Whitehead: "Words and phrases must be stretched towards a generality foreign to their ordinary usage; and however such elements of language be stabilized as technicalities, they remain metaphors mutely appealing

---

[18] Meland, *Faith and Culture*, p. 40.
[19] Bernard Meland, "Analogy and Myth in Postliberal Theology," *Perkins Journal* 15 (1962) in Delwin Brown, Ralph James, and Gene Reeves, eds., *Process Philosophy and Christian Thought* (Indianapolis: Bobbs Merrill, 1971), p. 124.
[20] Meland, *Realities of Faith*, p. 158.
[21] Meland, "Can Empirical Theology Learn Something from Phenomenology?" p. 289.
[22] Meland, "Interpreting the Christian Faith," 90-91.

for an imaginative leap."[23] The method of discovery is like the flight of a plane. "It starts from the ground of particular observation; it makes a flight into the thin air of imaginative generalization; and it again lands for renewed observation rendered acute by rational interpretation."[24] Meland concludes, "there is both tentativeness and bold, imaginative exploration in this mode of generalization, accepting the elusiveness and complexity of the data of immediate experience, yet venturing a formulation within the scope of adequacy that seems available and presently justifiable."[25]

In his early writings Meland discusses metaphysics more as of a piece with poetry rather than as analogy. Metaphysics and poetry are similar ways of thinking in that they use the language of imagination and indirection. Each is "a way that creates overtones and backdrops and coloring in scenes that might be descriptively drab or shorn of extending dimensions. When poet and metaphysician work, they employ a kind of medium that goes beyond description, beyond literalness or exactness. They employ a language not unlike that of the myth."[26] Whitehead himself recognizes this when he employs poetry in advancing his metaphysical discussion, not only for emotive interest but also to use imaginative meanings to carry on technical formulations.[27]

C. The Use of Metaphysics

How does Meland employ such a vision in his work as a theologian? He claims that if he were not asked to address this question directly, he would not even discuss it. Rather, he prefers in setting forth his theology to let these conceptual matters work on more hiddenly. The process orientation is implicit in his assumptions and spontaneous responses and provides some of the fundamental notions that inform his thinking. But his employment of these notions suggests "not so much a system of ideas as a structure of meaning in which one's experiences occur and take on intelligibility."[28] They serve primarily as "a mode of perceiving events and of expressing one's self through language."[29]

---

[23] Meland, *Realities of Faith*, p. 158.
[24] Ibid., p. 159.
[25] Ibid.
[26] Bernard Meland, *Seeds of Redemption* (New York: Macmillan, 1947), p. 155.
[27] Meland, *Higher Education and the Human Spirit*, p. 97.
[28] Meland, "Interpreting the Christian Faith," 88.
[29] Ibid.

His use of process philosophy, then, has more to do with predispositions and habits of thought than with interpreting faith within a philosophical framework. Propositional faith is rejected in favor of brooding over the elemental stance. His disciplining of thought is more the disciplining of the psyche—of acquiring sensibilities and sensitivities, discriminations and judgments, awareness and appreciation, and of subjecting these to whatever intelligibility can be wrested by way of brooding and interpreting within the predispositions and conceptuality of process modes of thought—than the interpretation of faith within a philosophical framework, with or without remainder. Thus, any discipline that can enhance the structure of meaning implicit in lived experience is employed by him. Indeed, the significance of process philosophy as such comes to assume major importance for him belatedly, accidentally, and unexpectedly, a sort of "summit view" following his use of other disciplines.

> My philosophical orientation is more in the nature of a structure of mind and feeling which forms the depth of my conscious experience and which brings to play upon the accumulations of experience, insight and brooding upon the problem of faith the full light of day, the sustained view, because the discrepancies, the broken meanings, the fragments of faith, the hit-and-miss turnings of thought which had no connectedness, no order, no symmetry, could now assume a pattern of relationships.[30]

Process philosophy, then, serves more as a larger perspective and a set of fundamental notions than as a set or system of propositions that provide a literal description of the world and a means by which to interpret the meaning of faith.

One never finds Meland explaining or defending Whitehead or process philosophy as such. His understanding and usage of the process vision does not make such a task even occur to him as important. Furthermore, for him such a procedure would be analogous to a pianist who would exhibit and concentrate on piano technique instead of playing a piece as an expression of her own sensibilities and an expression of certain moods, settings, events, or patterns. Such a display diverts the theologian from her primary task as theologian, namely, interpreting the realities of faith in their depth and rich fullness of meaning.

---

[30] Ibid., p. 90.

Another way to approach the question of the status and use of metaphysics for Meland is to see how he describes his approach to metaphysics autobiographically. A person is predisposed by early conditioning to habits of thought which never become uprooted or dissipated in later mature thought. In his own case, there persists "a Lutheran heritage in my thought processes despite all the intellectual somersaulting I have gone through."[31] He takes this to mean, in part, that in all his thought there is "too much of the subjectivist speaking in me."[32] Memory and brooding claim too much authority in his thought to permit a propositional faith.

Philosophical notions play some role in his thought from his college and graduate school years. But his explicit concern for philosophy comes only after he returns to Chicago during the Loomer era when a sort of Whiteheadian orthodoxy reigned. He describes his philosophical interests before that time as "the disciplining of the human psyche, of participating in various ways in a discriminating response, of acquiring sensibilities and sensitivities which partook of discrimination, of judgment, and of awareness that opened the mind to a fuller appreciation of meanings and to understanding of a discerning kind."[33] This orientation persists into his explicit concern with philosophy and its role in his thought after 1945. It makes philosophy more "a structure of mind and feeling which forms the depth of my conscious experience and which brings to play upon the accumulations of experience, insight, and brooding upon the problem of faith the full light of day,"[34] and prevents philosophy from becoming a closed system.

D. Meland's Relation to Whitehead

Meland's appropriation of Whitehead's thought can be understood only if we see that for Meland, Whitehead's metaphysics is to be interpreted not primarily as a rationalistic scheme but as the continuation and completion of the task begun by Bergson and James, namely, of giving some conceptual order and clarity to the "thickness" of experience. In Meland's own view, *Process and Reality* brings radical empiricism to a stage of conceptualization Bergson and James dared not

---

[31] Ibid., p. 89.
[32] Ibid.
[33] Ibid.
[34] Ibid., p. 90.

envision.[35] The problem for that vision is "the problem of achieving greater sensibility in discerning the dimension of thought and feeling which extends beyond clear observation, without abandoning intellectual rigor in the pursuit of observable meanings."[36]

As we noted above, in Meland's view there are two distinct dimensions to Whitehead's metaphysics, the rational and the empirical/aesthetic, the latter referring not only to artistic expression but to feeling and sensitivity.[37] Meland's primary interest is to see and appropriate the empirical and aesthetic dimensions of Whitehead's "rational empiricism." Further, he insists on interpreting the latter within the former, as when he argues that it is a distortion of Whitehead's thought for his followers to make him too rationalistic.[38]

Two elements of Whitehead's vision appeal to Meland and shape his use of it. First, Whitehead, as we have noted, is, in one regard, an empiricist. This empirical side of Whitehead dominates Meland's understanding and usage of Whitehead from beginning to end. Indeed, the new metaphysics is important because it gives radical empiricism a metaphysical interpretation. He persistently understands Whitehead's intention to be an extension of James's own efforts to establish the perceptive dimension in thought. Whitehead's metaphysical writings are "an attempt to generalize this notion of 'relations' beyond the amorphous stage of James's radical empiricism."[39] Whitehead does this by employing imagery from modern physics instead of introspective psychology to elaborate the depth of immediate awareness.

Second, Meland also sees the aesthetic side of Whitehead's thought. Not only is his thought grounded in and returned to the depth of lived

---

[35] Meland, "Can Empirical Theology Learn Something from Phenomenology?" p. 289.

[36] Bernard Meland, *Reawakening of Christian Faith* (New York: Macmillan, 1949), p. 50.

[37] For a similar view, although critical, see Arthur Murphy, "Whitehead and the Method of Speculative Philosophy," in Paul Schilpp, ed., *The Philosophy of Alfred North Whitehead* (New York: Tudor Publishing Company, 1951), pp. 353-380.

[38] Meland, *Realities of Faith*, p. 120. Meland himself sometimes thinks this is true of Whitehead. "Whitehead begins quite boldly declaring his recognition of the limits of human thought in his *Process and Reality*...but by the time his formulation of precise categories has been completed, one feels that confidence in the adequacy of these categories has noticeably risen, almost to the point of taking these forms at face value as being descriptive of the realities to which they point." "Analogy and Myth in Postliberal Theology," p. 124.

[39] Meland, *Higher Education and the Human Spirit*, p. 60.

experience. His thought is an imaginative generalization projected as a vision of how the world might be seen as a whole. In my own memory of Meland in class, he almost always refers to the introduction to *Process and Reality* when describing what he understands Whitehead to be up to in his metaphysics. Basically he understands the vision as an aesthetic venture of the imagination, not as a literal description of reality based on rational necessity and issuing in clarity and certainty.

Meland, therefore, is hesitant to take Whitehead's structure too uncritically. For Whitehead, the sense of structured meaning in the creative flow or living situation is too marked, even though that makes it less suspect of being a detour into mysticism. In Meland's view one needs the corrective of Bergson and James at times in reading Whitehead, lest the formative notions of the new physics implicit in his imagery make one's understanding of the creative nexus more external and rationalistic than it actually is.[40]

The rationalistic bent in Whitehead, Meland believes, has its roots in the source of his imagery. Whitehead borrows from the new physics with its notion of a field of energy. This makes his imagery more cosmological in its orientation than the Jamesian imagery borrowed from introspective psychology.[41] The imagery, though, leads to a kind of externality and to a kind of rationalism that is too much for Meland. Thus, although Whitehead's systematic formulation is a "formidable resource," "to use this magnificent resource as a closure upon thought, compelling all other insight to be brought within its purview or rejected as being irrelevant to rational experience, is to profane this vision and to forfeit the creative stimulus of its imaginative venture."[42]

Meland concludes that his own efforts "parallel" Whitehead's vision and "at crucial points" partake of it, but his own thought does not stem directly from it. The reason is highly significant. Meland's thought and Whitehead's thought depend in the beginning on two different sources. Meland draws from a faith "long held by a community of faith" and "formative of the cultural experience of Western history," while Whitehead draws from the "logos" character of reality. We will explore the significance of these two sources below.

---

[40] Meland, *Realities of Faith*, p. 120.
[41] Meland, *Higher Education and the Human Spirit*, p. 61.
[42] Meland, "Can Empirical Theology Learn Something from Phenomenology?" p. 291.

IV. MELAND AS A PROCESS THINKER

Of the postliberal theologians associated with the process perspective, Meland is the most ambiguously related to this school. Although he employs process categories, he neither defends nor utilizes the process scheme as a whole with the tenacity and thoroughness of other representatives, such as Bernard Loomer, John Cobb, Lewis Ford, Schubert Ogden, and David Griffin. One reason is that he is more critical of all metaphysical schemes than adherents to process metaphysics usually are. The other reason is that one of the most elusive of the many elusive dimensions of Meland's thought is the precise status he assigns to metaphysics as a cognitive discipline.[43] These two reasons are not unrelated. As we shall see below, Meland considers metaphysics to be cognitively significant, but he does not consider it to be the unique way cognitively to transcend the relativities of culture by way of a speculative metaphysical vision.

We will argue in the next chapter that Meland is the most important internal critic of the contemporary process school of theology. The way he employs "process philosophy" as a metaphysical vision is unique to his own elementalism and to his understanding of both the nature of the realities of faith with which the theologian deals and his own task as an interpreter of the realities of faith. Above all, he is the most insistent internal judge of the direction toward a new rationalism the process school takes after mid-century.

There is a sense, however, in which Meland employs process philosophy in a way *similar* to the theologians who constitute the school

---

[43] One of the basic criticisms of Meland's thought is that he employs process categories without ever defending process metaphysics as a true metaphysical scheme. To employ the concepts of creativity, concretion, and internal relations as Meland does, one must derive the meaning and truth of these from the entire scheme. When Meland does try to argue for the meaning and truth of such categories, he appeals to experience and the other sciences instead of the scheme. Therefore, we are never sure exactly what he is arguing, i.e., whether process categories are equivalent to the experience pointed to, or whether process categories have an analogous meaning, or whether experience illuminates the metaphysical concept which is true on other grounds as a metaphysical concept. Things and events are internally related: this statement can be defended as an intimation of experience or as a metaphysical truth. One can even begin from the former and move to the latter. But no such argument is made by Meland. Instead, he uses both interchangeably, so we are to never know whether they may be meaningless or false because they are metaphysically wrong or experientially dubious.

of process theology. Several primary categories, specifically some process neologisms and phrases, are employed by Meland in their technical Whiteheadian sense. His later writings frequently employ such process concepts as feeling,[44] prehension,[45] internal relations,[46] creativity,[47] concrescence,[48] and "causal efficacy."[49] Such categories have their full Whiteheadian intention of being descriptive of reality. He takes these terms to be explanatory of what he means to describe. There is a fundamental sense, then, in which it is fully appropriate to count Meland as a representative of process perspective in theology.

A. Temporalizing the Great Chain of Being

One of the great shifts in the modern West from premodern thought is the temporalizing of the great chain of being.[50] Change is recognized not only as a fact of existence but as characteristic of reality in its most fundamental character. It is common to identify process philosophy as a primary expression of this mode of thought in twentieth century philosophy and theology. However, that is not an adequate ascription. Most modern philosophical movements temporalize the great chain of being, at least since Hegel, in significant if not decisive ways.

What is called process thought is simply more explicit and thoroughgoing in its reconception of reality than most other philosophical movements. It has its own distinctive ways of speaking that distinguish it significantly from all other forms of philosophy which partake of this great cultural shift, including idealism, pragmatism, existentialism, phenomenology, personalism, deconstruction, and humanism. Its realism differs significantly from these various post-

---

44 Meland, *Faith and Culture*, p. 186.
45 Meland, *Realities of Faith*, p. 120; *Fallible Forms* and Symbols (Philadelphia: Fortress Press, 1976), pp. 55, 80.
46 Ibid., p. 227.
47 Meland, *Fallible Forms and Symbols*, p. 80.
48 Ibid., p. 43.
49 Meland, *Reawakening of Christian Faith*, p. 72; *Fallible Forms and Symbols*, pp. vii, 114, 185.
50 Arthur Lovejoy, *The Great Chain of Being* (New York: Harper Torchbooks, 1936), esp. Chapters 9-10. See, also, Franklin Baumer, *Modern European Thought: Continuity and Change in Ideas: 1600-1950* (New York: Macmillan, 1977), in which he describes the 17th century as the triumph of being over becoming, the 18th as being and becoming, and the 19th as becoming over being, and the 20th as the triumph of becoming.

Kantian dualisms. My argument is that Meland does not only merely partake of the temporalizing of the great chain of being in the way that has been characteristic of process thinkers. He is in some important ways a distinctive and indeed paradigmatic representative of the fundamental intuitions and insight of the orientation known as process thought.

Meland is a process theologian in the sense that he does theology utilizing the process way of temporalizing the great chain of being. Throughout his career, from beginning to end, he not only accepts as background and presupposition the basic insight into the "changing mentality of the West" and the resulting "cultural reorientation." He keeps in the foreground and elaborates in his own way the primary process metaphors with such clarity and persistence that he represents the process *orientation* toward the temporalizing of the great chain of being more explicitly, fully, and faithfully than most process philosophers since mid-century. Meland's life work is more to explore the meanings and implications of this process orientation than to contribute to the scholastic elaboration and application of the scheme.

One can see the distinctiveness and thoroughness of his way of formulating the basic process orientation by analyzing the way he reconstructs liberal theology. Early liberal theology adopts the modern Kantian framework, but that framework is essentially an idealism in which the human being itself, and specifically the human structure of consciousness (mental events) is taken as the most basic characteristic of reality. Any larger context is truncated from view. This is clear in the Kantian methodology adopted by most liberals, in the Darwinian view of evolution shared by most liberals, and in the Newtonian fundamental notions of the sciences that control liberal thinking. All modern philosophy—and we should include idealism, pragmatism, existentialism, phenomenology, personalism, deconstruction, and humanism—temporalizes the great chain of being. But most do so according to a modern Kantian strategy of thought and do not reflect fully the "wider cultural upheaval" embraced by process thought. This wider upheaval is decisive for Meland's conception of a postliberal theology.

What we want to argue now is that there are three specific concepts from the process framework that are employed in Meland's thought. These basic terms, which are integral to the process orientation and the context for the formal categorial scheme, are constitutive of Meland's thought and remain in the foreground of his thought throughout his career. These notions are important for all process thinkers. However, among many contemporary process philosophers and theologians, these insights tend to be submerged to the superstructure of process conceptuality. In Meland's thought these basic intuitions were explicit, public, focused, to the forefront, and directly explored for their richer meaning at the elemental and perceptual level as well as their conceptual implications. His process theology is more a brooding on, an exploration of, the deeper dimensions and implications of these basic process insights than an exegesis of the superstructure which assumes but largely ignores the richer and more ambiguous ranges of the basic intuitions.

B. Creativity

For Meland, as for all process thinkers, creativity is the most fundamental characteristic of reality as experienced. Creativity in its most basic feature is sheer ongoingness.[51] It is bare, brute force, which is essentially the coming into being and perishing of each droplet of experience. Creativity is, on one side, the advance into novelty which characterizes reality as such. It is, on the other side, the tragic process of dissolution which attends all actuality. Gushing out like a stream of turbulent water, it is without form and void. It is the ceaseless ongoing of coming into being and perishing. It is the most assured of all processes.

Sheer creativity, however, does not assure that the future is to be a preferred value. The perpetual process of coming into being and perishing implies only that ongoingness is a basic feature of reality and that the advance into novelty is the inevitable consequence of that ongoingness. "Presumably this endless creativity could go indefinitely as a formless void having no meaning, no purpose, no end in view; but it does no such thing."[52] Instead, there is a happening in creation by which feeling is infused into brute process, chastening, sensitizing, directing the process toward more tender meaning, toward more complex, subtle, and communal relations than the brute force would imply. "The creative act, wherever it occurs, is process yielding to a tender working, such that the power implicit in the process becomes creative and sustaining of the

---

[51] Bernard Meland, *Seeds of Redemption* (New York: Macmillan, 1947), pp. 51-59; *Faith and Culture*, pp. 105-106.
[52] Ibid., p. 59.

value that emerges."[53] Creativity is attended by a fusing of sensitivity among the events of existence.

Instead of developing a philosophical doctrine of God as the logically necessary implication of such an understanding of existence (the principle of concretion), Meland designates the objective side of this process the Creative Passage.[54] On its subjective side existence is a stream of experience; on its objective side it is a creative passage. Although this phrase points to the becoming which is characteristic of all process thinking, the phrase also points to what persists, giving to every moment of becoming its identity. Existence is not simply becoming but is the interplay of creativity and sensitivity working to infuse feeling and thus value into existence. Reality is both becoming and being or ground of being (something persisting) and their interplay. It is a Creative Passage in which all life is lived. As we shall see in chapter six, the reality of God is of a piece with this creative passage. God is not so much the logically necessary principle of concretion as the Ultimate Efficacy within relationships which works for qualitative attainment within sheer creativity.

Meland does not simply develop a theology of creation from this notion of creativity. His own employment of the term is distinctive, for his emphasis is continually on creation as interpreted by redemption and by the new creation. Nevertheless, the process concept of creativity provides the backdrop of his theology. He elaborates and deepens what this means within the Christian mythos.

C. Organicism

When experience is interpreted by radical empiricism and sheer ongoingness is interpreted as creative passage, other fundamental notions also change. In Meland's case, as among all process thinkers, dimensional, contextual, and relational thinking replace atomistic thinking. Organicism is his early way of designating this new tendency, and he never relinquishes this preferred way to identify the new mode of thinking which replaces earlier atomistic thought. Indeed, at times he calls this new mode of thinking process/relational instead of simply process thought.

---

[53] Meland, *The Reawakening of Christian Faith*, p. 92.
[54] Bernard Meland, *Fallible Forms*, pp. 150-152. See also *Seeds of Redemption*, p. 57.

There are two main sources for the new organismic thinking. One is the new awareness of depth in experience; the other is the new way of seeing the world which has resulted from the new sciences. Basic in the shift to organismic thinking is the notion of a depth in experience. Experience is deeper than conscious experience. There is a depth of feeling and a surplusage of meaning that attend all conscious experience. Specifically, relations are experienced and experienceable. They are not superimposed on experience or reality by the conscious mind but are conveyed in experience as such. Experience is thus textured, which means it conveys a complexity of meaning which defies ready observation or clarity of analysis. Reality is a configuration of events deeper than conscious awareness. This implies that every concrete individual event is part of a contextual and relational ground which serves as the primal context of all events. This communal ground of relations is the nexus from which all specific contexts emerge, including the human structure.[55]

Such a view of the depth of experience implies the relativity or interrelatedness of all reality. All living and thinking is cast in the concrete relatedness of all events in the primal ground or context. This implies internal relatedness, individual in community, not only in the sociological sense that each person has existence in relation to a social group, but in the primal sense that all individual existence arises from a wider communal ground and derives its meaning in continual activity within that ground. "It means that relations are not merely external, formal, subject to dissolution; but they are internal, intimate, and indissoluble by reason of the texture of existence itself."[56] Life is marked by an inevitable solidarity. In order to illustrate his theme of individual in community Meland is fond of amending John Donne's claim that no one is an island. Each person is an island, Meland says, but islands are not what they appear to be. Beneath the ocean surface each island is part of a vast interconnected continent. The organicism or relationalism conveyed in the depth of experience provides a fundamental notion in all

---

[55] There are many places where Meland discusses this idea, but the most complete is *Higher Education and the Human Spirit*. Good secondary discussions are William Dean, "Fireflies in a Quagmire," *Journal of Religion* (October, 1968), 384-388; and Larry Axel, "The Root and Form of Meland's Elementalism," *Journal of Religion* 60 (1980): 472-490.

[56] Meland, *Faith and Culture*, p. 132.

process thinking which replaces the external and mental relations characteristic of all atomistic thinking.

The dimensional thinking implied by the depth of experience is represented in disciplines far beyond the philosophy of radical empiricism. Indeed, early in his career and throughout Meland maintains that dimensional thinking had come to dominate all of the disciplines in their creative expression. Speaking of a new intellectual climate, he says, "What is common here is a fresh awareness of the concept of relations which greatly extended and widened the meaning of existence."[57] He is referring to such diverse disciplines as biology, physics, government, economics, literature, cultural anthropology, depth psychology, as well as the new metaphysics.

In biology the contextualism implied in the notion of emergence is key. In the new physics the interrelatedness evident in the concept of physical reality as a field of force instead of matter is to the fore. Relationships loom as dynamic, experienceable realities. The relativity theory of Einstein points to the loss of a fixed base of reference and the recognition of a variety of frames of reference. The quantum and indeterminacy of modern physics point to a depth and novelty unacknowledged in earlier physics. The net effect of all of this is to confirm a depth and communal ground that replaces earlier atomistic thinking. When one adds to this the rediscovery of the root metaphor of the Judeo-Christian faith by recent biblical studies, namely, the covenant, as well as the imaginative elaboration of the new depth and relationalism in the new metaphysics, one can see how central the notion of organicism is to Meland's process thinking.

D. Causal Efficacy

While most process theologians have appropriated Whitehead's metaphysical scheme as a resource for a developed doctrine of God, Meland draws on Whitehead's elucidation of experience, and particularly his notion of causal efficacy, as a key to elaborating and enriching his notion of creaturalism and elementalism not only as a mood but also as a context. Whitehead describes two modes of experience, presentational immediacy and causal efficacy.[58] Experience in the first mode is the perception of brute physical fact, such as sizes,

---

[57] Meland, *Reawakening of Christian Faith*, p. 35.
[58] Alfred North Whitehead, *Symbolism: Its Meaning and Effects* (New York: Macmillan, 1927).

shapes, and colors with no regard for the past or future. This is Whitehead's equivalent to the classical empiricists notion of perception. Experience in the mode of causal efficacy, however, "is heavy with the contents of things gone by, which lay their grip on our immediate selves."[59] Elements of the past remain, as if at the bodily level, to affect elements of present and future experience. Whitehead's notion of causal efficacy is a key to Meland's concept of the structure of experience. It shows how the present is dependent upon the power of the past and how events inhere to affect our perception in an organic, prediscursive manner. Causal efficacy, as "the hand of the settled past in the formation of the present,"[60] makes the relational context efficacious in the constitution of the experience of the present.

Although Meland never enters the scholastic debates about the meaning, relation, and application of technical Whiteheadian terms to philosophical debates,[61] he employs the notion of causal efficacy in its full metaphysical sense to undergird what he wants to say about the depth and structure of experience, language, spirit, faith, ethos and mythos, and culture. In practice, Meland does not defend and use the Whiteheadian metaphysical scheme as a whole as the grounds for theological claims. Rather, he uses selectively certain metaphysical notions and concepts from the Whiteheadian metaphysics, assuming their power as a vision and employing them to explicate and enrich his theological vision.

V. THE ABSOLUTE AND THE RELATIVE IN METAPHYSICS

Does Meland's concept of metaphysics offer a different solution to the problem of cultural relativism than he offers in his concept of culture? No clear-cut answer can be given to this question, at least not the kind of answer some Whiteheadians, such as Schubert Ogden and Philip Devenish, offer. For them, although metaphysics is *shaped* by cultural contexts, the *kind* of knowledge metaphysics provides transcends the limitations of cultural perspectives in the sense that any true metaphysical knowledge is necessarily true regardless of cultural

---

[59] Ibid., 86.
[60] Ibid., 50.
[61] See, for example, Lewis Ford, "Nancy Frankenberry's Conception of the Power of the Past," *American Journal of Theology & Philosophy* 14 (September, 1993): 287-300.

context. Although Meland eschews this kind of confidence in metaphysical thinking, he is not a skeptic about the possibility and significance of metaphysics, nor does he thoroughly historicize metaphysical thinking in the way contemporary deconstructionists do. Indeed, he insists, against all thoroughly relativistic views, that metaphysics does provide us with a certain kind of knowledge. The question is what kind of knowledge metaphysics is and to what degree does Meland think metaphysics is reflective of a culture perspective.

Metaphysical knowledge is neither absolute certainty nor knowledge that has transcended the limitations of cultural or individual perspectives. This is true of metaphysical claims because it is true of *all* claims to knowledge. There is no absolute certainty in any knowing because of (1) the limitation inherent in the human structure, (2) the depth dimension of all events and its conceptual elusiveness, and (3) the relativity (relatedness) of all reality and knowledge. This means that there is no knowledge as literal description in any field of knowledge. Recognition of this contextuality has occurred in the sciences, as relativity theory and the disclosure instead of picture character of scientific language attest. Metaphysics is no exception to these limitations because it too employs imaginative vision and subjective generalization in its thinking. However, this does not prohibit metaphysicians from making cognitive claims. In so far as metaphysics deals with reality and deals with reality in a way that gives comprehensive scope and rational structure to it, metaphysics is a unique sort of cognition. Although metaphysical knowing, like all knowing, must have its foundation in experience, and must be aware of its character as imaginative projection and not literal depiction, it is one of the cognitive fields.

Meland does not carry on a diatribe against metaphysics in the way contemporary analytical philosophy, historicism, neo-pragmatism, and deconstructionism do. Within its proper limitations, it is a particular kind of knowledge that is as much knowledge as any other cognitive field. However, the eminent question is this: If he does not claim necessity, finality, and certainty for metaphysical knowledge, on the basis of non-falsifiability, rational necessity or some other criterion for establishing certainty, what is his criterion for deciding between two or more competing metaphysical visions? Why has he chosen "the new metaphysics" over other metaphysical visions? The answer to this question is crucial for understanding Meland's resolution of the problem of relativism. He never argues that he or anyone else should accept the new metaphysics because of the rational necessity or even the rational consistency of the categories and principles. He finds the Whiteheadian scheme clear and coherent, but he never advocates it on that basis at all, let alone on that basis alone. His answer is that one chooses any metaphysical scheme over another because the fundamental vision is more "persuasive."

That criterion, however, only poses the obvious question: What makes, or could make, any vision "persuasive"? Meland, perceptively and candidly, recognizes and acknowledges that one factor in selection is autobiographical. "One is predisposed, through his early conditioning, to certain habits of thought which never really become uprooted or dissipated, despite one's maturing in thought."[62] However, no defender of metaphysics in general or of a specific metaphysical vision in particular can leave the answer here. Metaphysics is more than autobiography. There must be criteria other than that one alone.

As one examines closely Meland's understanding and use of metaphysics, it becomes clear that in the end his criterion for accepting the vision of the new metaphysics is *the predominant and persuasive mythos of our culture*. The metaphysical vision of Whiteheadian philosophy has persuasive power for Meland, not primarily because of its clarity or its rational coherence or its rational necessity or its non-falsifiability, but because of its "rapport" with the primal Judeo-Christian *mythos* of Western culture and its ability, beyond alternative visions, to express in universal categories and principles the fundamental insight and imagery of that cultural mythos, thereby giving that mythos greater generality and applicability.[63]

Myth, therefore, as the cultural bearer of the deeper resources of faith, is critical as a criterion for selecting a metaphysical vision. Faith and myth not only precede and underlie the structuring of a metaphysical vision. They are the *criteria* for judging the adequacy and persuasiveness of a metaphysical vision.[64] Further, when the metaphysical vision overreaches its limits, mythical thinking calls to mind the limits of rational thought, reminding the metaphysician of the depth of reality that escapes the coherent conceptual vision.

These points become even clearer when one contrasts Meland and Whitehead. One of the fundamental differences between them lies in

---

[62] Meland, "Interpreting Christian Faith within a Philosophical Framework," 88.
[63] Meland, *Faith and Culture*, p. 19; *Realities of Faith*, pp. 227-228.
[64] Meland, "Interpreting the Christian Faith," 89.

what myth they understand to be basic in informing and measuring their thought. In Meland's view the West has been presented with two basic and somewhat incompatible myths, namely, the Platonic myth, with its basic insight of *logos*, which Whitehead takes as definitive, and the Hebraic, with its basic imagery of creation, covenant, and recreation, which Meland takes as definitive. Whitehead thinks the latter too primitive as a basis and guide for metaphysical speculation, but Meland takes it as decisive.[65] In his view the compelling reason for embracing the new metaphysics is that it gives wider generality to the Hebraic myth, especially the notions of creativeness and community. Conversely, the weakness of Whitehead, for Meland, is his too heavy reliance on the vision of *logos* in the Platonic myth, a reliance which leads him too close to rationalism.

Meland never launches a deconstructionist diatribe against logocentrism or the idea of logos. However, when faced by what he takes to be the fundamental divergences between these two myths, Meland goes so far as to say he prefers not only the content of the Hebraic to the Platonic myth, but also the mythical form of thinking itself when the metaphysical way of thinking is identified with the basic logos metaphor of the Platonic myth.

> My concern with myth has been motivated, in fact, by the realization that analogy as employed in metaphysics appears unable to hold back the floodwaters of rationalism, once the tenuous "appeal for an imaginative leap" gives way to a more definitive mood of logical analysis. This may be because analogy stresses the note of continuity between thought and being, and does not stress sufficiently the discontinuity that exists. Myth, on the other hand, at least registers the shock of disparity between my thoughts as a human formulation and the reality that is other than my thoughts.[66]

Myth, a *cultural*, not a *rational*, category, is the *decisive* criterion in determining which metaphysical vision is best and in qualifying elements of the metaphysical vision selected. His argument for process philosophy consistently is that it shares, more than any other philosophy, the major elements of the Judeo-Christian *mythos* and that it confirms this *mythos* in its generalized categories in the sense that it gives more universal meaning to it.

---

[65] Meland, "How Is Culture a Source for Theology?" 12.
[66] Meland, "Analogy and Myth in Postliberal Theology," 124.

The question we are left with is this: Can speculative metaphysics, whose fundamental criterion is rationality, i.e., rational necessity or coherence, depend on the myth of a culture? And if it does, can metaphysics finally transcend the relativity of culture? Does the metaphysician not need to defend metaphysics on a different basis than the claim that it has "rapport" with or "is confirmed by" the dominant myth of Western culture? How can myth serve as the criterion in a discipline where rational coherence or logical necessity is normally the privileged criterion of selection?

This question leads us to a second question which is important for understanding Meland's view of metaphysics: What is the criterion for his theological thought as a whole? If it is not metaphysical judgments, in the sense that theological symbols and concepts must be exhaustively translated without remainder into the rationally necessary or coherent framework of a metaphysical system, what are the decisive criteria for his theological thought?

We might suggest that, since Meland is a radical empiricist, *experience* is the answer to this question, but experience is the occasion for thought, not the criterion of thought, at least not apart from some theory of experience. Experience presents no ready-made imagery or categories for knowledge. These come from the mind, which is formed by language and culture. Experience does function as a transcending authority or justification in the sense that experience, and what is perceived in experience, especially the *More*, is deeper than the symbolization of a culture. But what provides the authority *cognitively*? Experience in its *discriminative* aspect may, but that also is culturally relative in the sense that the fundamental notions in shaping and interpreting experience are culturally derived.

We may suggest that *faith* is decisive, but as we noted earlier, for Meland faith is a resource which, although in certain respects a transcultural psychical response of wonder and trust, is nevertheless a resource inseparable from the characteristic responses and the *mythos* of a culture. Faith, therefore, is a cultural energy and product. For Meland, in contradistinction to the neoorthodox understanding of faith as the final theological criterion, faith is not a transcendent confirmation beyond the relativities of history and culture, but is itself a cultural resource and therefore culturally conditioned and relative.

But if faith as conveyed in the *mythos* is decisive for Meland's thought, as we have been arguing, we must ask, What is the basis for accepting any *mythos*? Among some philosophical theologians we get a metaphysical defense of the *mythos*, by means of the correlation with (Tillich) or even the determination of the meaning and truth of the *mythos* by (Hegel) philosophy. However, as we have noted, for Meland mythos has place of privilege, even for metaphysics. So we are left with the myth as the authority and criterion for theology. What is the basis for accepting the mythos as authoritative if it is not on the basis of faith as a transcendent resource (neoorthodoxy), or the authority of Church or Scripture (traditionalist and conservative theologians), or reason (metaphysians)?

Meland's answer is a thoroughly postliberal answer. In the end *the only answer to our questions is that the basis for the acceptance of the myth is cultural.* "The Hebraic myth, I would hold, is not only more basic to Western forms of thought and sensibility than the Greek myths, but it has been more persuasive in its influence in shaping the human psyche of the West as well as its religious institutions."[67] The historical context is decisive for what myth is selected.

> Once the revelation of God in Jesus Christ had become a concrete historical fact of Western experience, there was no concealing it, not even from philosophers. Or to state it differently, no thinking or feeling of man's being within its orbit of meaning and experience was immune from its shaping. A philosopher may not say, "Jesus Christ is Lord." He may not even acknowledge the name, or think of it. He will still feed upon the sensibilities of thought that issue from its nurturing matrix. Thus to say that a philosopher, even when he is Heidegger, all by himself sees what the New Testament says, is to appear to have no sense of historical context.[68]

But if, in the end, the myth, conveyed both through the cult and the culture, is decisive for theology, what authority or criterion keeps the theologian from slipping, willy nilly, into historic*ism* and cultural relativ*ism*? Meland says explicitly that he has chosen the Hebraic-Christian mythos as decisive "not on philosophical grounds, but on grounds indicated by hints from cultural anthropology."[69] One could argue that philosophy, in its process form, and the faith conveyed in the cultural mythos of the West, are correlates, one being *compatible* with the other. Clearly this is Meland's conviction, and he succeeds in balancing

---

[67] Meland, "How Is Culture a Source for Theology?" 12.
[68] Meland, "Analogy and Myth in Postliberal Theology," 125-126.
[69] Meland, "How Is Culture a Source for Theology?" 12.

both of these more than most other theologians in "the process school." But when the question of final authority or criterion is forced, Meland offers two alternative myths (Hebraic and Greek) as fundamental options and defends his choice on *cultural* grounds.

Does Meland resolve the modern debate between certainty and relativism? What, if anything, keeps him from retreating to a radical postmodern historicism or a thoroughgoing relativism? Although I do not believe that Meland fully resolves this dilemma (and it is probably irresolvable given what is admissible as argument or evidence in our current context), I do believe he makes some real contributions which advance the discussion and he offers an answer which we can test on pragmatic grounds.

Meland makes some significant contributions to a resolution of the problem of certainty and relativism. His analysis of the role of the idea of "the Absolute" in modern philosophy and theology is illuminating. He maintains that the certainty implied in the idea of "the Absolute" is more akin to the certainty sought in the Enlightenment period of Christianity than to periods antedating the seventeenth century or to our postmodern context.[70] Indeed, he argues, "the Absolute" is a creation of the modern, liberal period to supplant the authority of the Church and the Scriptures. "For the Absolute implies a rational certainty established by logical argument out of concern to find points of fixity and ultimate reference in a world of change."[71] For Meland, however, such certainty is not available, even though the search for it legitimately arises out of the attempt to cope with "the mind's allegiance to despair." The Absolute has "dissolved," not because moderns have disproved or neglected such an idea but because of the nature of existence itself.

What is needed is an "alternative to absolutes." The alternative to modern absolutism and radical historicism and relativism is a postliberal empirical realism in which all concrete historical reality is cradled in a rich ultimate context of depth and relationship which surpasses any adequate interpretation. The alternative to these two false dichotomies is the awareness that experience and existence are thicker than thought, that existence involves depths of occurrences which affect and qualify our conceptual awareness but which do not yield wholly to conceptualization. Neither absolut*ism* nor relativ*ism* is adequate to our

---

[70] For a discussion of this point, see Stephen Toulmin, *Cosmopolis: The Hidden Agenda of Modernity* (New York: Free Press, 1990).
[71] Meland, "Structure of Christian Faith," 553.

lived experience. The only workable resolution of the dilemma is a postliberal contextualism which is open to the full dimension of existence.

> The dissolution of the Absolute as a controlling concept in philosophy and theology, and the accompanying increase in relativistic thinking, I would assert, must be seen alongside of this more sensitive probing into the meaning of context as it affects perceptual thought. Otherwise, the word "relativism" in the current idiom will be exalted to the status of an ontological notion, and made to convey the impression that because absolutes have been dissolved, *all* is relative. What are relative are the perspectives with which men view existence and the events of history. Existing, as a succession of lived experience, participates in a context that may have far more to commend it as an ultimate stratum of passing events than our forms can convey. For this context is not for us to lift up and abstract as a manageable notion. It is, however, a dimension of the act of existing of which we need to be aware, to which we need to be responsive, about which we need to have a sense of wonder, if not a sense of apprehension.[72]

Meland's own distinctive way to phrase his resolution of the dilemma is to say that *"ultimacy and immediacy traffic together."* The search for the Absolute can give way to an awareness of the rich contextual relationships within the relativities of experience and existence, an awareness of the sense of ultimacy within our wider context, a sense of the *More* within the relativities of history. The substance of meaningfulness is grounded in our experience of ultimacy within relationships (relativity). Without reference to ultimacy there is no stature of meaning. What is not axiomatic for some contemporary theologians is his contention that the ultimate is operative within and indigenous to the relativities and immediacies of concrete human experience. Ultimacy is a context of relationships within immediacy. What is equally important is that ultimacy qualifies immediacy, and immediacy qualifies ultimacy, so that ultimacy is not a dimension apart invading as something alien, and immediacy is not simply the flat, insignificant occurrent of many modern truncated views of existence. What is empirically available is the experience and interpretation of ultimacy as the ground or context of all concrete immediacies. The reality of ultimate contextuality is the only "absolute" of existence.

---

[72] Meland, "Alternative to Absolutes," 347.

Meland, therefore, does not propose a radical historicism. Experience within its full context is a more fundamental notion for him than culture and its language. Experience has depths and dimensions to it that are transcultural and that transcend the limited perspective of fundamental notions and frames of meaning of every culture. That is, knowers can transcend their culture because experience is inclusive of culture, and experience is not *merely* a product of a culture. Further, experience transcends culture in the sense that it has features that are relevant to cognition in any culture, such as "surplusage of meaning" and sensitivity to the *More* of experience. These are dimensions of experience as a human phenomenon that transcend conceptual and cultural confinement, even though they are conveyed only through cultural formulation and expression. To the degree that experience is more than conscious experience and cognition is more than conceptualization, to that degree cognition transcends the limits of culture. Indeed, conscious experience and conceptualization are historical, cultural, and relative components of cognition. The non-relative elements refer to the primordial dimensions conveyed in the appreciative consciousness, not in conceptualization.[73]

We are still left with a conundrum. Cognition involves some degree of conceptual clarity, even if the appreciative dimension is cognitively relevant in terms of making the cognitive act richer and less precise than is frequently assumed. Yet, cognition does not, in Meland's view, transcend the culture because conceptual clarity depends on the frames of meaning and the fundamental notions of particular cultures, and these in turn depend on the unique, concrete experiences of cultures in

---

[73] The questions arise here as to how Meland claims to know this and how his definition of experience, with its "fringes" and "relations," is not simply his own cultural frame of meaning. The answer to the first question is that Meland thinks that the deeper dimensions of experience attend experience as such regardless of culture (namely, the act of experiencing the world as a human being), and that these primal experiences which occur in all cultures are expressed in the images, symbols, and myths of every culture. We know this by examining the multifarious mythological expressions of the cultures. In regard to the second question, Meland would not claim that his own frame of meaning (derived from James) is any less relative than other frames of meaning. Rather, he is arguing that from the point of view of the need to conceptualize, James's description comes closer to a "precise" (schematic) scheme than others he or our culture knows. However, he would make a distinction between the universal qualities of experience pointed to in the myths and conceptual schemes of every culture and the schemes themselves, including his own.

different ages. Meland is a thoroughgoing postliberal in this respect. Experience persists, but the meaning of experience depends on language. Thus, in the end, all dimensions of knowing depend on culture. Although knowledge cannot be reduced to culture, cognition cannot escape the relative frames of meaning given by a culture and its experience.

Is there any higher court of appeal for Meland than this one? Is there any cognition that transcends this limit? Can metaphysics transcend the relativities of faith and myth and the relativities of less general forms of cognition? This last question is not a casual one, because if Meland is identified with any one theological-philosophical "school," he is identified with process theology. If he is as thoroughly a process theologian as is popularly assumed, we might expect to find an unqualified, even enthusiastic, affirmative answer to this question. But we never find such a claim in Meland's thought. Although his understanding of human experience, and the dimension of depth conveyed in experience, save him from a *radical historicism* or *absolute relativism*, he nevertheless has a contextual, historical, cultural, and relative understanding of all human knowledge, including metaphysics and theology. Meland is not a liberal theologian in the sense that he appeals to experience, subjective or rational, as a ground of knowledge that transcends culture. He is, rather, a postliberal theologian in the sense that all forms of knowing, though not reducible to culture, are cultural, contextual, and so relative to the core.

5

Meland as a "Rebel Among Process Theologians"

Charles Harvey Arnold, an historian of The Divinity School of The University of Chicago, refers to Bernard Meland as "one of the three odd men" of the Chicago School. Along with George Burman Foster and Henry Nelson Wieman, Meland does not easily "fit" into the school. Meland himself, in an apparently casual comment, refers to himself as "a rebel among process theologians."[1] This chapter is an analysis of ways Meland's thought is a critique of the main line of development in process theology since mid-century.

It is important to remember, as was shown in chapter four, that Meland is also a major representative of recent process/relational thought. Although he understands and employs the vision and the conceptual scheme of process philosophy in his own distinctive way, his thought is nevertheless determined by the fundamental insights and orientation of modern process thought. Indeed, he can be described as the paradigmatic process thinker in the sense that the insights and orientation of the movement not only undergird and inform his thought but remain explicit and at the center of his theological work. His work is devoted more to the application of the process orientation to theological interpretation than to the defense and elaboration of process metaphysics for theological usage.

In that role, however, Meland is also one of the most persistent internal critics of the movement, particularly of the direction the movement has taken since mid-century. In addition, there are themes in

---

[1] Bernard Meland, "Analogy and Myth in Postliberal Theology," in Delwin Brown, Ralph James, and Gene Reeves, eds., *Process Philosophy and Christian Thought* (Indianapolis: Bobbs-Merrill, 1971), p. 124.

his thought that put him at odds with prominent themes of the movement. These criticisms and counter themes are so significant that it is appropriate to designate him as "a rebel among process theologians." It is this side of Meland's thought that we examine in this chapter.

There are some significant, though not decisive, ways in which Meland's thought ought to be distinguished from the process school. Given the direction process theology takes among the students and disciples of Whitehead after WWII, Meland's theology should not be cast as representative of current process theology. First, he prefers designations other than "process" for the larger context of his thought.[2] Second, the major influences on his relational thinking predate the second phase of the Chicago School of Theology from Wieman through Loomer, viz., the philosophical phase, and are broader than the metaphysics of the process movement. I refer not only to the fact that he finished most of his graduate residency work prior to the impact of Whitehead at Chicago. The persistence of the socio-historical method (and its assumptions) and of the mystical mode of thought (from Smith) is evident throughout all of his writings, not only his earliest writings. Third, Whitehead is very seldom appealed to in a direct and authoritative way in his publications. Indeed, Whitehead is appealed to less frequently than Bergson, James, the emergent thinkers, or even cultural anthropologists as "evidence" or as "authority" in his reflections. In his early books and essays, process metaphysics (he usually refers to it as "the new metaphysics") is almost always listed as one among many expressions of a change in fundamental notions that reshapes liberal theology.

These considerations, of course, do not mean that Meland is not a process theologian. As was shown in chapter three, the process conceptuality is crucial in his thinking. Yet, his thought is too rich, nuanced, and complex to be adequately described as "process theology." Process philosophy is but *one* of *many* cultural resources which are useful for the "reawakening" of the witness of faith. He draws upon "mystical naturalism," myth, literature, cultural anthropology, and the history of religions as much as he draws upon the "new metaphysics" in interpreting the realities of faith. An elementalist in his understanding of faith and a theologian of culture in his effort to interpret the expressions

---

2 Bernard Meland, *Fallible Forms and Symbols* (Philadelphia: Fortress Press, 1976), p. xiii.

of faith within the structure of experience of a culture, he does not fit the narrower conception of the process theologian as one who interprets the Christian faith within a process philosophical framework.[3]

The following recurring motifs in Meland's thought point to fundamental ways in which he is a "rebel" among process theologians. They represent themes that cut across the characteristic style of thought of most process theologians today. Some who knew Meland personally may be surprised to see him use such strong critical language in describing his evaluation of the process school and his relation to it. He is described by more than one student at the Divinity School as "one of the few true gentlemen" the place produced during the first two phases of the Chicago School. His sensitive temperament, gracious spirit, restrained style, and open wonder make the term "rebel" seem harsh or at least inappropriate when applied to him, especially when he himself suggests the term. Yet there is in him a proud independence of thought, and above all a non-negotiable loyalty to the rich and nuanced data of experience, that make the designation appropriate.

Although his critique of process theology becomes increasingly explicit and forceful, even strident, in his later writings, especially his trilogy on methodology and most explicitly in the final volume of the trilogy, his restraint in the use of process philosophy and his resistance to any overreaching by metaphysics is present very early. It is, perhaps, present as early as his break with Wieman but clearly as early as his first book. The following considerations point to some fundamental ways in which Meland is a "rebel" among process theologians and introduce themes that challenge the characteristic assumptions and modes of thought of most process theologians today.

I. THE LIMITS OF METAPHYSICS

Meland insists that metaphysical thinking can proceed only with a restraint consistent with empirical demands and with the limitations of our human powers of inquiry. He criticizes some followers of Whitehead for not remaining sensitive to the empirical grounding of Whitehead's own philosophy, ignoring the primacy of perception for the clarity of the

---

[3] For a discussion of the way he intends to employ process philosophy in his theological work, see "Interpreting the Christian Faith within a Philosophical Framework," *Journal of Religion* 33 (1953): 87-102.

categorical scheme. Process philosophy, he thinks, could learn restraint in this respect from phenomenology. "Strange as it may seem, one finds in the writings of present day phenomenologists such as Merleu-Ponty the very corrective which process thinking sorely needs in order to bring it back to a more empirical orientation in its procedures. For the preoccupation here is the perceptual field."[4]

The preoccupation with conceptual matters among process thinkers has led some process theologians away from the realities of faith to a preoccupation with semantic clarity. In the shift from appealing to lived experience within a specific context to appealing to a scientifically tested or a rationally defensible scheme, presumably distilled from experience, a metamorphosis has occurred. In this shift of perspective, theological words such as love, revelation, or forgiveness are given an ontological meaning and thereby are taken to be meaningful simply as words, simply as linguistic realities. The experienceable realities of faith as events somehow become obscured or lost from the theological discourse as inquiry assumes more and more the status of semantic and logical explication.[5]

Meland expresses his primary criticism of this move by asking whether rationalists, modernists, and process theologians have not forfeited the very empirical base upon which religious faith ultimately rests

Regardless of whether his critique of the direction process theology has taken is wholly fair, Meland is clear about what emphasis and direction process theology should take following its development throughout the fifties. "In so far as it pursues the empirical and organismic side of its mode of thought, instead of capitulating to conceptualism with its logical and semantic demands, [it] can reformulate this primal nexus in its own terms as an inescapable elemental fact of lived experience, expressive both in terms of human subjectivity and in terms of creaturely objectivity."[6]

A second criticism by Meland of process metaphysics is related to this one. He criticizes the overconfidence in reason exhibited on the part

---

[4] Bernard Meland, "What Can Empirical Theology Learn from Phenomenology?" in Bernard Meland, ed., *The Future of Empirical Theology* (Chicago: University of Chicago Press, 1969), p. 291; see, also, *Higher Education and the Human Spirit* (Chicago: University of Chicago Press, 1953), pp. 29-30.

[5] Ibid., p. 293.

[6] Ibid., p. 295.

of some process metaphysicians. For example, "I sense in Schubert Ogden, especially, a degree of confidence in the formulations of human reason comparable to that of Professor Hartshorne, which I am unable to share."[7] The basis of his criticism is not only a critique of reason as such, which Christian concepts of the fallibility of human nature convey, but the judgments of relativity theory in the sciences which place limitations on the powers of human observation and reason in dealing with the realities themselves. As a result, for Meland, the canons of reason play a far humbler role than in earlier liberalism or in present day process theology. This limitation is not observed as some understandings of the purpose and task of process metaphysics become increasingly rationalistic.

> By the time Whiteheadians begin to distribute this new crop of fundamental notions, process thinking takes on the air of a new rationalism. Thus the demon dogmatism begins to plague us again. I have been a rebel among process theologians, protesting this very tendency to close the gap between manageable and unmanageable aspects of experience. My concern with myth has been motivated, in fact, by the realization that analogy as employed in metaphysics appears unable to hold back the floodwaters of rationalism, once the tenuous "appeal for an imaginative leap" gives way to a more definitive mood of logical analysis.[8]

A third criticism of metaphysics grows out of this one. Overconfidence in reason leads to a view of literal language which metaphysics, in Meland's view, does not possess. Because the living situation resists precise formulation, the imagery of the process vision cannot be taken literally.[9] This overextension of its view of language is what leads process metaphysics into its rationalism. Instead, the imagery must be understood as metaphors or analogies rather than literal description. He reminds process theologians that Whitehead, aware of the audacity of the undertaking to which he commits himself, insists that the categories and principles metaphysicians use "remain metaphors mutely appealing for an imaginative leap. As such they are as words

---

[7] Meland, "Analogy and Myth in Postliberal Theology," p. 123.
[8] Ibid., p. 124.
[9] Bernard Meland, *Realities of Faith* (New York: Oxford University Press, 1962), p. 120.

listening for a truth that is given, not as one defining or describing that truth."[10]

II. RADICAL EMPIRICISM AND RATIONAL EMPIRICISM

In his first book, *Modern Man's Worship*, Meland anticipates a criticism of process metaphysics that is to come to full clarity and force during the third period of his writing, namely, a critique of the rationalism inherent in "the new metaphysics." Process metaphysics, to be sure, is pluralistic in the sense that the ultimate constituents of reality, actual occasions, are viewed as plural. But it is monistic in the sense that it proposes a unitary actuality to ground the coherence and unity of reality. Meland advances early on in his first period of writing a thoroughgoing pluralism that is expressed as a version of the conceptual theism of Ames and Mathews in distinction from the monism implicit in cosmic theism (the "first phase" of the Chicago School) and process theism (the "second phase" of the Chicago School).[11]

Criticizing both Whitehead and Wieman, Meland argues that the forces or sustaining activities working for a good not our own in the universe are not synthesized through one activity or unified in one actuality but are plural realities unified only in each actual occasion or individual event.[12] A unitary concept is useful to symbolize these pluralistic elements taken together and so aid in our adjustment to them in worship. But the realities are themselves many, diverse and plural. Every rationalism implies an ontological unity beyond what the empirical realities permit. Furthermore, every rationalism implies an overreaching of the mind beyond the actualities of lived experience. His phrase "mystical naturalism" is intended early on to qualify the overreaching of the mind by supplementing the discursive and analytical approach to reality with the appreciative response to reality in its richness and thickness. This critique of rationalism, including rational empiricism, is to persist throughout his career and will become the

---

[10] Meland, "Analogy and Myth in Postliberal Theology," p. 123.

[11] I am following Charles Harvey Arnold's development of the Chicago School here. *Near the Edge of Battle* (Chicago: Divinity School Association, 1966), pp. 28ff and 60ff.

[12] Bernard Meland, *Modern Man's Worship* (New York: Harper, 1934), p. 179.

primary focus of our analysis of his critique of process theology in the latter two periods of his writing.

Since Meland's response to the rationalism of process metaphysics is our focus here, we must recognize from the outset that process philosophy is rationalistic in a distinctive sense. It is not classical rationalism, even though it has some affinities with that form of rationalism. It is of a piece with classical rationalism in the sense that the construction of a system is central, coherence is the test of truth, a denial of these truths is seen to result in incoherence, truth is a unity of logically independent structure, the failure to falsify is an indication of truth, and the world is ultimately a place of unity and beauty.

The differences between the rationalistic version of process metaphysics and classical rationalism, however, can be seen more clearly when one contrasts Whitehead's rationalism with classical rationalism. In classical rationalism Euclidian geometry provides the controlling model for the system. Whitehead, however, reconceives mathematics on a non-Euclidian basis so as to include all types of formal, necessary, and deductive reasoning. Specifically, his rationalism is a speculative vision which proposes to interpret every element of experience, namely, to provide the most general principles exemplified in all experience. Reason is not so much a guide from certainty to certainty as it is a vision to enlarge possibilities. It is what one might call an imaginative rationalism, expressed most clearly in the Introduction to Whitehead's *Process and Reality*, a characteristic of rational speculation which is acknowledged in all process views of reason even though it is less apparent or explicit in the subsequent developments by Hartshorne and his followers.

Regardless of the novelty inherent in the Whiteheadian vision of metaphysics, though, it is still rationalistic in the sense that it is a system of thought, a system based on logical consistency, a system in which coherence among concepts is basic, and a system that purports to provide an adequate interpretation of experience and reality. When Meland advances his criticism of the rationalism of process metaphysics, he is not submitting it to the usual critiques of classical rationalism as such. He is making an internal criticism of the rationalistic side of the system that has come to dominate the process orientation to thought and its vision.

Seldom do direct criticisms of Whitehead appear in Meland's writing. In fact, it is not until the third period of his writing, from *Realities of Faith* through *Fallible Forms and Symbols*, that direct substantive criticisms of Whitehead or of process philosophy appear. Rational empiricism in the process mode is the attempt to take the relativity of the event and see if there is "a generality of meaning issuing from each concrete occurrence that can be formulated as a true vision of experience. Such a vision is a venture in imagining first principles which will adequately express the world in its essence."[13] Meland is sympathetic with the imaginative vision that results. It provides informative or guiding insights as to how one might view things as a whole. However, by appealing to the new physics as the model for grounding the new vision, specifically the vision of internal relations, Whitehead's thought, in designating the nexus of events, exhibits more externality than he really means to convey. One needs the corrective of Bergson and James in reading Whitehead lest the formative notions of the new physics render one's understanding of the creative nexus more external and rationalistic than the depth in the living situation actually is.[14]

For all his use of Whitehead's vision and the process conceptualities, Meland, throughout his career, holds that the depth of the lived situation is more evident in the radical empiricism of James and Bergson than in the rational empiricism of the process metaphysicians because the structured meaning in process conceptuality overwhelms and obscures the depth and complexity of the lived reality. But even beyond the fact that the empirical ground tends to be obscured by the metaphysical framework, Meland insists that the radical empiricists who precede the rational empiricists and provide essential elements in the vision should continue to contribute something to the process orientation that must be maintained amidst the systematic formulations of the system.

When rational empiricists forget or systematically ignore the surplusage of meaning inherent in concrete actuality, they turn its vision away from its radical empirical base. This misleads the process philosopher to overreach the limits of reason to clarify the richness of events and to underplay the complexity and ambiguity of the concrete realities. "The real objective here is to ask whether, in defending religious thought against such maudlin excesses, rationalists, modernists, and process thinkers have not forfeited the very empirical base upon which religious faith, in sickness or in health, ultimately rests."[15] When lived experience is merely the beginning point for a speculative vision,

---

[13] Meland, *Realities of Faith*, p. 158.
[14] Ibid., p. 120.
[15] Meland, "Can Empirical Theology Learn from Phenomenology?" p. 294.

subsequently to be lost to a conceptual scheme seeking clarity for understanding, the scheme itself replaces lived experience and becomes an abstraction apart from the richness of the full reality.

The primacy of perception among some process philosophy gets replaced by a scientifically tested (Wieman) or rationally defensible (Hartshorne) system of thought. A new rationalism results in the fifties and sixties in process thought when the perceptions of the process perspective are overwhelmed by the conceptions of the process scheme. Philosophy as an imaginative voyage to larger generalities becomes a literal depiction of cosmic existence. Confidence in the adequacy of the categories is raised "almost to the point of taking these forms at face value as being descriptive of the realities to which they point. By the time Whiteheadians begin to distribute this new crop of fundamental notions, process thinking takes on the air of a new rationalism."[16]

Meland's designation of process philosophy as a "new rationalism" is to be taken as a criticism of the direction the new metaphysics has gone toward rationalism at the expense of empiricism in recent years, not a repudiation or even subordination of its basic affirmation and vision. For him, the emphasis among most recent process thinkers unfortunately falls on the rationalistic system and not the novel vision of the perspective. The reason for his hesitation to support the new direction is that rationalism of any sort, new or old, even if the new has an empirical base and is an elaboration of the general principles inherent in the self as experience, is an overreaching of the human structure and a reduction of the unmanageable to the manageable.

Meland's explicit criticism of both restrictive empiricism (positivism) and rationalism begins to appear in the second period of his writing, from *Seeds of Redemption* through *Higher Education and the Human Spirit*. Any focus on "intellectually clarified concepts" at the expense of the "emotional rootage of man" leaves the deeper realities of experience "uncalculated."[17] A literalist of any sort "simply will not be reverent before ideas or emotions that transcend his understanding; or stretch his mind to become sensible to them.... His thought moves in a single key— that to which his restricted mind has become accustomed."[18] Focus on

---

[16] Meland, "Analogy and Myth in Postliberal Theology," p. 124.
[17] Bernard Meland, *Reawakening of Christian Faith* (New York: Macmillan, 1949), p. 47; also *Seeds of Redemption* (New York: Macmillan, 1947), p. 135.
[18] Ibid, p. 70.

fact, exactness, and certainty results in a shrinkage and reduction of human experience.

Although speaking during this middle period primarily of scientism and pragmatism as the direct objects of his criticism, Meland includes any form of thought that would reduce or restrict knowledge of humankind and the world to exact certainty or clarity of concepts. The critical analytical temper employed exhaustively at the expense of the appreciative consciousness as a way of knowing reduces reality to only what is clearly and certainly available to the mind in its focused activity as concepts and bars the surplusage of meaning available in the elemental response of the organism to reality that is deeper and more complex than the mind in all of its functions is capable of focusing. The criticism is made not in order to dismiss the significance of the quest for clarity of meanings. But the overly focused mind can too easily dismiss complexity as if it were non-existent or irrelevant to our perception of reality.[19]

This shrinkage is the result of the overreaching mind in the quest for exactness and certainty. For Meland, we live more deeply than we think. We "participate in this Creative Passage as bodily event at a depth and fullness not manageable at the cognitive level; for in the conceptual act, the limiting purview of our own fallible human structure intrudes with a sharper focus and assertiveness than occurs simply in the act of living."[20] Thus, the "ballooning" of our minimal perceptions into systems of ideas conveys more of our abstractive genius than of the realities experienced. The focus on the critical instead of the elemental consciousness and the creatural stance creates the illusion of precision, the illusion that reality is not the complexity and depth of the living situation but is our conception of it. The lure of certainty has been with us in biblical and creedal forms. Now it was just as present in scientific and philosophic forms. Such a lure, Meland believes, is present in much of the process philosophy of

---

[19] "We have our choice, then. We may say, as some of our contemporaries have said, that we shall ignore all discourse, save as it moves within the logic and syntax of recognizable and meaningful speech. This is to dismiss the complexity of existence as if it were nonexistent, and to remain, at all cost, within the prim world of intelligible discourse. Or we may choose to live on the boundary of meaningful discourse, and the depth of reality which is ever present, yet resistant to our constantly seeing eye, except as our formulae or formulations of meaning accomplish the unexpected and thus receive in structured form what is otherwise denied to formulation." Meland, *Realities of Faith*, pp. 159-60.

[20] Meland, *Fallible Forms and Symbols*, p. 28.

the forties, fifties and sixties. Although Hartshorne is the primary object of his critique, Wieman also is subject to the same criticism.

> The question that I find persisting as I contemplate his impressive efforts in relation to process theology is, does Hartshorne project his efforts as an *adventure of ideas* in the spirit of attaining a provisional overview? Or does he employ analogical thinking in such a way as to close the gap between imagery and reality? Is the intent, in other words, more definitive in producing certainty of belief than such an adventure implies or affords?.... I would insist that, theologically, neither the ontological security to which this rationalistic effort aspires, nor the degree of empirical certainty which Professor Wieman sought to establish through the years, is available to us. Both efforts seem to me to draw upon intellectual assumptions, or upon assumptions concerning the status of our intellectual powers which our present imagery of thought will not sustain.[21]

When the philosopher or theologian proposes to translate the symbol or myth into ontological statements "without remainder," she is overreaching the ability of the mind to know the depth of meaning conveyed by the symbol or myth. The challenge to any overconfidence in reason is one of Meland's persistent themes in his own work among the process theologians. Although he is educated, works, lives, and identifies himself with the process philosophers and theologians of the Chicago School throughout each of its three phases, he prefers to speak of his own version of process theology as process thought as modified by an empirical realism.

It is an irony for Meland that in a philosophy that stresses becoming, experience, and relativity, the search for the Absolute had continued among some of its representatives. Absolute space and absolute mind are supplanted in Hartshorne by "a sense of absolute assurance concerning the ultimate goodness of God by meticulously developing his logic of perfection." The Absolute dies hard, "for the shadow of ultimate certainty, first initiated in the dogma of authority, to be followed by biblical literalism and an appeal to reason, has a strange hold upon the human mind."[22] The search for the absolute, therefore, is not confined to supernaturalism or classical rationalism. A similar search for clarity, certainty, and the Absolute (absolute goodness) persists in a Calvinistic form, instead of a rationalistic form, in Wieman's thought about God and

---

[21] Ibid., pp. 140-41. Italics original
[22] Meland, *Fallible Forms and Symbols*, p. 72.

in Hartshorne's own form of rationalistic speculation. In Meland's view, the rationalistic bent has won the day among most process thinkers in the recent developments within process theology.

Meland's postliberal empirical realism by no means repudiates the role of philosophical construction (or other forms of analytical and critical thinking) in theology. The human being has access to partial knowledge and partial understanding.[23] Although Meland consistently insists on the primacy of faith in theology,[24] he is no fideist and no irrationalist. He accepts the obligation to give "cognitive meaning" to faith. This, however, is quite different from reducing faith to reason. It is rather setting the outreach of faith in an intelligible context such that the language of faith, its hopes and aspirations, become continuous with the reasonable discourse of the culture.[25] The theological task consists of the restoration of meaning to the Christian myth, and that restoration includes the intellectual problem of seeing these valuations of faith in the cognitive context, a context provided by the structured meanings found in the critical thinking of our age.[26] His elementalism is always accompanied by a search for empirical grounding and meanings as clear as one can establish in faithfulness to the realities of experience.

Meland proceeds by insisting on the dialectic of depth or complexity and clarity. Mystery and clarity are held together in tension in the life of faith.

> When we acknowledge that complexity forms the basis and starting point of our inquiry, that we think out from deep involvement in a nexus of relationships which hold us in existence, we are immediately alerted to the fact that the word "reality" conveys a more profound and deeper context than can be expressed or formulated by reason. This is not to reject reason or to deprecate its role in the life of faith. On the contrary, given this basis of complexity, the concern for intelligibility in the exercise or affirmation of faith is made all the more insistent.... But intelligibility in faith is not to be equated with the complete rationality of faith. The concern for intelligibility in faith is a more modest recognition of the role of reason in religion. It

---

[23] Bernard Meland, *America's Spiritual Culture* (New York: Harper, 1948), p. 152.
[24] Meland, *Reawakening of Christian Faith*, p. 85; *Fallible Forms and Symbols*, p. 73.
[25] Meland, *Reawakening of Christian Faith*, pp. 70-1.
[26] Bernard Meland, *Faith and Culture* (London: George Allen & Unwin, 1953), p. 59.

assumes that, at best, we can aspire to but a margin of intelligibility in the face of depth of relationships which form the complexity of our existence.[27]

Conceptual meanings provide "sanity," not rationality, or "a margin of rationality in the midst of irrational and unpredictable factors which, nevertheless, assures sufficient order and meaningfulness to enable us to function intelligibly in a context of related disciplines."[28] Although depth and fullness are not fully manageable at the cognitive level, the venture in intelligibility is valuable so long as we do not think the full truth is the framework. "The truth is a truth of actuality (revelation), received from the witness of faith, or out of the depths of experience."[29] Truth is the lived experience in all of its depth and complexity. Conceptualization is the manageable margin of intelligibility that can be wrested from within this larger unmanageable reality. There is a divergence between these. Any vision, including a philosophical one, that claims absolute clarity and certainty has overreached the human measure. Reality is deeper than we can think.

III. THE PRINCIPLE OF LIMITATION

Underlying the critique of some process philosophy as a rationalistic overreaching of the human mind is a complex of other notions which provide the basis for this basic critique. Fundamental to this cluster of notions is Meland's idea of the "principle of limitation."

Our inability to grasp the full import of the lived situation arises from a limitation more basic than the mechanistic character of the intellect or the formalistic character of disciplined thought. Basically, it stems from limitations inherent in the human structure itself, given its level of emergence.[30] All human life is lived in the primal context, the elemental condition of being creatures of the Creative Passage that is not made by us. But we also live in a specific context, namely, the human structure, the particular dimension within which our creaturely existence

---

[27] Bernard Meland, "For the Modern Liberal: Is Theology Possible? Can Science Replace It?" *Zygon* 2 (June ,1967), 185
[28] Meland, *Faith and Culture*, p. 37.
[29] Ibid., pp. 130-131.
[30] Meland, *Realities of Faith*, p. 178.

occurs. This provides both the range of our possibilities and the limitations under which we exist.[31]

As part of this emergent structure we share a basic continuity with all other life that precedes us. Sea water still flows in our veins. We have marginal apprehensions of the More. But there are structural limits to our access to the range of occurrences within the Creative Passage. "We participate in this Creative Passage as bodily event at a depth and fullness not manageable at the cognitive level; for in the conceptual act, the limiting purview of our own fallible human structure intrudes with a sharper focus and assertiveness than occurs simply in the act of living."[32] The principle of limitation is applicable not only to the sciences "but to every form of human inquiry and response, including that of the religions.... One need simply acknowledge that, because a man is human in the exercising of his religion and his art, as is the scientist or philosopher, he is limited in vision and understanding to what is available to the human structure, under conditions that influence and shape that structured experience."[33]

Meland applies the principle of limitation explicitly to his understanding of language. Language is a fallible human form. Language is not reality. "Reality" is the depth and complexity of the lived context. He begins to emphasize this point very early in his second period of writing. All language is suggestive of reality rather than descriptive of it. Therefore, we need to cultivate indirect discourse in religion, including theology, rather than a direct, self-conscious language about religion as such which was so common in the era of our earlier liberalism. Indirectness puts distance between speaker and audience and where the distance is felt, something of an objective mood comes over us. What is conveyed is less described than depicted. It is less pointed to than acknowledged.[34] In his chapter on the poet and the metaphysician in *Seeds of Redemption*, where he speaks of the idea of the creation, he says it is not exact knowledge of origins that the poet and metaphysician seek, but a way of apprehending the idea of creation as a continual event in the primal context.

---

[31] Bernard Meland, *The Secularization of Modern Cultures* (New York: Oxford, 1966), pp. 119-20.
[32] Meland, *Fallible Forms and Symbols*, p. 28.
[33] Meland, *Secularization of Modern Cultures*, p. 151.
[34] Meland, *Seeds of Redemption*, p. 48.

This same theme of the limitation or fallibility of all language continues throughout his writings, refocused and culminated in his chapter on the relation of language to reality in his last book.[35] Theology and philosophy have come to think the word—the right word—is the thing. "But, since we live more deeply than we can think, no formulation of truth out of the language we use can be adequate for expressing what is really real, fully available, fully experienced, within this mystery of existing, in the mystery of dying, or in whatever surpasses these creatural occurrences of such urgent moment to each of us."[36]

Another way Meland makes his point is to insist that language does not picture reality; it serves to disclose reality. Language is not used to describe the structures or processes of reality. It is a series if "formulas projected," never certain what the outcome will be. It is not only the language of the poet that functions in this way. All language, including the so-called precise language of science, serves to disclose some meaning to our awareness of the mysterious universe. All users of language who presume a literal or direct usage misunderstand or ignore both our fallibility and the depth of mystery in which we exist.

The question of the status of language raises the specific questions of the role of reason and logic in Meland's understanding of the human structure. This is an especially significant question in an analysis of his place among process philosophers and theologians. Many process philosophers have come to see logic, specifically modal logic, as exempt from the principle of limitation and the fallibility of language in the way Meland describes it. The logic of necessity and contingency provides a literalism and certainty not available to other forms of language.

A consideration of the crux of this issue will have to remain until our discussion of the notion of coherence and dissonance in Meland's thought. In anticipation of that discussion we can say here that for him a high degree of congruence between any vision of the mind and reality itself remains only a hope because ultimate coherence itself remains a vision and hope. Here, though, we want to stress that for Meland logic stands under the judgment of lived experience with all of its complexity and mystery as much as does any other function of the mind. Logic is susceptible to the same fallibilities as science and art.

---

[35] Meland, *Fallible Forms and Symbols*, chapters 2 and 3, "Language and Reality in Christian Faith," and "Language and History."
[36] Ibid., p. 24.

In his own use of reason, Meland employs it within the limits of the human structure, but above all directs it to serve the ends of whatever clarity disciplined thought can provide. This means that the end of reason is not to discover or delineate rational certainty but "to create and promote the art of life."[37] Thus, even though reason and logic are employed for whatever margin of intelligibility is available within the human structure, when inquiry and the immediacies of existence are both in focus simultaneously, the structure that emerges is not so much the structure of a logically necessary or coherent system but the structure of a symphony. "There is a logic implicit within its minor themes, but the overall movement of its affirmations presents a dissonant situation in which contraries are simultaneously acknowledged and disavowed, in which resolution and peace are somehow attained, but not without the price of conflict, pain, and suffering."[38] In short, the resolution of the unclarities or uncertainties of faith is not a logical argument into which everything reasonably fits, but an arduous negotiation in which conflicting claims are brought into a livable correlation without achieving uniformity of meaning.

In light of the role myth plays in Meland's use of process philosophy, we have already noted that for Meland there are at least two distinct modes of rationality in the West, the Greek and the Hebrew. It is common to set the moral law of the Judaic heritage against the Greek concept of a logos at the heart of things. But the contrast is exaggerated when it is taken to imply commitment to form and structure in the one instance, and an indifference to form and structure in the other. The law in Judaism is more than a social law. It is an "underlying mode of rationality stemming from the covenant between man and God, thus providing the backdrop to man's ordered existence."[39] Thus the option is not rationality in the Greek mode or irrationality of the working of the spirit transcending form and structure in the Hebrew. In a viewpoint from which rationality is seen as the structure of covenant instead of logos, creativity and form are characteristic of reality. Logos within covenant becomes a conceptual approach to the living reality rather than a substantive explication of it. When reason is understood as a mode of apprehending structure in the lived situation instead of a description of the order of reality, it is given a crucial place in theological thought and

---

[37] Meland, *Realities of Faith*, p. 161.
[38] Meland, *Fallible Forms and Symbols*, p. 75.
[39] Ibid., p. 110.

not set over against the mystery and depth of a dynamic and relational reality.

Within this context philosophy for Meland is not so much metaphysics in the mode of clear and distinct ideas and their logically necessary presuppositions or implications. It is a "vision" of rationality, a "venture in understanding, abstractly considered."[40] This venture says: this is how things could be, given certain presuppositions we are willing to make at this point. It is a bold though highly disciplined projection extending the lines of continuity from the original premises toward larger meaning. Christian theology itself stands midway between philosophy so understood and art, partaking of the more subtle and indirect usage of language of the one while attempting to lift the themes of Christian myth to more explicit, cognitive expression as in the other.[41]

> [The theologian's] language, if relational, is never simply metaphysical; for he operates at a level of imaginative thought which, as yet, has not yielded to extensive abstraction.... His language, if aesthetic or poetic, is never simply poetry; for he seeks to interpret and to communicate mythical meaning with more direct, cognitive concern than the poet can exemplify.... Theology, in its function of interpreting myth, thus carries forward two seemingly contradictory modes of inquiry: the one, definitive with a view to explicit clarification; the other, imaginative, with a view to insinuating the fuller range of meaning implicit in the adumbrations of experience which can never be fully borne by explicit language.[42]

The Christian theologian, then, does not use philosophy to translate the Christian myth into a philosophical framework in order to establish its literal meaning without remainder. The object of theological language differs from that of philosophical language. The philosopher attends to the meanings that arise in consciousness from its starting point. "The theologian, on the other hand, must attend to the intimations of an ultimate reality which, presumably, persistently sustains existence, but which intermittently arrests his attention as a work of grace and

---

[40] Ibid., p. 77.
[41] His view of theology is similar to the one expressed by Sallie McFague in which theology as metaphor stands somewhere between image on the one hand and clear concept on the other, in *Metaphorical Theology: Models of God in Religious Language* (Philadelphia: Fortress, 1982), chapter 1, especially pp. 22-23, or between poetry and philosophy, in *Models of God: Theology for an Ecological, Nuclear Age* (Philadelphia: Fortress, 1987), chapter 2, especially p. 32.
[42] Meland, *Faith and Culture*, pp. 94-5.

judgment."⁴³ The language appropriate to the theologian, then, is not a discursive language of utter clarity. She faces the less manageable task of serving the witness of faith and bringing whatever meanings can be insinuated from her more precarious stance. "[T]heology represents a depth of inquiry into what ultimately claims us, a depth not necessarily of cognitive inquiry but of existential or experiential inquiry; a mode of inquiry motivated not so much by a concern for comprehension as by a concern with apprehension."⁴⁴ Theology is not the concern for the rationality of belief so much as a re-presentation of the cultural witness of faith in an idiom that conveys whatever structured meaning is available to the theologian within the predominant images and metaphors of the day.

Theological thinking proper cannot dispense with mythological thinking. The practice of employing human personality or the human organism metaphorically or analogically to extend our understanding of existence is inescapable as a mytho-poetic way of speaking or thinking. However, to the extent it presumes or pretends to be a serious undertaking in literal description or logical construction, it becomes a dubious venture. What is metaphorically imagined is given the weight of literal meaning, but in fact the literal and imaginative elements then become so intermingled as to produce a new mythology. The fact that the philosopher does not acknowledge this effort to be mythological makes it all the more dubious as literal description, for one then assumes that one is really speaking literally and logically, when as a matter of fact, one is simply marshaling an intricate system of logical arguments behind a mytho-poetic assumption and representation. The enterprise as a whole rests upon mythical apprehension and expression.⁴⁵

Whitehead himself acknowledges that his own vision can be traced back to Plato's *Timaeus*. He selects that myth as the basis for his thought instead of the Genesis myth because the latter is "too primitive" to provide a basis for metaphysical construction.⁴⁶ Meland's own choice of a myth is otherwise. He chooses the Hebraic myth of creation and redemption, "not on philosophical grounds," as we noted in chapter three, "but on grounds indicated by hints from cultural anthropology."⁴⁷

---

43   Meland, *Fallible Forms and Symbols*, p. 137.
44   Meland, "For the Modern Liberal," 167.
45   Meland, *Fallible Forms and Symbols*, p. 129.
46   Meland, *Seeds of Redemption*, p. 156.
47   Meland, *Fallible Forms and Symbols*, p. 153.

The import of this choice is highly significant for Meland's relation to and evaluation of subsequent developments in process philosophy and theology. First, as a theologian in the sense defined above, he understands his first responsibility to be a re-presentation of the fundamental myth underlying the various myths of our culture. Thus, his criterion is in part the compatibility of the myth with metaphysical construction, specifically, a myth that shares the basic assumptions of metaphysical construction, and vice versa. He also selects the myth that he thinks has shaped the sensibilities, sensitivities, and vision of our culture, since that is the one most significant for the realities of faith in our culture.

Second, this means that whereas the Hebraic myth has been more influential than the Greek myth in our culture, themes of dissonance, grace, and redemption carry major import and authority in his thought, themes that are less readily accommodated to the Greek myth of logos, especially in its philosophical expressions.[48] The Hebrews, Meland believes, were empiricists of sorts, looking to history and so redemption as much as cosmic process and so creation for their directive.[49] Most process theologians tend to focus on creation and to subsume the whole of the redemptive story under the notion of creativity. This procedure is much more compatible with the Greek myth of logos and order. However, because the Christian mythos and myth also carry the themes of grace and redemption, a new dimension of renewal and hope, as central to their vision, he employs the process vision in some significantly different ways and with distinctive emphases in contrast to many process theologians.

Stated theologically, Meland is in some significant ways a theologian of grace and redemption more than a theologian of creation. Stated more precisely, he understands creation as a process of redemption, the infusion of sensitivity into sheer creativity, within the Creative Passage. This puts him theologically at odds with much of the older liberal tradition and with parts of the contemporary process movement in

---

[48] "The redemptive act is a defining motif in the cultural experience shard by the Judaic-Christian history in a way that creation is not. Creation is a universal myth. But creativity, presupposing a context of the covenant relationship in which the redemptive concern is primordially intended, provides a distinctive setting in which relations between the human and the divine occur." *Fallible Forms and Symbols*, p. 97. See, also, pp. 99-100.

[49] Meland, *Seeds of Redemption*, p. 41, 67.

theology. This is not so much because of a fundamental disagreement with process philosophy, even its emphasis on creativity, but because of the theological themes of grace and redemption which cause him to focus on themes of the Hebrew as well as the Greek myth, and so to be selective in his use of the scheme of process metaphysics.

One final point regarding Meland's criticism of process theology in its overreaching developments needs to be made. He stands as a rebel among process theologians also because of what I call his "consequentialist argument." Specifically, some process theologians tend to ignore or play down some of process theology's original insights in ways that mute themes that are essential to an empirical and organismic view. The rationalistic note predominates at the expense of other notes which would qualify its rationalism. It is not so much that process theologians explicitly deny some of the themes and emphases Meland makes. Many of these points would be formally acknowledged. But after being acknowledged, their significance for the nature and limits of the philosophical and theological tasks is forgotten in favor of points which lead to clarity, certainty, and rational necessity. This has the consequence of playing down, ignoring, or even implicitly denying some of the major themes of a process perspective.[50]

Meland acknowledges that we usually contend most intently on particular issues with those with whom we agree fundamentally, as did, say Barth and Brunner or Niebuhr and Tillich. A common "neoorthodox" vision is shared among these contenders, and a common postliberal process vision is shared between Meland and the

---

[50] "Now it is possible that the process theologian may assume that, because there is this acknowledgment at the base of process metaphysics, he is free to assimilate theological statements and statements of faith to this framework without committing any misrepresentation of the witness of faith, or the ultimate reality to which it points. However, even if this practice were legitimate, it is made such a cumbersome procedure that the sensibility of thought necessary to maintain this distance between imagery and reality is dissipated. For in order not to misrepresent the theological explication on the metaphysical level as saying more than one intends to say, the philosophical theologian would have to remind himself and his listeners periodically with the caution, 'Understand, I am speaking analogically, not logically in a literal sense.' The fact that this procedure is cumbersome means that the process thinker tends to fall into the habit of assuming that what he expresses at this ontological level is, in fact, not only intelligible but true in a definitive and adequate sense of that term. And because of the seductive nature of this habit of mind, one will soon speak theologically within this framework as if the framework itself were normative of meaning for ultimate reality itself." *Fallible Forms and Symbols*, pp. 134-35.

contemporary generation of process theologians he critiques. Yet he is quite explicit that his approach "reflects reservations concerning the spirited inquiry into conceptual forms now dominant in that [process] school of thought."[51] It is, in part, then, more a problem with the "temper and prevailing mood" of some process thinkers that leads to an overreaching of the limits of the task than it is a disagreement about the importance of philosophy in the theological task.

This is not to say at all that Meland's critiques of the direction of process theology are strictly internal and are only tactical. There are some ways in which, given the present understanding of the nature and status of process metaphysics among some of its adherents as well as the prevailing temper and mood among some process theologians, Meland is on the fringe of the movement as a whole. This claim, though, implies a judgment which is, I think, incorrect. One could just as persuasively argue, as I am, that it is he who remains faithful to the full scope of the Whiteheadian viewpoint, or at least to the process-relational orientation of thought, and it is some of the recent advocates of this perspective who have gone beyond the empirical ground and more modest claims in their use of this framework of thought in theology.

Even if this is not conceded, at least I would argue that it is he who remains most faithful to the realities of lived experience and to the radical dimensions of the empiricism that underlie all process-relational viewpoints. Lived experience is basic to all process thought, but the depth, complexity, and ambiguity as well as the mystery conveyed in lived experience have been muted in much contemporary process thought. It is Meland's task, as "a rebel among process theologians," to maintain the centrality and depth of lived experience in any process perspective. The total datum of reality—the sheer event of existing, the actuality of occurrences as lived rather than as generalized or conceptualized—is his preoccupation and his contribution to the process-relational mode of thought in theology.

One may say that the radical empirical and organismic sides of process thinking are best represented in the theology of Meland while the direction most current process thinkers have taken lifts up the rational empirical side and its conceptualism with its logical and

---

[51] Bernard Meland, "Grace: A Dimension of Nature," *Journal of Religion* 54 (April 1974), 120.

semantic demands.⁵² "Process thought as *modified* by an empirical realism" describes the program for Bernard Meland's theological method.⁵³ (italics added) The truth of faith as lived experience is the ultimate source for his theology, not church, or individual, or culture. As to the probabilities of process theologians overcoming the "problems inherent in the process methodology," he is not very sanguine. The direction of process theology today leads him to be "less confident about such explorations occurring, especially within the theological discipline, itself."⁵⁴

IV. COHERENCE AND DISSONANCE

All theologians who employ a metaphysics in the theological task, including process theologians, assume a view of coherence which is essential for the metaphysics to work at all. In order for the rationalistic character of some contemporary process philosophy to emerge and to predominate, the philosopher must assume that the mind has the power to know reality as it is and to delineate its real and not merely apparent structures, and that there is an ultimate identity or at least correlation between reality and the structures of thought. Only if reality follows the patterns of thought and is in fact a coherent system—a rational order giving form and coherence—can the rationalistic elements of process philosophy be sustained.⁵⁵ That theme—ultimate coherence—is one of the most basic presuppositions of process philosophy in its rationalistic mode that Meland challenges. He qualifies it in such a significant way that his critique makes him a rebel among contemporary process theologians.

There is a "darker" vein in Meland's thought than in that of most process theologians (late Loomer excepted), and it is this "darker" strand that we shall finally explore. The shadowy side of Meland's thought is not simply his acknowledgement of the fact of evil and his attempts both to account for it and respond to it as an empirical, realistic, and Christian

---

⁵² Meland, "Can Empirical Theology Learn Something from Phenomenology?" p. 295.
⁵³ Meland, *Fallible Forms and Symbols*, pp. 121, 150.
⁵⁴ Bernard Meland, "Response to Paper by Professor Beardslee," *Encounter* 36 (1975), 331.
⁵⁵ Langdon Gilkey, *Naming the Whirlwind: The Renewal of God-Language* (Indianapolis: Bobbs-Merrill, 1969), pp. 212-14.

theologian. The murkier side of his thought—reflected more perceptively in Archie Lieberman's photograph of Meland than in much of the writing about him[56]—is a strong tragic sense of life that is not resolved by a formal theodicy or in his theology as a whole. There is no theodicy in Meland's thought in quite the same way there is in Hartshorne's, Odgen's, Cobb's and Griffin's.[57] Indeed dissonance is such a significant theme in Meland's theology that the very concept of coherence which underlies the rationalistic side of process theology, including its theodicy, is challenged. He insinuates a note into process thought that is not characteristically found it in its more recent expositions.

That I am not the only one to detect this characteristic and to note how important it is in Meland's role among process thinkers is evident from a significant review of *Fallible Forms and Symbols* by David Hall. Noting that Meland adopts in his own way Whitehead's notion of causal efficacy as well as Eros and Peace, Hall says,

> What is lacking in emphasis in Meland's theological understanding of cultural experience is the third notion which would complete a Whiteheadian vision of the philosophy of culture—viz., the Unity of Adventure, the harmony of experience due to the consequent functioning of God. Meland agrees that "presumedly there is a resolution of all conflict and striving in the final destiny of God," (p. 76), but wishes to avoid any philosophic conceptualization which becomes, instead of a "form of inquiry to mitigate 'the mind's allegiance to despair,'" an *answer* to despair.[58]

The superficial problem with Hall's criticism of Meland is that he tends to identify Meland's thought more with Deweyan pragmatism than Jamesean elementalism with its themes of depth and dissonance. But more significantly, Hall misses the fact that Meland simply does not share the commitment to metaphysical unity and coherence common to most process philosophers and theologians. Or better stated, Meland's commitment to coherence as a vision and a hope, persistently qualified by the theme of dissonance, makes him unique among contemporary process theologians.

---

[56] *Criterion* 6 (1967), 5

[57] See my "Religious Empiricism and the Problem of Evil," *American Journal of Theology & Philosophy* 12 (January, 1991): 35-48.

[58] *Process Studies* 7 (Summer, 1977), 118. Italics original. See, also, William Dean, "Fireflies in a Quagmire," *Journal of Religion* 48 (1968): 376-395.

This dimension of Meland's thought will be elaborated under three themes: the predominance of the tragic sense of life in his thought, the note of "ontological peril" in his thought, and the critique of coherence as the fundamental notion in the critical analysis of experience that persists in his thought.

All process theologians respond theologically to the reality of suffering, tragedy, and death. Indeed, process theodicy is one of the genuinely creative new ventures in theodicy.[59] The centrality of perpetual perishing in the metaphysical vision makes evil in all its dimensions a reality in a way not characteristic of most other classical theistic theodicies. Yet, in the end, evil "fits" into a coherent scheme in all process theodicies. It is seen as a necessary accompaniment of the structure of the world. The tragic sense is subordinated to its appropriate, if not its inevitable and necessary, place in the framework. Even though the reality of tragedy is more acknowledged here than in most classical theodicies, the "sting" of tragedy is muted by making it rational, coherent, necessary.

There are variations on many of the process themes in theodicy in Meland's own thought. But there is a predominance of the sense of suffering, tragedy, and death and the mystery of these which sets him apart from most process theologians. The "tone" is different in Meland's reflection on the problem of suffering. Despair is a real option for him, and the meaning that emerges within that threat is a negotiated event which does not negate or overcome the tragic sense of life. The "significance" amidst the reality of suffering he discovers and promotes remains characterized as much by dissonance as by coherence. The tragic sense of life does not loom within the purview of most process theologies in the same stark and overriding way it looms in Meland's life and thought. Although not as stark as the later thought of Loomer, it shares some of the same sense of doom and pathos which Loomer moved to the center of process-relational thought.[60] In speaking of the modernism of an earlier era, Meland speaks as truly of much contemporary rationalism

---

[59] See, for example David Griffin, *God, Power, and Evil: A Process Theodicy* (Philadelphia: Westminster Press, 1976); and Schubert Ogden, "Evil and Belief in God: The Distinctive Relevance of a 'Process Theology'," *Perkins Journal*, 31 (Summer, 1978): 29-34; and John Cobb, *God and the World* (Philadelphia: Westminster Press, 1969), chapter 4.

[60] Bernard Loomer, "The Size of God," *American Journal of Theology & Philosophy* 8 (January & May, 1987): 20-51.

when he says, "To be able to rest so confidently upon the rational support of a method was itself a confession that the tragic sense was unreal."[61]

The themes of suffering and tragedy begin to loom at the beginning of the second period of his writing with *Seeds of Redemption*. There he argues much as all of the process theodicies argue: the necessity of suffering for significance. "You cannot have significance without suffering.... I must nevertheless insist that when all these efforts to relieve humankind have been fulfilled, suffering with a capital S remains inescapable—if the human being is to be fulfilled.... There is no human life of any depth or vigor that is without its tragic sense.... Living is suffering."[62] The darker mystery of human evil also appears.[63] The problem of death in particular is that in the perishing of the person, the life lacks fulfillment. "We speak glibly of the fulfillment of life; but every life remains ultimately unfulfilled, so far as the span of years is concerned.... All life is lived toward its consummation. Yet every life must of necessity, so far as these eyes can see, remain unfulfilled."[64]

These themes are common among process theologians who write theodicies. What is not so common is that despair in the midst of suffering is a real possibility for Meland. The problem for him is not how to establish the certainty of preserved value within the framework of a metaphysical vision, as in most "official" process theocidies. His problem is one of faith, viz., how significance can be negotiated out of the tragedy of living. The answer to tragedy is not assurance but is faith, and faith is trust, not the certainty of preserved ultimate value. Religious faith tempers, but it cannot rout, the threat of despair within the tragic sense.

The problem of faith does not haunt the modernists and does not haunt many contemporary process theologians; it is given, assured, necessary, unavoidable. These thinkers pursue the problem of value with singularity. The problem of faith for Meland, as for all process thinkers, is the meaningfulness in existence, given the fact that both life and death are our lot. But for Meland this meaning is negotiated, neither automatically given and inescapable, nor assured and preserved by necessity. In addition, all negotiated meanings are collectively a partial

---

[61] Bernard Meland, "The Genius of Protestantism," *Journal of Religion* 27 (1947), 286.
[62] Meland, *Seeds of Redemption*, pp. 105-06.
[63] Meland, *Faith and Culture*, p. 34, chapter 9.
[64] Meland, *Reawakening of Christian Faith*, p. 56.

vision of meaning, not a comprehensive one. Meaning is a vision selected from experience. Insofar as it is rational, it is at best a margin of intelligibility distilled from the maze of experience and events that tumble around us, seemingly absurd, fraught with anxious moments and enigmatic instances. But even this margin of intelligibility that we may glean serves only to allay the "mind's allegiance to despair," not to give us full assurance. Without this degree of intelligibility, we may be driven to dissipate into cynicism, or be tempted to wallow in sentimental assurances. But Meland rebels against cynicism and sentimentalism in the name of the human spirit.[65]

The alternative to the tragic sense, then, is not certainty but trust. "I have ceased to use the word 'hope.' In its place I put the word 'trust.' That may seem an even more optimal term than hope. For a process thinker it can be otherwise. It can be a measured stance within the margin of intelligibility afforded by the critical sense, joined with an elemental, creatural response to what is apprehended in our life in God."[66] His response to the tragic sense is constructed partial meanings within the context of a faith that tempers despair. He could not affirm the assured meanings derived from a metaphysical doctrine of God, objective value, and ultimate coherence.

Meland's challenge to the theme of coherence in process philosophy, though, goes even deeper than his sharpened awareness and account of the tragic sense of life. There is a surd of insensitivity in reality that introduces a sense of ontological peril. There is an abyss of disorder and irrationality, and this abyss is so deep and so pervasive that we must say that dissonance is as much a characteristic of reality as is coherence.

There is an enigma in existence "whose depth and complexity resist ready analysis and comprehension."[67] Thus, dissonance refers both to the divergence between our visions of order and rationality, and the dimensions of reality that negate or surpass those visions, on the one hand, and the dimensions of disorder and irrationality in reality, on the other. There is a surd of insensitivity in creativity itself which results in an ontological peril in existing not evident in ontological visions where

---

[65] Bernard Meland, "Narrow Is the Way Beyond Absurdity and Anxiety," *Criterion* 5 (1966), 8.
[66] Bernard Meland, "Response to Paper by Professor Beardslee," 337.
[67] Meland, "For the Modern Liberal," 181, 185.

ultimate coherence reigns.[68] What predominates in Meland's thought, then, in contrast to that of most contemporary process philosophers and theologians, is the "persisting dissonance within experience" which defies all efforts at establishing rationality and coherence as final and recognizes it to be "an accompaniment of and persistent, even irresolvable surd within our rational experience."[69] This dissonance creates a peril both in existing and in thought.

Underlying this note of dissonance, however, is Meland's most basic criticism of the rationalistic theme in process philosophy. He develops a fundamental critique of the concept of coherence itself. Dissonance does not mean irrationality or chaos, but it does qualify "the universalizing of the notion of coherence."[70] Stated directly, Meland rejects the notion of coherence that underlies process metaphysics in the way most contemporary metaphysics understands and uses the notion. Below we shall see that Meland walks a thin line between rationality and despair, and the notion of coherence as it is employed in rationalistic metaphysics is qualified by his notion of dissonance described above and his understanding of the role of the concept of order in thinking and living.

---

[68] Meland, "All existing, as we have implied, is fraught with peril as well as with possibility and promise. The peril of existing derives in large measure from the surd of insensitivity that intrudes upon all relationships with varying degrees of defeat and destructiveness, ranging from the anguish and evil of isolated existences among individuals to explosive encounters between individuals and groups. As an empirical datum, this surd of insensitivity appears to derive from pathological conditions within the human structure itself and, conceivably, among other structures within nature. There is no assurance, however, so it would seem to me, that this surd of insensitivity is confined to conditions within these created structures. Speculatively speaking, there is the possibility that it may extend to conditions accompanying creativity itself, that it impairs the creative process, or, in any case, sets obstacles to the creative act, thus persistently offering a threat to that act and to conditions consonant with it as implied in the terms sensitivity and negotiability. To the degree that this peril assumes ontological proportions, say as an abyss of disorder and irrationality, or as an aggressive distaste for or disregard of creativity, it becomes a threat to the Ultimate Efficacy attending existence as well as to existence itself. I see no way of affirming or disavowing such an ontological peril categorically; but the tendency of my thought is to assume its possibility to the extent, at least, of acknowledging that the creativity, sensitivity, and negotiability that bring meaningful and redemptive events into existence do so at a price—at the price of an ultimate encounter with suffering and anguish, consonant with qualitative attainment," *Fallible Forms and Symbols*, pp. 45-6.
[69] Ibid., p. 67.
[70] Ibid., p. 198.

Meland says, "It has become increasingly insistent in my own reflections during recent years that the creative matrix itself inclines to suggest that coherence, taken by itself or comprehensively, tends to be a false motif."[71] Again, "In my aging years I have become enamored of that dirty word [dissonance] to the point of wanting to stress the tough-minded implication of the formula; lest process thought become encapsulated in a more optimum view of coherence than the stuff of its insights warrants."[72] Meland is no irrationalist by any definition of the term. Order is a part of the datum of experience as understood in radical empiricism. His critique, instead, is directed toward the sense of comprehensive order and of ultimate order expressed in rationalisms of any sort. The datum of experience does not support "inherent rationality at the heart of things" and "the legacy of an inherent coherence" as it persists in Western thought in general and the process mode of thought derived from the rationalistic side of Whitehead's writings in particular.

Meland insists throughout all his criticism on the relevance of the note of coherence along with the note of dissonance, on order along with the surd of insensitivity. Indeed, as we have noted, he accepts the notion of order as a vision and as a goal. What he rejects is the notion of ultimate order as part of experience or as a necessary idea derived from experience itself. Coherence as ultimate order, including the idea of God, is a working vision amidst the dissonance of experienced reality.

That Meland holds this modified view of coherence becomes clearest in his discussion of ultimate order as it emerges in the revolution in modern physics. Specifically, quantum physics and indeterminacy point to chance in nature, upsetting the idea of absolute order implicit in pre-relativity physics. The metaphysical issue posed in this context is that of chance verses ultimate orderliness, of the relation of discontinuity and continuity in reality. Two views on this metaphysical issue emerge within modern physics. In one, discontinuity and probability predominated. Ultimate order is eschewed. In the other,

> [w]hile these men are not able to affirm an order of nature as Newton and the nineteenth-century mechanists envisaged it, they see a rationality at work in its processes; or more precisely, they find the formulation of thought a useful instrument in apprehending and exploring instances of orderly events and the projection of experimental inquiry effective in

---

[71] Ibid., p. 65.
[72] Meland, "Response to Paper by Professor Beardslee," 336.

verifying some of their expectations. To this extent orderly occurrences are experienced and known.... Yet, as Einstein has said in speaking of the question of an ultimate order of nature and reality, it is his faith that such an order of laws exists. It is a faith that the experimental scientist must assume, he would argue.[73]

Thus, ultimate order is "a faith," a mode of thinking and living for which there is evidence in experience, but which, balanced by the evidence of dissonance, remains a vision of orderliness toward which we struggle. "Order in this ultimate sense can be said to be a structure of meaning toward which inquiry and thought continually strive."[74] It is a venture in understanding, not a presupposition of experience as such or a logical implication of experience. This working vision of reality is a goal, a dream to explore with reservation and hesitancy as well as risk and boldness. "But if an emphasis must be declared, it is clear that, while the abstract vision of God in his ultimacy is a kind of lodestar holding inquiry and the act of living forward in their courses, the disclosures of this ultimate vision as a fact of experience in the concrete pathos and promise of existence, as these loom in individual and communal instances, form the burden in inquiry."[75]

Meland's alternatives are not coherence or structurelessness, rationality or irrationality, rationalism or despair. He affirms coherence and rationality, but these themes in their ultimate dimensions are taken as faith, risk, and task, and they include dissonance even if achieved. "Coherence as such is not denied, or ignored; but it is sought in a context of inquiry in which acknowledgment is made of a self-evident condition of dissonance between what man's own structure of experience can report and affirm and what may in fact be true of existence as a total phenomenal fact or as ultimate reality."[76] Coherence is a project for living and thinking. And congruence between that project and the reality it envisions remains a hope.[77]

Whether process thought as such requires an ultimate coherence, a literalism, and a certainty of its own distinctive sort, remains a matter of debate and an issue of temperament, of personal need, of interpretation of what experience delivers, and of "the boggle point" to which one is

---

[73] Meland, *Realities of Faith*, pp. 151-52.
[74] Ibid., pp. 154-55.
[75] Meland, *Fallible Forms and Symbols*, p. 81
[76] Ibid., p. 112.
[77] Ibid., p. 135.

willing to push one's imagination. What process philosophers as metaphysicians think the system is and does, what linguistic status it has as literal, factual, certain, and final knowledge of what is "really real," how it resolves matters of faith and doubt, security and despair, depends more on the judgments one makes on these preliminary issues than on arguments resulting in certainty. Hall sees that Meland implicitly raises this issue for process theologians.[78] But as Hall himself notes, the degree of literalism and certainty is higher in most process philosophers than it is in Meland. His own hesitation to advance the status of the system beyond what is given in experience remains to the end. The path between rationalism and despair is a narrow one, but it is, according to Meland, the one truest to experience and can be satisfactorily negotiated by the truth of faith as it is lived.[79] Significance, not coherence, is what human living is about.[80] And the truth of faith provides that significance without a kind of coherence that surpasses the realities of lived experience. The truth of faith resides more in our lived experience than in the vision of the mind in understanding.

Meland understands theological inquiry to be more than religious utterance, more than emotive utterance, more than indirect expression. It is a critical effort to wrest whatever meaning, whatever clear and direct understanding is available to faith in its several forms. But as an elementalist in theological inquiry, the sense of creaturehood precedes and qualifies the ambitious project of creating and sustaining a world view, a systematic cosmology. Meland, the theologian, understands himself to be interpreting the meaning of Christian faith, but that meaning must reflect the ambiguity of existence and faith if it is to be faithful to the realities of each. Faithfulness overrides clarity. He understands clearly the role played by temperament in this understanding of the realities and ambiguities of faith.

> People differ in their responses to ambiguity. Getting clear about something seems to some the most important objective in life. And of course it is in confronting certain demands and decisions. But in probing the depth of realities that form our very lives and speak to elemental depths of our

---

[78] Hall, review of *Fallible Forms and Symbols*, 120.
[79] Meland, "Narrow is the Way between Absurdity and Anxiety."
[80] Here Meland's view is very close to Loomer's on Size or Stature instead of perfection and certainty as the goal of all life, including the life of God. See Loomer, "The Size of God."

creaturehood, or of our meaning as human beings, can we hope to move swiftly or even confidently simply by sharpening our tools of thought?[81]

---

[81] Meland, "Grace: A Dimension Within Nature," 123-124.

6 | Meland's Naturalistic Interpretation of God

Meland's approach of the concept of God throughout the entire corpus of his writings is ironic. On the one hand, he says, "[t]hinking about the meaning of God has occupied a major portion of my professional life."[1] On the other hand, he never offers a clearly formulated concept of God, an argument for the reality of God, or a systematic statement about the place of the concept of God within the scope of his thinking. He is not a direct participant in the discussion of "God the problem" rekindled in the sixties and seventies among theologians influenced by analytic philosophy and process philosophy. Renewed among process theologians by the speculative work of Charles Hartshorne, and epitomized in the early work of such process thinkers as John Cobb and Schubert Ogden, establishment of the meaning and truth of the concept of God is at the center of the theological agenda of many theologians who in the sixties and seventies were influenced by process philosophy. "God the problem" moves back to the center of the theological agenda. As Schubert Ogden says,

> Faith in God of a certain kind is not merely an element in Christian faith along with others; it simply *is* Christian faith, the heart of the matter itself. Therefore, the very thing about the expressions of faith in Scripture and tradition which makes a properly *secular* interpretation of them possible and even necessary also makes a *secularistic* theology impossible. The issue here

---

[1] Bernard Meland, "In Response to Loomer," *American Journal of Theology & Philosophy* 5 (May and September, 1984), 144. For two essays on Meland's view of God, see Bernard Loomer, "Meland on God," *American Journal of Theology & Philosophy* 5 (May and September, 1984): 138-143; and Edgar Towne, "God and the Chicago School in the Theology of Bernard Meland," *American Journal of Theology & Philosophy* 10 (January, 1989): 3-19.

is indeed either/or, and all talk of a Christianity *post mortem dei* is, in the last analysis, neither hyperbole nor evidence of originality but merely nonsense.[2]

Although Meland does not share to the same degree the apprehension about using "God language" which has characterized some of the empirical theologians of the eighties and nineties, such as Donald Crosby, Jerome Stone, Nancy Frankenberry, and, to a degree, Wiliam Dean, he nevertheless is circumspect and modest in his claims about the importance of the concept itself within the scope of his religious inquiry.

The reason for Meland's reticence to discuss a concept of God is clear. The limitations of the human structure make any clarity and certainty about the ultimate mystery of existence impossible. The principle of limitation, however, implies more than a methodological caution based on a disparity between language and reality. Uncertainty about "the nature of the affirmation itself" implies a "reverent skepticism accompanying belief" and causes him to "move very close to the skeptical attitude."[3] Yet he is from time to time "emboldened by some effort at a minimum designation of deity."[4] As a theological empiricist, however, his focus is not on the rational necessity or clear formulation of the concept of God as a unique idea. His focus is on "the fact of God" which can be empirically located in experience and can be described with some margin of intelligibility,[5] on what in the environing reality the term "God" points to, on how this designated reality works, and on the character of this God.[6]

---

[2] Schubert Ogden, *The Reality of God and Other Essays* (New York: Harper & Row, 1966), pp. 14-15.

[3] Bernard Meland, "Prolegomena to Inquiry into the Reality of God," *American Journal of Theology & Philosophy* 1 (September, 1980), 77, 76.

[4] Ibid., 77.

[5] Meland, "In Response to Loomer," 144.

[6] "I have recoiled from trying to envisage or to define God in any complete, metaphysical or ontological sense, preferring instead to confine attention to such empirical notions as the creative act of God and the redemptive work of God in history." Bernard Meland, *Fallible Forms and Symbols* (Philadelphia: Fortress Press, 1976), p. 151.

I. GOD AS A CONSTRUCTIVE IDEA

Meland's empirical approach to the concept of God, however, should not be read as a naive assumption that the reality and character of God can simply be read off experience, history, or nature. His empirical description of the reality and nature of God, like an empirical description of anything whatsoever, occurs within the framework of a set of assumptions, images, and perspectives. What Meland offers is a description of what the term "God" means within a naturalistic framework.[7]

In his and Wieman's *American Philosophies of Religion* Meland identifies himself with the "empirical theists" who offer "a theistic interpretation of the universe along the empirical and naturalistic lines" of Ames, Dewey, Mathews, and Smith. "The key insight into this mode of thought lies in the idea that man has been produced by the natural universe, and that through healthful relations with its environing processes, he may fulfill his life."[8] For an empirical theist, the appeal is to what deity means as experienced within a naturalistic perspective.

Meland's idea of God is "constructivist" in a double sense. It is constructive in that it moves beyond strictly methodological preoccupations to an interpretation of the given realities within which the human structure exists. It is also constructive in the sense that God is a construct of the human imagination. In the latter sense his thinking is similar to the current interpretation of the idea of God among historicists, neopragmatists, and deconstructionists.[9] What is distinctive is that his constructivism is set within the perspective of empirical realism instead

---

[7] For a summary of key empirical concepts of God, including Macintosh, Wieman, Meland, and Loomer, see William Dean, "Empiricism and God" in Randolf Crump Miller, ed., *Empirical Theology: A Handbook* (Birmingham: Religious Education Press, 1992), pp. 107-128. See, also, William Dean, "Pluralism and the Problem of God: A Sketch of an American Predicament," in Creighton Peden and Larry Axel, eds., *God Values, and Empiricism: Issues in Philosophical Theology*. Highlands Institute Series I (Macon: Mercer University Press, 1989), pp. 42-51.

[8] Henry Nelson Wieman and Bernard Meland, *American Philosophies of Religion* (Chicago: Willett, Clark & Company, 1936), p. 272.

[9] For one of the most thorough explorations of a constructivist concept of God, see the work of Gordon Kaufman. *An Essay on Theological Method* (Missoula: Scholars Press, 1975), chapter 2; *The Theological Imagination* (Philadelphia: Westminster Press, 1981), chapters 1, 4, and 10; *Theology for a Nuclear Age* (Philadelphia: Westminster Press, 1985), chapter 2; *In Face of Mystery: A Constructive Theology* (Cambridge: Harvard University Press, 1993), Parts I and IV.

of the neo-Kantian dualism which shapes so much postmodern theology. This orientation marks his interpretation of the idea of "God" as both similar to and distinctive among contemporary imaginative and constructivist doctrines of God.

The similarity between a radical empiricist, like Meland, and a neo-Kantian constructivist, like Gordon Kaufman, is a shared sense of mystery.[10] To the extent constructivists hold that the referent of the term God is something more than merely a construct of the mind, they offer an awareness of the environing mystery within which the notion of God is set. However, some contemporary constructivism is based on a neo-Kantian dualism in which the split between mind or language and mystery is nearly thorough. Mystery remains remote, beyond the immediacies of experience. As a result the mind constructs an idea of God, but any correspondence, correlation, or connection between the mind or language and the environing mystery is severed or is inaccessible. The dualistic assumption of the bifurcation between mind or language and reality locks out assurance of any correlation or even connection between the construct and the mysterious context. Mystery is something which supervenes the world, is cast like a shadow from beyond the world, and so is itself an inaccessible "reality." All we have access to is a construct of the mind, which, insofar as it is presumed to be more than thoroughgoing subjectivism, rests on the assumption, which the framework cannot underwrite, that somehow the supervening reality breaks into the world of mind or language and provides some access to itself through the imagination.

Meland, too, has a strong sense of how thoroughly any concept of God rests in a sense of ultimate mystery. However, the mystery of which he speaks is not a reality which supervenes the phenomenal world of nature and culture and casts its shadow or looms as a horizon (Karl Rahner). Rather, mystery is a depth of ultimate relationships within the immediacies of experience. This understanding of mystery, too, is a construction, a reading of reality within a specific interpretive framework. Meland acknowledges "empirical realism as a metaphysical interpretation of human existence."[11] It is no more an objective mirror of

---

[10] Bernard Meland, "'Ultimate Mystery' and Structured Thought," *American Journal of Theology & Philosophy* 10 (September, 1989): 153-157. Compare Kaufman, *In Face of Mystery*, especially Chapter 5.

[11] Meland, *Fallible Forms and Symbols*, p. 123.

reality than that which any neo-Kantian version of constructivism offers. As Nancy Frankenberry argues,

> The determination of what is to count as "empirical" has always been a highly theoretical matter. This is no less true of the school known as empirical theology. The major themes taken as "empirical" by this theology, as well as the various appeals it makes to "experience," are already effects produced by the particular theory it has adopted to render the "empirical" epistemically accessible to reflection in the first place.[12]

Since for Meland ultimate mystery is set within the interpretive framework of empirical realism instead of neo-Kantian dualism, ultimate mystery as it traffics with the immediate experience is given more an empirical than a dualistic meaning.

Meland's understanding of ultimate mystery and his notion of God, then, combine both constructivism and realism. Furthermore, he moves beyond both subjectivism and objectivism. On the one hand, the imagination is free to construct infinite variations on the reality of God according to the perceptions and conceptions offered by the linguistic context out of which the theologian lives. At the same time, the concept of God is derived from and shaped by an ultimate mystery. This mystery is an environment of relationships which exists outside the subject and is a richer context than language alone. One might call Meland's viewpoint a "constructive realism" or a "soft realism." Every concept of God is a construct of the mind, but that concept, although it is not "read off" of experience directly and unambiguously, can nevertheless be shaped, enriched, revised, or even vetoed by the ultimate mystery of the environing realities in which we are set.

II. THE RELIGIOUS MEANING OF THE CONCEPT OF GOD

The most compelling evidence for how thoroughly Meland understands "God" as an imaginative construct is his claim that the primary meaning of the term God is religious, and that its religious meaning is its capacity symbolically to gather certain realities in our environment into an object of devotion. "God, as a religious concept, is a

---

[12] Nancy Frankenberry, "Major Themes of Empirical Theology," in Randolf Crump Miller, ed., *Empirical Theology: A Handbook* (Birmingham: Religious Education Press, 1992), pp. 36-37.

collective representation of certain sustaining relations having cosmic implications."[13] There are, Meland maintains, two different approaches to the world, the contemplative and synthetic, on the one hand, and the theoretical and analytic, on the other. The primary meaning of the term God resides in the former approach to reality. God is first and foremost a religious symbol used for contemplation, not an idea to be used for reflection. It has to do with our adjustment and devotion to the environing forces that sustain us. Thus, God is primarily a synthetic concept instead of an analytic concept.

In an early discussion with John Dewey, "Is God One or Many?" Meland again argues that "the term God is essentially a religious or contemplative concept."[14] In worship the mind synthesizes the multiplicity of experience into a oneness and is devoted to that vision. To believe in God is to make into a single object of devotion the many sustaining activities of the universe. Even though empirically experienced and analytically considered the reality of God may not be One or a personality, the religious meaning of God as a synthetic concept is an idealized and synthesized construction of the pluralistic reality of sustaining behaviors of the universe. Thus God is "a collective term" which refers to those most important conditions of our environment upon which life depends for its sustenance and meaning. It is primarily used not as a theological term but for purposes of adoration and address.[15] God, therefore, is a regulative notion synthesized by the religious person for religious purposes of devotion.

III. THE REALISTIC MEANING OF THE CONCEPT OF GOD

Although the primary meaning of the term God is a collective term of devotion to the most important conditions upon which human life depends, the meaning of the term is not exhausted by purposes of devotional commitment. When the concern is about practical adjustment to these conditions and theoretical reflection upon them, the language of worship, including an unambiguous and confident use of the term God itself, must be set aside and in its place a more empirical language

---

[13] Meland, *Fallible Forms and Symbols*, p. 176.
[14] Bernard Meland, "Is God One or Many?" *Christian Century* (31 May 1933), 725.
[15] Bernard Meland, *Modern Man's Worship* (New York: Harper & Brothers, 1934), pp. 171-174.

employed. Meland's method of distinguishing between the religious meaning of the term God, on the one hand, and the practical and theoretical consideration of the meaning of the term, on the other, is clear. "In reflective tasks, where the objective is avowedly that of discerning the empirical nature of sustaining reality; and in practical tasks, where the objective is that of adjusting to those empirical conditions of supreme importance, the preliminary method at least would seem to be analytic, and would therefore call for terms expressive of the empirical phenomena thus encountered."[16]

In his earliest writings it is clear that Meland shares the view of the early Chicago School that the function of the religious concept of God is adjustment to objective reality. Countering the themes of subjectivity and mentalism in liberalism, he says, "The distinctive religious dimension, then, is awareness and appreciation of reality. Religion is reality-centering."[17] This objective sense of reality of which he speaks refers to the larger environment which supports the human venture and prompts the creatural response of appreciation and devotion. Even the religious meaning of the term God is not reduced by Meland to subjectivism or constructivism. God as a religious symbol can also be explored in practical and reflective thought as a concept which has some connection to an environment which prompts, cradles, judges, and nurtures the religious response of appreciation and devotion.

The term God, then, also is an empirical concept. It has some correspondence to the mystery and depth of the environment, and thus has a "realistic" reference as well. When viewed analytically, that is, in terms of the kind of language which seeks some margin of intelligibility within an empirical and naturalistic framework for understanding the world, not only does the singular focus and focused meaning of the term God dissipate, the meaning of the term becomes more vague and ambiguous than either traditional theism or the neoclassical theism of process-relational theologies suggest in their elaborate doctrines of God. When empirically approached from the point of view of what a rich view of experience offers and what a naturalistic construction of the world permits, God as an empirical and realistic concept refers to particular behaviors or structures of reality within the total environment that sustain us.

---

[16] Meland, "Is God One or Many?" 726.
[17] Meland, *Modern Man's Worship*, p. 185.

In his early discussions of the concept of God, which are primarily a critique of the liberal christocentric description of the character of God in terms of personality, Meland argues that to understand the idea of God in terms of the analogy of personality overstates the case. The "cosmic reality" cannot be understood in terms of personality, for personality is itself an emergent synthesis so is not of absolute or even ultimate significance. The mystery of lived experience cannot be reduced to a Oneness. Instead, all sustaining behaviors, complex and ambiguous as they are, must be included in any concept of God. "The very assumption, in fact, that there is a single organic tendency at work in the universe which may be designated God, seems an over-simplification of the facts.... The richest reality may not be the One, but the Many."[18] When approached empirically, then, the term God has a pluralistic meaning. Finally, Meland stands with Ames, Dewey, and Mathews, against Wieman, acknowledging pluralistic elements which, taken together, describe God.[19]

The certain sustaining relations having cosmic implications are not One, simple, single, unified. Empirically apprehended and reflectively comprehended, these elements of the world and of experience are many. The impulse of religious devotion cannot, in reflection, reduce objective reality to an empirical Oneness. Fully experienced reality vetoes any assumption that reality can be so conceived as one in any direct or indirect way. Instead of designating this activity as One, or one aspect of this activity as God, as did Whitehead and Wieman, Meland opts early on for an explicit pluralism in his concept of God on the grounds of what is empirically required.

> It would seem to me...that these many sustaining activities, so important to life, attain synthesis in each individual event, person, or concrete object. These many activities so work together as to produce events in synthesis and to sustain them, just as associated activities in any system, organization, or institution work together to sustain the good of its members. But that *working together* in the cosmos cannot be abstracted as a single behavior and term God any more than the working together in organizations and institutions may be abstracted and termed the head of the system or the initiator of the system. The many activities come to synthesis in specific events, and there is this working together of the many activities which issue

---

[18] Bernard Meland, "Toward a Valid View of God," *Harvard Theological Review* 24 (July, 1931), 202-203.
[19] Wieman and Meland, *American Philosophies of Religion*, p. 274.

in the synthesis of the many; but the empirical character of these sustaining realities, when theoretically conceived or practically approached, is pluralistic, even though these pluralistic elements be correlated into harmonious operations. To state it simply, reality thus conceived gives the effect of a *community of activities,* rather than a single behavior.[20]

God, then, designates "a reality in the creative passage bent on qualitative attainment, winning the creative passage for qualitative emergence."[21] This reality is empirically described as particular behaviors and structures within the creative passage. Early on, when emphasizing the pluralistic character of the forces within the environment which produce and shape us, Meland speaks of God as a "community of behaviors," an efficacious complex of forces or powers within the natural world which produces whatever meaning emerges out of the sheer ongoingness of nature.

By 1937 Meland expands his description of the human relation to the environing forces of nature to include a structured order among them. He begins to move beyond the thoroughgoing conceptualism in his notion of the divine toward a naturalistic theism in which God is the growth of organic unity within the cosmic environment. This is apparent when he begins to claim that there are two facts that seem persuasive: the human species has been sustained and promoted through organic interaction, and "through disciplined devotion to what appears to be an *order of life,* humankind, in certain of its forms, has achieved a high degree of fulfillment."[22] These activities within the natural sphere he calls "the Creative Order." The activities which constitute this Creative Order suggest a growing organic unity in the world.

> The mystical naturalist views this growth as a more-than-human functioning; not an extra-human or supernatural activity, but a wider-than-human pattern, including the human, but extending beyond his efforts, weaving and shaping the many inter-related human behaviors toward a richer integration of activity. This Creative Order thus envisioned, growing

---

[20] Meland, *Modern Man's Worship,* p. 179.
[21] Bernard Meland, "The New Language in Religion," in Perry LeFevre, ed., *Bernard Meland, Essays in Constructive Theology* (Chicago: Exposition Press, 1988), p. 141; and *Faith and Culture* (London: George Allen and Unwin, 1955), p. 126.
[22] Bernard Meland, "The Faith of a Mystical Naturalist," *Review of Religion* (1937), 270.

toward increasing organic unity, the mystical naturalist terms *God*, believing that this reality is worthy of man's full devotion.[23]

In a later credo statement he speaks of God as "a structure of infinite goodness and incalculable power," and of "the transcendent structure of meaning which is beyond our comprehension" and says that "God stands to man as one structure of meaning stands to another."[24]

Meland's notion of God as a pluralistic structure of qualitative goodness stands between Wieman's monism and Loomer's pantheism.[25] His empirical realistic concept of God stands between the sharper concepts of God as a singular structure of good (monism) and God as the world (pantheism). Unlike Wieman, he is unable to designate God as one behavior or structure. The assumption that there is a single, organic tendency at work in the universe which may be designated God is an over-simplification of the facts.[26] The richest reality may not be the one but the many, an idea which puts him closer to Loomer's than to Wieman's concept of God. On the other hand, Meland "will not make a devil out of God"[27] by identifying God with sheer ongoingness, or creativity as such, or, as Loomer did, with the whole world.[28] If one identifies God with the world instead of with a term of selection within the world, such as behaviors or structures of sensitivity within the nature which have some correspondence to human interests, as Meland does, one has no basis on which to identify and to be devoted to the good, which is the object of the religious life.[29]

Meland's empirical realistic approach to God also stands between a strictly constructivist and a strictly objectivist interpretation of God. He does not treat divinity either as an objective being which is singular or as a subjective construct which is an illusion. On the grounds of the wider

---

[23] Ibid., 271.

[24] Meland, *Faith and Culture*, p. 195.

[25] A critique of Loomer's pantheism in the light of Meland's thought will come later in this chapter. For a critique of Wieman's monism in a similar light, see my "How Empirical Is Wieman's Theology?" *Zygon* 22 (March, 1987): 49-56.

[26] Meland, "Toward a Valid View of God," pp. 202-3.

[27] The phrase is Meland's and is from a taped conversation between him and Loomer at a conference at Purdue University in October, 1982 on "Bernard Meland and the Future of Theology."

[28] Bernard Loomer, "The Size of God," *American Journal of Theology & Philosophy*," 8 (January & May, 1987): 20-51.

[29] See my "Radical Empiricism and the Problem of Evil," *American Journal of Theology & Philosophy* 12 (January, 1991): 35-48.

theory that experience and language even though disparate nevertheless interpenetrate,[30] Meland insists, on the one hand, that the concept of God is a linguistic construct both in the broad sense that it is a strictly functional or linguistic concept of devotion and in the narrower sense that all of experience, including realism, is interpretation from within a perspective. On the other hand, the surrounding mystery proffers behaviors and structures which nourish certain constructs and qualify or veto others as abstractions or inadequate, and it proffers other constructs as worthy of pragmatic exploration. "The nexus of relationships that forms our existence is not projected; it is given. We do not create these relationships; we experience them."[31]

Meland's view of God is as William Dean describes it: "God, like any entity, is the creature of current interpretation; equally, God is historically creative just as any historical force is creative."[32] Meland himself is quite explicit about including these dual components of constructivism and realism in his meaning of the term God as a practical and reflective term. "From one angle, we might say that what the organismic philosopher designates God, namely the integrating process, is part and parcel of the very activities which are so integrated."[33]

As noted earlier, Meland's caution, resistance, or downright skepticism about the possibility of developing a proper doctrine of God causes him to focus most of his discussion on the workings and character instead of the definition of God. Therefore, one never finds an "argument for the reality of God" in the writings of Meland. Insofar as he offers an argument, his argument focuses on what we might be required to affirm on the basis of empirical evidence.

> Gushing out like a stream of turbulent water, is the brute process of creativity. It is without form and void. It is a ceaseless ongoing of coming

---

[30] Nancy Frankenberry, *Religion and Radical Empiricism* (New York: State University of New York Press, 1987), 136-144; William Dean, *History Making History* (New York: State University of New York Press, 1988), p. 142; Tyron Inbody, "Meland's Post-Liberal Empirical Method in Theology," in W. Creighton Peden and Larry Axel, eds, *God, Values, and Empiricism*, Highlands Institute Series I (Atlanta: Mercer University Press, 1989), pp. 99-108.
[31] Bernard Meland, "How Is Culture a Source for Theology?" in *Bernard Meland: Essays in Constructive Theology A Process Perspective*, ed. Perry LeFevre (Chicago: Exploration Press, 1988), p. 3.
[32] William Dean, "Pluralism and the Problem of God," p. 49.
[33] Meland, *Modern Man's Worship*, p. 180.

into being and perishing, coming into being and perishing. Presumably this endless creativity could go on indefinitely as a formless void having no meaning, no purpose, no end in view; but it does no such thing. Instead, it issues in events of meaning, in beauty, in concrete objects with character and pattern, in cycles of history, in a drama of triumph and tragedy. Whence all this character and meaning rising from the formless void?[34]

This is an "argument" for God something like the principle of concretion in process philosophy. Creativity itself is sheer brute process, coming into being and perishing. However, because of the ultimate solidarity of existence, existence has this character because God, like a presence in every event of emergence, stands over the brute process with tenderness and patience, holding up to it all possibilities of meaning and value. One has to distinguish between what is brute force in creativity and what gives to creation meaning and character. God is that gentle working. The empirical datum is the abundance of concrete good that is in each situation which is beyond each individual's perception and even apprehension.[35]

IV. GOD AS A DESIGNATIVE IMAGE

Instead of offering a definition or doctrine of God, Meland provides a series of images in his effort to point to that which, within the surrounding mystery of existing, the term God designates. God is both an imaginative construct which focuses the religious devotion and a reality within the creative passage.[36] Since that reality is a mystery deeper than we can think, we can denote that structure only through images which specify that structure within the creative passage. One can

---

[34] Bernard Meland, *Seeds of Redemption* (New York: Macmillan Company, 1947), p. 59.

[35] Ibid, pp. 51, 53, 57, 59; also *Faith and Culture*, p. 180.

[36] A similar argument has been made by Gordon Kaufman. In his earlier writing about God as a constructive idea, the term God was discussed almost exclusively as a "regulative concept" analogous to "world" or other strictly Kantian metaphysical ideas. In his more recent writings, the term God comes close to referring to (at least certain) cosmic forces at work within the evolutionary process for relativizing and humanizing purposes. See, for example, *Theology for a Nuclear Age*, pp. 35, 37, 42-44. He even speaks of his emerging concept of God as "conceived in this narrowly naturalistic way," p. 40.

trace the development of Meland's thought about God as a structure within his empirical realism by examining the primary images he uses.

In *Modern Man's Worship* the primary image is "sustaining process."[37] In *Write Your Own Ten Commandments*, the final chapter on "The Supreme Reality" designates this sustaining activity as "a Silent Process." He speaks of God as "a growth in our midst, a Silent Process making us what we are and shaping us into what we shall become."[38] In *American Philosophies of Religion*, this community of activities which sustains and promotes life is specified as "a Creative Order in the universe." "Wholly apart from its wider implications, it is clear that it fulfills human ends. This Creative Order, the mystical naturalist calls God."[39]

Clearly, however, the predominant two images are "the sensitive nature within nature" and "depth and ultimacy within the creative passage." The former of these two recurring images appears when emergent evolution, the new physics, and organismic thinking force his reconception of nature.[40] The new cosmology provides a new set of imagery for thinking about God.

The significance of the new cosmology for his image of God is most apparent in *Seeds of Redemption*. The distinctive significance of the new metaphysics lies in its distinction between that which is brute force in creativity and that which gives to creation meaning and character, a gentle working that is the redemptive influence upon force. "This is the thesis we return to again and again, which gives metaphysical ground for the assertion that a situation is right, religiously right, only when force and process yield to the shaping of a sensitive working which can issue in meaning and character."[41] Creativity as sheer ongoingness, as brute force, is modified by a structure of sensitivity within nature. In *The Realities of Faith* he speaks of "a matrix of sensitivity in which all life is

---

[37] Meland, *Modern Man's Worship*, chapter XII. Images such as "wealth of sustaining activities and relationships," "the portion which is sustaining," "many sustaining activities," "those most important conditions upon which life depends," "sustaining reality," "the system of progressive integration," and "the integrating system" also appear.

[38] Bernard Meland, *Write Your Own Ten Commandments* (Chicago: Willett, Clark & Company, 1938), p. 140.

[39] Wieman and Meland, *American Philosophies of Religion*, p. 294.

[40] Meland, "In Response to Loomer," p. 145.

[41] Meland, *Seeds of Redemption*, p. 57.

cast."[42] What this sensitive nature within nature reaches for is qualitative attainment.

> Creativity is, on the one hand, the tragic process of dissolution. It is made good only as its perishings are transmuted into meaningful events....Bare Creativity is advance into novelty.... Creativeness, or the creative act, issuing in event, implies turning the reproductive process toward meaningful ends by transmitting to each event the burden of actuality, which is to make it, in some sense, the bearer of attained value. God is on the side of qualitative attainment, pressing its demands upon the impulse toward novelty.[43]

Sensitivity rather than mind or will is a better designation for God, for what gives significance to mind is precisely its capacity for sensitiveness.[44] The sensitive nature within nature is the ultimate efficacy. Countering the dissociation of sensitivity from causal efficacy and the implication that sensitivity is weakness and impotence lacking efficacy, Meland stresses that sensitivity as a mode of being attentive and caring is a form of efficacy within nature.

Following his return to the Divinity School as a member of the faculty, Meland broadens the scope of his images of God. He adds the notion of depth and ultimacy within the Creative Passage as a proper designation of God. The context for the talk about the sensitive nature within nature becomes Ultimacy as a Creative Passage within which our immediacies transpire.[45]

Creative Passage is Meland's term for being. It is his term for envisioning ultimate reality processively and for expressing the depth and ultimacy that pervade and sustain every moment of our immediacies. "On its subjective side I see existence as a stream of

---

[42] Bernard Meland, *The Realities of Faith* (New York: Oxford University Press, 1962), p. 184.
[43] Meland, *Faith and Culture* (London: George Allen & Unwin, 1953), pp. 105-6.
[44] Meland, *Seeds of Redemption*, p. 60.
[45] Meland, "In Response to Loomer," p. 151. "The path in between has been to broaden the base of inquiry by viewing the dimension of ultimacy not simply as being terminal, nor exclusively as a dimension of depth in the sense of earlier conceptions of immanence, but as being processively present and immediately operative within our immediacies as a Creative Passage. Within that broader conceptualization of a processive depth of ultimacy, I have envisioned the impelling efficacy of a Sensitive Nature within Nature effecting its qualitative attainments."

experience; in its objective aspect, as a Creative Passage."[46] The term Creative Passage refers to both being and becoming in their interplay. It is the most fundamental characterization of existence. Although he does not identify God and the Creative Passage, "I have come to see the reality of God as being of a piece with the Creative Passage."[47] So designated, God is the ultimacy efficacy within relationships. This sensitive working and efficacy inheres within the creative passage.[48]

V. THE AMBIGUITY OF GOD

Toward the end of his career the theme of dissonance or ambiguity within the creative passage and thus within God begins to appear more prominently. "It has become increasingly insistent in my own refections during recent years that the creative matrix itself inclines to suggest that coherence, taken by itself or comprehensively, tends to be a false motif."[49] The creative matrix, rather, is ambiguous.

Part of the problem in understanding the subtlety of Meland's concept of God is focused on his use of the term ambiguity with reference to God. The term itself can mean either conceptual imprecision or conflict within and between commitments. Clearly God is an ambiguous idea in the former sense, and necessarily so because the locus of the empirical meaning of the term God is at the fringes and depth of experience which escapes clear and precise conceptualization. The issue, rather, in understanding Meland is how he uses the concept of the ambiguity of God in the aesthetic and moral senses.

Here again Meland stands between Wieman and Loomer. He rejects, on the grounds of empirical evidence, Wieman's devotion to a structure or behavior of singular goodness abstracted from the rich range of sustaining behaviors or structures in experience within the creative passage. However, he is not about to worship nature or "to make a devil out of God," as he believes Loomer's pantheism licenses when he makes nature in the widest range of its creative power identical with God. In one of his earliest books he writes,

---

[46] Meland, "How Is Culture a Source for Theology?" p. 2.
[47] Ibid., p. 3.
[48] Meland, *Fallible Forms and Symbols*, p. 151.
[49] Ibid., p. 65.

> To those who are not committed to an either-or doctrine—either a perfect world, or a chaos of demonic intent—this growth of the ages gives evidence of an emerging organic reality; not inevitable and omnipotent, but persistent and potent, as mighty as the growth of the fields and of the higher creatures of the earth; a Silent Process of unfathomable scope and possibility, shaping the course of our days in so far as we are able to yield intelligently and effectively to its shaping.[50]

Because God is of a piece with the creative passage, the reality of God is ambiguous to the extent that the creative passage is itself rugged and hazardous. This means the power of God is tragic. "We do not understand this silent working of a creative God in our midst if we think of it as wholly beneficent. Growth involves destruction if it is to be creative."[51] Growth as the creative advance of life also means suffering. Indeed, in a footnote reminiscent of much scripture, of some themes in classical theism, and of Gordon Kaufman's discussion of the complexity of the love of God,[52] Meland rejects the notion of the evil God but advances the notion of the ambiguous God, if ambiguity be defined as a power which in its moral and aesthetic dimensions is more complex than a singular goodness or a singular unitary structure abstracted from the richness of the creative passage.[53] Referring to counterthemes, Meland says, "These reveal sensitiveness that knows wrath and justice as well; but the wrath of a patient, long suffering deity differs from the ruthless deity revealing its power."[54]

This does not make God evil, nor does it make ambiguity something to be celebrated or worshipped. Meland accepts the naturalistic theist's point that in order to apply the term ambiguity to God one must assume the term God has meaning with reference to human interests, for nature is not ambiguous in itself but only from the point of view of the

---

[50] Meland, *Write Your Own Ten Commandments*, p. 143.
[51] Meland, *Seeds of Redemption*, p. 63. See, also, "The Tragic Sense of Life," *Religion in Life* 10 (1941): 212-222; and "The Breaking of Forms in the Interest of Importance," *Criterion* 10 (Winter, 1971): 4-11.
[52] Gordon Kaufman, "Empirical Realism in Theology: An Examination of Some Themes in Meland and Loomer," in *New Essays in Religious Naturalism*, ed. Creighton Peden (Macon: Mercer University Press, 1993).
[53] For a discussion of the ambiguity of God, see Bernard Loomer, "The Size of God,": 20-51, and James Poling, *The Abuse of Power: A Theological Problem* (Nashville: Abingdon Press, 1991), pp. 51-52, 164-166, 190-191.
[54] Meland, *Seeds of Redemption*, p. 147n.

commitment to the human good.[55] But God is implicated in the ambiguity of the creative passage in the sense that God as the structure of sensitivity within the creative passage is interdependent with it and so is affected and limited by the creative passage. Meland's idea of the character of God, then, is shaped by the concrete complexity of the historical creativity and love of God, witnessed to in much Scripture and historical experience, instead of the monopolar unity of God and the singular goodness of God in any form of theism, whether it be classical theism, neoclassical theism, or even some empirical theisms, viz., any kind of theism which sees God as a cosmic individual or as a discrete unitary entity or force.

Meland's view is that tragedy and ambiguity stand at the very "heart" of God. This tragic element, however, is not what we worship and serve. Religious commitment should not be given as some form of natural piety to the ambiguous whole within which God is included, but to the sustaining concrete behaviors or structures within the creative passage which produce value, as a form of religious and ethical devotion. Meland is a naturalistic theist in the sense that he believes that mature religion is devotion to what increases meaning. But any empirical accounting of the meaning of the term God requires that the situation within God is more ambiguous than theism of almost any sort acknowledges. Nor does ambiguity require the spirit of pessimism. "Religious pessimism, in short, is not simply required by the fact that there may be no omnipotent, unambiguous, extrahistorical, and evil-eradicating historical process."[56]

Meland is a *theist* in the sense that the human imagination does not create the latent possibilities of value but discovers them, and human effort does not contrive the relevance of natural conditions but responds to them and serves them. He is a *naturalist* in the sense that he hypothesizes no extrahistorical reality and he assumes a naturalistic construction of experience. He is a *naturalistic theist* in distinction from a pantheist in that he sides with the priority of human interests instead of nature as a whole and with the ways human effort itself is undergirded by the grace of nature in his construction of the concept of God.[57] In that

---

[55] Marvin Shaw, "The Romantic Love of Evil: Loomer's Proposal of a Reorientation in Religious Naturalism," *American Journal of Theology & Philosophy* 10 (January, 1989), 40.
[56] William Dean, "Pluralism and the Problem of God," p. 51.
[57] Shaw, "The Romantic Love of Evil," 35.

fundamental sense, then, Meland's use of the term God is a term of selection and places him in among such naturalistic theists as Ames, Mathews, and Wieman.

As a *naturalistic constructivist*, Meland carves out a place to stand between the fallacies of the extreme options of objectivism, where there is a permanent matrix or framework and God is an objective being or unitary force or structure to be discerned and described, and relativism, where there is no higher appeal than a language game and God is nothing more than a regulative notion of the imagination offered by linguistic communities as rules of belief and behavior. His position may be described best as *contextualism* or *soft realism*, in which the human mind constructs reality but in which that construction can be suggested, guided, revised, and even vetoed through the reciprocity between the imagination and nature. William Dean describes his contextualism as one in which the imagination "is both free to construct subjective variations and is derived from and determined by environmental possibilities outside the subject."[58]

VI. MELAND ON GOD AND EVIL: AN EVALUATION

In order to judge the adequacy of Meland's concept of God, one must evaluate it in relation to his basic purpose. His quest is not for clear knowledge of a transcendental absolute which casts its shadow upon the finitude world. Nor is his effort to establish an irrefutable proof for the existence or reality of God. Nor is his project to salvage theism from the trilemma of theodicy. His primary interest is to understand the religious life and to ask, as a constructive theologian, whether, to what degree, and how religious sensibilities and humane living can be supported and nurtured within a naturalistic understanding of the surrounding environment.

The adequacy of a concept of God can be judged by its clarity and its conceptual coherence. On the basis of these two criteria, Meland's concept of God does not match the doctrines or descriptions of God offered by many other process philosophers and theologians. But these two criteria are not the only criteria for an adequate concept of God. An adequate concept must interpret and be interpreted by the richness and complexity of lived experience. This does not mean criteria of clarity and

---

[58] William Dean, *History Making History*, p. 142.

coherence are not relevant to judge the relative adequacy of a concept of God. But the final criterion finally is the religious serviceability of a concept of God, namely, its capacity to enhance sensitivity to meaning within the mystery of our surrounding environment.[59] One might even call this an empirical instead of a conceptual criterion for evaluating the relative adequacy of a concept of God. If one begins with a naturalistic vision of the world, with the assumption that reality and meaning are confined to the experienced world and not superimposed upon the experienced world from a more ultimate reality, then the truth of the term God must be measured by its success in increasing the richness and complexity of meaning within the borders of the experienced world.

Meland's constructivist-realistic concept of God, it seems to me, better serves this religious need than many alternative concepts of God. His version of the naturalistic God stands between Wieman's singular and undifferentiated goodness and Loomer's undifferentiated power of nature. His less precise and more subtly constructed God is more adequate both to account for the experienced complexities of the natural world and to support the humanizing needs of religious devotion. Though modest in fullness and precision, his concept of God is adequate and appropriate to the experienced mystery, richness, and complexity of the environing world. Precision and certainty are sacrificed on the alter of faithfulness to the richness of lived experience. Amidst all his convoluted twists and turns and his diffuse and amorphous language, Meland pursues with a "singleness of heart" the vision of making theology faithful to the depths of lived experience. By using the perspective of empiricism and process thought, he is able to go beyond the exploratory efforts of earlier empiricists, such as James and the Early Chicago School, to construct a thoroughgoing radical empirical concept of God.

His naturalistic view of evil, also, is the best of the three process alternatives. Rationalistic, speculative, and empiricist forms of process thought provide alternative approaches to evil as a religious and theological problem. To be sure, the beginning point of all three differs radically from classical theodicies. None of the three is engaged in

---

[59] For a similar argument about the religious criteria for evaluation, see David Conner, "A Functional-Empirical Approach to the 'Whitehead Without God' Debate," in *New Essays in Religious Naturalism*, ed. Creighton Peden (Macon: Mercer University Press, forthcoming). See, also, Tyron Inbody, "Paul Tillich and Process Theology," *Theological Studies* 36 (September, 1975): 472-492.

theodicy proper, namely, the attempt to make rationally consistent the three concepts of genuine evil, omnipotence, and moral perfection. Instead of attempting to explain the reality of evil as an idea consistent with the ideas of a wholly good and omnipotent deity, ending either with an "evil" but all powerful God (for example, Frederick Sontag[60] and John Roth[61]) or an all good but limited God (self limited, as in Hick[62], or ontologically limited, as in the process theologians[63]), radical empiricists begin with our experience of this world as the only appropriate beginning point and attempt to understand good, evil, and God within that context alone without any preconception of the nature of the power and goodness of God.

As I see it, the primary strength of Meland's contribution to theodicy is that he reframes the entire question. In the strictest sense of the term, radical empiricism is a theology without a theodicy. If one begins with our experience of the natural world instead of a preconception of the meaning of the terms God, good, and evil, and asks what our experience implies about these three concepts instead of how the conceputal trilemma can be resolved, that is, asks how good and evil fit within an empirical and naturalistic understanding of God, then the whole problem is recast.

One of the significant consequences of this reframing is that the problem becomes as much "the problem of good" as "the problem of evil." By this I mean to say that if Meland is correct in his description of sheer creativity, complexity, and ambiguity as fundamental characteristics of this world, then the whole problem of traditional

---

[60] Frederick Sontag, *The God of Evil* (New York: Harper and Row, 1970); *What Can God Do?* (Nashville: Abingdon, 1979); *God, Why Did You Do That?* (Philadelphia: Westminster Press, 1970), and in Stephen David, ed., *Encountering Evil* (Atlanta: John Knox Press, 1981), pp. 137-166.

[61] John Roth, *A Consuming Fire: Encounters with Elie Wiesel and the Holocaust* (Atlanta: John Knox Press, 1979), and in Stephen Davis, ed., *Encountering Evil* (Atlanta: John Knox Press, 1981), pp. 7-38..

[62] John Hick, *Evil and the God of Love* (New York: Harper & Row, 1978).

[63] David Griffin, *God, Power and Evil* (Philadelphia: Westminster Press, 1976, and Charles Hartshorne, "A New Look at the Problem of Evil," in F. C. Dommeyer, ed., *Current Philosophical Issues: Essays in Honor of Curt John Ducasse* (Springfield: Charles C. Thomas, 1976), Marjorie Hewitt Suchocki, *The End of Evil: Process Eschatology in Historical* Context (Albany: SUNY, 1988), and Barry L. Whitney, *Evil and the Process God* (New York: The Edwin Mellen Press, 1985).

theodicy is cast in a different framework and the problem to be understood is different than in traditional theodicies.

All radical empiricists have some form of the doctrine of the ambiguous God. However, the closer an empiricist such as Loomer comes to identifying God with the world, the closer she comes to embedding qualities of evil within the character of God. Clearly there are persons in scripture and the tradition for whom God cannot be identified either with the benign goodness of much piety or the univocal goodness of traditional theism. Here the empiricists speak not only for a consistent empiricism and naturalism but for certain dimensions of the biblical tradition and Christian piety.[64] Nevertheless, questions must be raised about the adequacy of some empiricists' understanding of good and evil as a theological problem. One of the most important of these is the issue of the religious adequacy of a radical empirical concept of God. Is the God of the radical empiricists worthy of our loyalty and devotion?

The answer to this question is, I think, more complicated than it is usually considered to be. On the one hand, religious empiricism seems to me to be more religiously adequate than the typical extremes. At one extreme is the claim that what is religiously significant is solely the intuition of unity, harmony, qualitative wholeness, sheer well-being. At the other extreme is the claim that what is religiously significant is primarily the dark night of the soul, the sick soul, the descent into hell.[65]

One of the strengths of radical empiricists such as Meland, Loomer and Dean is that they eulogize neither intuition but acknowledge that full religious adequacy must somehow take into account the interplay between harmony and chaos in a religiously significant world, that a world full of significance is a world full of struggle in all of its aspects and elements, including whatever within it is to be designated as divine.

---

[64] Biblical examples include Exodus 10: 1-2, 2 Samuel 14: 1 & 10, Amos 6: 3, Lamentations 3: 38, Isaiah 45: 7, Job 40: 15-24, Matthew 27: 46, Acts 4: 28, and Romans 9: 18. In addition to Frederick Sontag and John Roth, theological examples include Robert McClelland, *God Our Loving Enemy* (Nashville: Abingdon Press, 1982); Jim Garrison, *The Darkness of God: Theology After Hiroshima* (Grand Rapids: Eerdmans, 1982); and Belden Lane, "A Hidden and Playful God," *Christian Century* (September 30, 1987): 812-13, and "God Plays Rough for Love's Sake," *Christian Century* (October 14, 1987): 879-81, and "Fierce Landscapes and the Indifference of God," *Christian Century* (October 11, 1989): 907-910.

[65] See Evelyn Underhill, *Mysticism* (New York: New American Library, 1955), William James, *The Varieties of Religious Experience* (New York: Mentor Books, 1958), and Thomas Altizer, *The Descent Into Hell* (Philadelphia: J. B. Lippincott, 1970).

There is something positive to be said for not identifying God wholly with human interests and with the concept of human value but rather with the larger whole in its many dimensions. One needs not claim that God is evil or evil is God when setting the concepts of good, evil, and God within a naturalistic, or one might even say a somewhat pantheistic, framework. One is claiming, however, that God's purposes and character are not exhaustively identified with human value or even with one aspect or another of human value.

However, the closer empiricists come to strict pantheism in understanding the relation or even identity of God and the world, the closer they come to abandoning any criterion of human good as the criterion of worshipfulness or devotion and to advocating a natural piety in which God promotes evil as well as good in the quest for stature. That conclusion, as I see it, is in the end neither religiously adequate nor tolerable. Natural piety and religious devotion are not convertible concepts. Religion, finally, is about devotion and not merely awesomeness and adoration. And this is the point where Meland's version of religious empiricism is a more adequate solution to the problem of religious devotion within an empiricist framework than is Loomer's.

When one asks the question of what we as human beings are to be devoted to if we are to serve what actually enhances life, one cannot finally abandon some criterion of correlation between human good and divine good. Is nature or some aspect of nature the source of human good? Even though God may be more ambiguous than traditional theism or neoclassical theism has taught, in the end God must be distinguished as some aspect or element of the world instead of nature as a whole or its essential structure, even within a naturalistic framework, or else the nerve of religious devotion and worthiness of devotion is cut.[66]

The strength of the kind of empiricism that veers toward pantheism is its recognition of the positive significance of some sort of "natural piety" for the religious life and the concept of God. Empiricists like Loomer have a keen awareness of how we live with a sense of creaturely dependence in a cosmic context which does not necessarily have only our own good in mind. A sense of awe and reverence frequently attend our experience of nature and its awesome beauty. We worship, that is,

---

[66] A version of this argument is also made by Shaw, "The Romantic Love of Evil," 33-42.

adore, bow down before, and are overawed in this experience of natural piety. Both the thoroughgoing pantheist and the radical empiricist have a strong and clear sense of what worship means in a naturalistic instead of a supernaturalistic context.

However, to *worship* God through a sense of awe and to *serve* God through loyal devotion are not identical. To serve God is to be selective from among the aspects of the world as a whole. In the religious life, piety as an experience of awe and service as a commitment to value must be distinguished. Devotion and moral commitment can be directed to only certain features of natural piety, for the awesomeness of natural piety frequently does not have much to do with, and can even be counter to, ethical devotion and religious service to that which in fact enhances life.

No radical empiricist, then, can or finally does abandon the criterion of human good in the effort to understand good, evil, and God as they relate to religious sensibilities, nor can radical empiricists be content to serve a morally ambiguous power or structure of nature if what they seek is to be devoted to what actually enhances life. This claim has both a negative and a positive aspect. Negatively, it must be pointed out that no radical empiricist claims that the ambiguity of nature and/or God is itself something to be worshipped or celebrated. Positively, what is to be celebrated is the creative good, the sensitive nature within nature, or stature.

What the empiricist seeks to do is to refuse to dichotomize the world and God, something classical theism and even some process theologians do. The claim is not that we should affirm evil as much as we affirm good. Radical empiricists introduce complexity into God, a more inclusive and so ambiguous complexity than most theists are willing to consider. But the ambiguity of good and evil is not celebrated. That is simply where we must start in our efforts to understand God and the world. All empiricists, in fact, finally bring religious and moral judgments to this given awesome complexity of God and the world.

Thus, in the end, Meland does not follow out the complexities of the naturalistic view of the world to a full blown pantheism, as does Loomer late in his career. Meland's concept of God is a form of naturalistic theism. God is a term of selection, viz., the sensitive nature within nature. God is not nature as such or an essential structure of nature, but the sensitivity working toward a more subtle and complex range of meanings within nature. It is this alone, ambiguous as it is within the complexities of the creative passage, that is adequate for religious devotion. Wieman's God is finally a God of monopolar goodness, and Loomer's God tends toward the pantheistic identification of God with nature as a whole. Meland stands between Wieman and Loomer on this question, and seems to me to be more satisfactory than either because his concept is more adequate both to the richness of experience and to the needs to the religious life.

Even Loomer, it should be noted, who explores the implications of theological naturalism to the edges of pantheism, finally ends with a tension in his own thinking on this issue. He advocates a pantheism in which God promotes evil and good with a wildness not measured by human good. Yet evil is evil precisely because it is measured by and serves the good, which is the increase in stature. Finally, Loomer, no less than a naturalistic theist like Meland, actually equates God with an aspect of nature. Although Meland's concept of the relation of God to evil is less focused than Loomer's (and most other process concepts of God, for that matter), Meland's empirical understanding of the relation of God to the evil of the world is to be preferred among theological empiricists because he takes account both of ambiguity and religious adequacy.

All radical empiricists, then, in fact, adopt some form of naturalistic theism, for each in practice uses the term God not as equivalent to nature but as a term of selection which has a direct bearing on religious devotion, that is, upon human value. Thus, God is, in fact, for them an aspect of nature. Even Loomer maintains we should resist the evil (the wildness) of God, that is, that which diminishes the opportunities for good, and be devoted to the increase in stature. Stated in terms of piety, we should be devoted to God as the growth of good within the total process, that is, to the increase in stature which integrates the realities of good and evil within nature, instead of to God as the ambiguous whole. Loomer, the empiricist who comes closest to pantheism, in the end selects for commitment one strand in the web of nature, and calls for us to work toward increasing the richness of interrelationships through our devotion to stature or size. To his natural piety which drives him to designate nature as a whole as divine he adds commitment to ever expanding experience which may be a part of nature but is nevertheless one function of nature and not the ambiguous whole.[67]

---

[67] Ibid, p. 40.

VII. MELAND AND THE FUTURE OF EMPIRICAL THEOLOGY

In the future, process theology may have to choose between 1) a process perspective that is primarily a philosophical theology, focused on clarity, coherence, necessary ideas, and speculative conceptual visions, 2) some form of revelationism, whether it be fundamentalism or dogmatism or some form of postliberal fedeism, which makes no appeal to lived experience, or 3) a view of faith and theology that is more radical in its commitment to the complexity and ambiguity of lived experience, and so selectively employs process conceptuality as the most useful tool to wrest some margin of intelligibility out of a reality that is fundamentally rich, deeep, and mysterious.

This third option implies a degree of untidiness, unclarity, uncertainty, and relativity of thought not characteristic of the predominant direction of process theology in the last generation. The future of process theology in terms of its adequacy for a quest after a rational and coherent viewpoint is not questioned here. That quest is perennial and persists as much in a postmodern, secular, this-worldly time as in more religious, otherworldly times. But the future of process theology as an articulator of the lived experience of reality in its many dimensions is more in doubt if Meland's way of employing process thought is submerged to the speculative impulses of the process movement.

Meland does, to be sure, leave some unresolved issues that exemplify divergences between him and some other process theologians. Because causal efficacy is so dim, there may be all the more cause to apply reason in an effort to understand experience and faith. That issue is part of the controversy between him and Wieman. Also, one can never set an arbitrary limit to what reason is capable of doing in determining the intelligibility of experience. Especially in *Fallible Forms and Symbols*, Meland's criticism of the overreaching zeal or at least confidence on the rationalistic side of the process perspective reaches an unflagging persistence that was not characteristic of his generous spirit. It is important for the future of empirical theology that it not become anti-rational. Finally, Meland seems to imply at times a split between reality and language that is problematic in the context of contemporary neo-pragmatic and deconstructionist discussions.[68] All three of these persisting issues continue to be discussed among those radical

---

[68] See Frankenberry, *Religion and Radical Empiricism*, pp. 134-144.

empiricists, such as Frankenberry, Dean, and Stone, who continue to develop Meland's own brand of empirical theology.[69]

In two significant ways Meland's empirical theology extends the liberal project in theology into the postliberal and postmodern period. First, he does not abandon the critical, post-authoritarian stance in theological method which liberalism initiated. Authority rests in reality itself in its depth and richness, not in an authority who can prescribe or proscribe beliefs about reality. The nature of his appeal to experience in its depth, to language, and to culture in its breadth and depth as sources in his empirical method continues the liberal orientation in theology, and is quite different from the current postliberal appeal to the authority of a specific religious community or of its language system as the sole basis and context for theology.

Second, Meland attempts to connect theology with experience. Our theological beliefs depend on a description of the depth and richness of reality as it is experienced in individuals, cults, and cultures. Although his concept of experience is more social, in both the ontological and cultural senses, than the older liberals' notion of experience as an isolatable ground of certainty within the consciousness of the individual subject, his theological method cannot be understood apart from the liberal appeal to experience as a source and norm in theology.

Nevertheless, Meland's liberal method is postliberal in significant ways. He speaks of his method as one which has moved through not back from liberalism.[70] Long before the current phrase "postliberal" becomes fashionable as a way of describing the pragmatic, cultural, historicist, linguistic, deconstructionist, and textual approaches to theology, Meland's empirical realism is critical of some of the basic characteristics and themes of liberal theology. Although he says in his last book, "I find myself moving into a post-liberal methodology," that statement could have been made as readily concerning his first book written in 1934, which is even then a challenge to the liberal restriction of theology to the experience and mental enclosures of the individual subject.

Meland's empirical method is postliberal in at least three senses. First, his stress on realism or otherness throughout the entire corpus of

---

[69] Two books on the future of empirical theology are important here. One is Bernard Meland, *The Future of Empirical Theology* (Chicago: University of Chicago Press, 1969), and Miller, *Empirical Theology*.

[70] Meland, *Fallible Forms and Symbols*, 142-43.

writing makes him a thorough, persistent critic of all forms of liberalism which reduce experience and reality to the subjectivity of the isolated individual, regardless of whether that subjectivity be rooted in the sense experience or feelings or ideas. From *Modern Man's Worship* through *Seeds of Redemption* and *Faith and Culture* to *Fallible Forms and Symbols*, the theme of objectivity or otherness (later referred to as realism) dominates his thinking.

Earlier, historic liberalism, which was basically Kantian in its philosophical method, can be characterized as an enclosure within self-experience, the result of this is the circumscription of every meaning to the mental sphere. Empirical realism, which "lifts up the simultaneous presence of an ultimate dimension of reality and the humanly available immediacies within the stream of experience,"[71] claims, like all forms of neoorthodox theology which also react against the limitation of reality to the human equation, that otherness is real. But unlike most other forms of postliberal theology which arise throughout Meland's career to try to replace the subjectivity and mentalism of liberal idealism with an otherness that cast its shadow upon experience, cult, and culture from beyond this world, "otherness" in Meland's thought is incorporated in the notion of "withness," so that ultimacy and immediacy traffic together as the depth of concrete experience.

Second, it must be granted that there is a sense in which Meland continues the kind of foundationalism characteristic of liberal methodology. His effort to ground theological method in experience, and particularly his appeal to the primal context of experience, not only sounds like the language of one who is searching for the foundations of faith and theology behind concepts and formulations but is an argument that faith and theology are indeed grounded in a natural context which is deeper and richer in context than feelings, language, ideas, text, cult, and culture. If any attempt to ground theology in something more than human language systems is foundationalism, then Meland is a foundationalist and grounds his appeal in "an experienceable base"[72] as conceived, both metaphysically and culturally, in radical empiricism.

However, if foundationalism is defined, as it is in much anti-foundationalism today, such as neo-pragmatism, linguistic theory, historicism, and deconstruction, as "the thesis that our beliefs can be

---

[71] Ibid, 123.
[72] Meland, "Grace a Dimension of Nature," *Journal of Religion* 54 (1974), 121.

warranted or justified by appealing to some item of knowledge that is self-evident or beyond doubt,"[73] then Meland's work is anti-foundational to the core. Not only is certainty denied as an impossible achievement because of the limitations of the human structure, the lure of certainty is eschewed as a search for the kind of ultimacy that is not available in a radical empirical understanding of lived experience. "The Absolute was a creation of this modern, liberal period, supplanting the authority of the church and Scriptures. For the Absolute implies a rational certainty established by logical argument out of concern to find points of fixity and ultimate reference in a world of finitude and change."[74]

Meland's relativism is nearly as thoroughgoing as many other postliberal theologies. He discovers no certainty in any human equation. However, his relativism rests not only on the fact of cultural plurality, but in the contextuality and relativity of reality itself as it is given in experience. His solution to the problem of relativism is not to appeal to the Absolute or certainty but to appeal to ultimacy within the immediacy of experience itself in its various dimensions, individual, cult, and culture. The answer to the problem of relativism is not absolutism or even foundationalism in the strict sense, but relativity itself.

> Relativity implies interrelatedness.... There is no immediacy in history or experience that is without its ultimate depth, its ultimate reference. The appeal from any religious witness, while it exudes the conditioning of its cultural environment, speaks also out of the depths of its own encounter with what sustains and judges its witness. Limitation and ambiguity imply an intermingling of our immediacies with ultimacy, not insulation from it. The fact that our human formulations in thought and effort are not to be taken as direct accounts or descriptions of what is ultimacy and real in experience is not to be understood to mean that we stand dissociated from these depths of reality in experience.[75]

Third, Meland is close to many of the postliberal methodologies in his emphasis on the relation of language and culture to experience. As we have seen above in analyzing his concept of experience, he does not conceive of experience as isolated within the conscious subject. It has both metaphysical depth and cultural breadth. His concept of experience places him closer to the postliberal theologies than to historic liberalism

---

[73] Frankenberry, *Religion and Radical Empiricism*, p. 4
[74] Meland, *Fallible Forms and Symbols*, p. 72.
[75] Meland, *Realities of Faith*, pp. 164, 168.

to the extent that the postliberals stress the reciprocity between language and culture.

Experience, for Meland, however, is not reducible to language and culture, a reduction which Kaufman and Lindbeck come close to making. Even when experience is not explicitly reduced to an epiphenomena of linguistic systems, this conclusion seems implied or at least possible or permissible because of a failure to develop any theory of the relation of experience and culture. Postliberal empirical realism offers such a theory in its concept of the reciprocity between language and experience.[76] The failure by many postliberal theologies to offer any account of the relation between language and experience leaves the most fundamental issue between liberal and postliberal theologies not only unresolved but even unexplored.

The genius of Meland's postliberal empirical realism is that he explores this problem in great detail. He maintains the liberal project to the degree that language and culture can offer metaphysical and empirical descriptions of experience. On the other hand, Meland does not preserve a concept of "pure experience" as an element of the human equation which can serve as a secure foundation for clear and certain knowledge independent of the ambiguities and relativity of all linguistic and cultural systems. Experience, for Meland, is not a "prior" or "autonomous" ground for knowledge independent of language but is a dimension of reality which partakes simultaneously of the depth of relationships that constitute reality itself and the human forms of subjectivity, language, and culture.

Meland eschews foundationalism to the extent that the term designates the search for a transcendental starting point, but he claims that to deny foundationalism is not to deny every form of realism. Empirical realism is a form of realism which does not appeal to monistic foundations. Experience makes contact with reality, and an empirical realistic account of experience points to a context and depth of relations beyond us on which we can count to produce us, support us, correct us, judge us, and redeem us. Unlike Kaufman and Lindbeck, who imply the kind of relativism which reduces experience entirely to linguistic worlds of the imagination, the empirical realist defends a kind of realism which simultaneously encompasses nature, the individual, experience, language, and culture in a reciprocal reality of interdependent

---

[76] See chapter two, footnote 80.

relationships. Meland is a relativist without subjectivism and a realist without foundationalism.

The significance of Meland's appeal to experience within a radical empirical framework for the various postliberal formulations of theological method, then, is that he provides a concept of experience which does not force one into an either/or choice, either the liberal appeal to pure experience or the postliberal claim that experience, both of immediacy and ultimacy, is simply a product of the language or texts or other forms and symbols of culture. These cannot be either/or choices for an empirical realist because experience is a richer and more relational concept than most liberal theologies proffer, including both a depth of relations and linguistic and cultural embodiments of that depth. And it is more realistic than most relativists conceive, including contextual relationships that exist beyond the world of language. Experience and culture have an inherent connection with the depth of reality and a structure of experience that grounds all our fallible forms. When postliberal theologians begin to take radical empiricism seriously as a mode of empirical orientation in theology, they may discover that empirical, linguistic, and cultural modes of theology are not discreet methods, perspectives, or options, but indeed are aspects or elements of a realism that provide a thoroughly empirical context for theology.

7
Postliberal Empirical Realism

Vackav Havel, President of Czechoslovakia, spoke at the World Economic Forum in Davos, Switzerland on February 4, 1992. He said that the end of Communism has brought a major era in human history to an end, not just the 19th and 20th centuries but the modern era as a whole.

> The modern era has been dominated by the culminating belief, expressed in different forms, that the world—and Being as such—is a wholly knowable system governed by a finite number of universal laws that man can grasp and rationally direct for his own benefit. This era, beginning in the Renaissance and developing from the Enlightenment to socialism, from positivism to scientism, from the Industrial Revolution to the information revolution, was characterized by rapid advances in rational and cognitive thinking.
>
> This, in turn, gave rise to the proud belief that man, as the pinnacle of everything that exists, was capable of objectively describing, explaining and controlling everything that exists, and of possessing the one and only truth about the world. It was an era in which there was a cult of depersonalized objectivity, an era in which objective knowledge was amassed and technologically exploited, an era of belief in automatic progress brokered by the scientific method. It was an era of systems, institutions, mechanisms and statistical averages. It was an era of ideologies, doctrines, interpretations of reality, an era in which the goal was to find a universal theory of the world, and thus a universal key to unlock its prosperity.[1]

---

[1] *New York Times*, Op-Ed, Sunday, 1 March, 1992, E 15.

I. POSTLIBERAL THEOLOGY

Bernard Eugene Meland's religious inquiry is a labyrinthine search throughout the second and third quarters of the twentieth century for a postliberal Christian theology. Near the end of his graduate student days at the Divinity School of the University of Chicago in the late 1920s, he detects his dawning awareness that in the twentieth century the liberal project in theology has become bankrupt. His thought travels for fifty years both the hidden trails and broad vistas of experience and culture in search of a constructive theology that would be faithful to the liberal orientation in theology while attuned to the requirements of the postmodern context. It endures with pain and stature the birth pangs of a new theology for a world in which the modern project has come to a crisis point if not to an end. For half a century his theology is an effort to revise the liberal orientation in such a way that the liabilities of liberalism and modernity could be overcome and the contributions of liberal Christianity to a postmodern world would be constructive.

Meland's theology is characterized throughout this book as postliberal. Nevertheless, his theology remains liberal in the sense that he seeks to advance the liberal perspective into a new cultural context. Liberalism is an imprecise term in theology.[2] At times it is used

---

[2] Historic liberalism has two meanings. First, it refers primarily to a political movement. There have been two types of political liberals, those who see "freedom as something which belongs to the individual, to be defended against the encroachments of the state, and those who see freedom as something that belongs to society and which the state, as the central instrument of social betterment, can be made to enlarge and improve." Maurice Cranston, "Liberalism," in Paul Edwards, ed., *The Encyclopedia of Philosophy* (New York: Macmillan, 1967), pp. 458-461. Political liberalism, however, entails a larger cultural agenda, "the modern liberal project," and is employed here nearly as a synonym for "Enlightenment modernity" as expressed not only in the political thought, but also in the economic, scientific, and philosophical thought of English, French, German, and North American intellectuals and cultural elites from the seventeenth century to the twentieth century. One of the best recent histories of modern liberal culture is Franklin Baumer, *Modern European Thought: Continuity and Change in Ideas, 1600-1950* (New York: Macmillan, 1977). Second, liberalism refers here also to liberal theology, the application of the liberal perspective to theological problems, primarily to theological method, and to a lesser extent to the theological conclusions of those employing a liberal methodology. Liberal theology encompasses the same time period and geography and includes the phases of the Rationalism, Romanticism, Modernism, and Existentialism in theology. See Bernard Meland, "Liberalism, Theological," *Encyclopedia Britannica*, Volume 13 (1968), pp. 1020-1022.

interchangeably with modernism, with the rationalistic mentality, with the disregard for historical structures, with the appeal to the rational or scientific grounds of faith, or with the mode of thinking which permits doctrinal latitude in contrast to orthodox thinking which adheres to a rigid formulation. As Meland himself recognizes, "The truth is that liberalism has undergone a series of historical transformations, expressing different emphases and objectives according to the demands or necessities of a given time."[3]

Liberalism is more a sensibility of thought than a specific set of conclusions or action. That sensibility is primarily an openness toward changing conceptions of nature and human existence and responsiveness to resources of inquiry which inform such a developmental view. As a generic term liberalism refers to resistance to the coercive control of external authority and structures, and a consequent concern for inner motivation in religious and ethical inquiry, along with their social nurture and application. Most forms of liberalism include a two-pronged interplay between both historic and innovating modes of thought, namely, an appeal to earlier or even ancient sources as a reaction against the status quo, and a thrust toward new demands in a new situation.

Liberal theology seeks the establishment of the authority of theology on the basis of something other than the authority of tradition. It is driven by the need to clarify the role of human experience and culture in establishing and formulating the religious response in distinction from

---

[3] Bernard Meland, "The Persisting Liberal Witness," *Christian Century* 79 (26 September 1962), 1158. Meland divides the history of liberal theology into four distinctive cycles: (1) rationalist (1650-1750), (2) romanticist (1750-1850), (3) modernist (1850-1930), and (4) existentialist (1930 to present). He sometimes refers to the fourth phase emerging during the twenties and early thirties countering what was then to the fore as liberal theology as "postliberal"; at other times he designated it a "new cycle of liberalism" or "liberalism revisited" or "neoliberalism" or "critical liberalism." "A Profile of the Theological Field," *Divinity School News* 24 (1 May 1957), 18. Stemming from the new vision of the sciences, particularly relativity theory, and from the literature of phenomenology and existentialism, this whole era of inquiry shared a poignant concern with "lived experience," vivifying, clarifying and fulfilling the promise and possibilities of lived experience. Thus, in some contexts he prefers to call this era more the fourth cycle of the liberal ethos, the existentialist era, than a postliberal era. Nevertheless, the new cycle is explicitly a thrust countering earlier cycles of liberal religious inquiry. It was a reaction against much of the methodological restrictions of the previous cycle. The most significant shift is from the idealistic humanism of the liberalism of the twenties to the realism of the post-idealistic period.

the traditional appeal to the supremacy of tradition, creed, or ecclesiastical structure. Meland sides with the liberals in seeking to establish a different ground of religious authority than revelation or ecclesiastical authority. In that sense he is one of the minority of representatives of classical liberal theology throughout the ascendancy of neoorthodoxy in Europe and North America in the middle half of the twentieth century. His career begins, though, during the collapse of the older liberalism and the rise of this major alternative to liberal theology. At the time when neoorthodox theology sweeps the liberal project off the agenda of Protestant theology, he works to reconstruct "the persisting liberal witness."

To the persisting traits of the integrity of personal decision, the will to be liberated from the coercive control of external institutions and forms, and concern for inner motivation and discipline, Meland adds a new dimension to liberal thinking which distinguishes his work so significantly from the older forms of liberalism that he must be called postliberal. What is new in his postliberal thought is his emphasis on the social basis of existence and his realism, both anti-optimistic and anti-subjectivistic, about the individual and society.[4] To be sure, the core of meaning in the liberal ethos is the focus on the human structure of consciousness and experience as the nexus of reality in terms of which objective realities are mediated. For the liberal there is no bypassing the human reality in speaking of the transcendent or of realities other than humanity.[5] In this respect Meland remains a liberal amidst the midcentury neoorthodox return to revelation and its recent developments and variants in newer forms of postliberal theology. But his empirical realism and his exploration of the role of culture and language in the religious response make him postliberal. He remains faithful to the liberal ethos while adopting the realistic themes of neoorthodox theology and the cultural and linguistic themes of contemporary postliberal theology.

From the beginning of his career in 1929 he serves both as a critic of the liberal witness in theology and as an advocate of themes and sensibilities that are not characteristically liberal. Although tradition as an arbitrary norm is displaced in his thought, the traditions of culture

---

[4] The term "realism" will be developed more fully in section three of this chapter. At this point, I will simply indicate that the term has two meanings, anti-optimism and anti-subjectivism. I mean to apply both of these meanings of the term to Meland.

[5] Meland, "The Persisting Liberal Witness," 1159.

and the religions are re-introduced into the classical liberal idea of experience to supplement if not to refocus this liberal orientation. Culture, language, symbol, and myth play a determinative role in his theology long before they have become predominant themes in the Kierkegaardian and Wittgensteinian theology of the current Yale School (Hans Frei, Paul Holmer, George Lindbeck, William Placher, Stanley Hauerwas), which has claimed the name "postliberal." At the time when reason and experience are the predominant themes in liberal theology existing along side the alternative neoreformation appeals to revelation and faith, Meland sets reason and experience within the larger context of culture, language, symbol, and myth.

Meland's criticisms of liberal theology run deep. The folly of liberalism, which led to its own pathology, lay in the excess of its zeal for liberation of the individual from coercive control.

> What, in fact, it accomplished was not the renewal of a covenant relationship but simply the inversion of tyranny. Insisting upon the primacy of the person led inevitably to an idealization of the human equation; and the basic Christian insight into the limitations and ambiguities of man's nature, giving rise to his sinfulness, faded from view. The idealization of man as a major premise is something quite different from upholding the dignity of the person.[6]

The liberals he criticizes include the pragmatic liberals and modernists of the early Chicago School as much as the continental and American Ritschlians, Personalists, and Religious Humanists.

There is a development in his criticism of liberalism. In his very first published essay in 1930,[7] he criticizes the christocentrism of liberals such as Albrecht Ritschl, Wilhelm Herrmann, Adolf Harnack, William Newton Clarke, George Burman Foster, Henry Churchill King, William Adams Brown, and Harry Emerson Fosdick. The problem is not that they are christocentric but that they introduce a new supernaturalism into their christology. In trying to locate the normative factor for ethics in Jesus, they conceive the conditions of the ethical life of Jesus, like the ethical life of every person, as having been determined by a supernatural end. The ethical task is to ascertain the revealed ideal and to apply it normatively to human living. Meland offers the alternative of

---

[6] Meland, "A Profile of the Theological Field," 18.
[7] Bernard Meland, "A Present-Day Evaluation of Christian Ethics," *Journal of Religion* 10 (1930): 378-393.

interpreting the ethical task pragmatically or experimentally instead of a priori with reference to moral needs arising out of the conditions of life within the natural world.

In 1931, still under the strong influence of the socio-historical method of the early Chicago School, he writes of a new appreciation of Jesus which sets Jesus in his context as a product of his social environment in contrast to the supernaturalism of the liberals who see Jesus as "a peculiarly individualist character, directly related to God in a supernatural fashion.... He shared a unique relation to God, not merely an unusually profound one, but a relation that set him apart from every other person in history. Christocentric theology made this assumption basic to its interpretation of Jesus."[8] Indeed, at the end of a discussion of Jesus in 1932 he argues that liberals do not differ from the orthodox in that liberal christocentrism is a new authoritarianism or new dogmatism.[9]

In addition, in the early thirties Meland begins to criticize liberals as neorationalists. Their preoccupation with keeping religion in line with the scientific method sustains a strenuous mood in theology that is suspicious of the emotional or appreciative side of religion. In its quest for intellectual respectability, "the whole liberal movement in theology is a counterpart of a neorationalism, based on the historical sciences, which has been affecting the currents of thought in all areas since the nineteenth century." He refers here not to the religious supernaturalists but to the early twentieth century modernists, who have made the scientific outlook and method so decisive that it must control emotion lest it become sentimentalist or excessive. The theologian, the modernists claim, must stay close to the scientist because religious adjustment involves coming to terms with the natural processes. But "keeping religious thought in line with scientific knowledge is the theologian's avocation, not vocation."[10] Theologians should not be afraid of becoming adventurously and aggressively religious. Religion includes sensibilities of awe and appreciation beyond strictly rational and ethical sensitivities.

---

[8] Bernard Meland, "Toward a New Appreciation of Jesus," *The Open Court* 45 (1931), 600, 608.

[9] Bernard Meland, "The Present Worth of Jesus," *International Journal of Ethics* 42 (1932), 326-27.

[10] Bernard Meland, "The Appreciative Approach in Religion," *Journal of Religion* 14 (1934), 200.

His most substantive critique of liberalism, though, is his rejection of the "mentalism" of liberalism, which veils both a hidden humanism and subjectivism. Meland casts his lot with the objective theme of the emerging postliberal thought of the neoreformation revival. One finds this criticism of liberalism in a very early review of Emil Brunner's *The Word and the World*. Although Meland thoroughly rejects Brunner's constructive theology as "supernatural absolutism," he nevertheless applauds his anti-subjectivist and anti-humanistic theme.

> The insight that impels his constructive efforts, and which he points to as "the core of the conflict" between Christianity and modern culture, is of immense importance, namely, the question whether man can insist upon his "self-sufficiency" or must acknowledge his dependence upon an objective order. This is by all means the crucial question in modern theology, and must be answered in terms of some new synthesis of thought.[11]

This theme of realism or objectivity stands at the center of his criticism of the liberal mood and method and is the most basic of all his criticisms of liberals. Indeed, it is the central theme in his first book and persists throughout his fifty years of religious inquiry.[12]

This persistent defender of the liberal orientation in theology, then, advances new perspectives and themes that have come today to be called postliberal. In the broader theological discussions of the time, the options seem to be either the older liberal appeal to individual and subjective experience or the neoorthodox appeal to revelation and faith. But stated in our contemporary idiom, Meland is both in sensibilities and themes "a postliberal liberal" before "postliberal" becomes a term of endearment in the theological community of scholars.

Although it is difficult (and not particularly important) to establish a genetic connection between Meland's theology and current postliberal developments in theology, the argument in the preceding chapters is twofold. (1) He has a much subtler understanding of nuances of liberal theology than the current 1990s critics of the liberal tradition recognize or acknowledge in their near parody of it. The fullness of his own theology does not begin to match the descriptions of liberal theology presented in a typology such as George Lindbeck's in *The Nature of Doctrine*. (2) More positively, he bridges the apparent gulf between liberal and postliberal

---

[11] Bernard Meland, "A Revolt Against Modernism," *Journal of Religion* 12 (1932), 314.
[12] Bernard Meland, *Modern Man's Worship* (New York: Harpers, 1934).

theology in an important way because he offers an option in his understanding of the interplay between experience, language, and culture between "postliberal fedeism" and "liberal subjectivism."

In North American theology "postliberal theology" has at least two distinct centers of development. Postliberal theology refers to the "distinctive approach to religion in its particularity and communality" represented by "the Yale School" (including Hans Frei, George Lindbeck, Stanley Hauerwas, William Willimon, Ronald Thiemann, and William Placker.)[13] This postliberal theological family has been influenced primarily by Soren Kierkegaard, Karl Barth, Thomas Kuhn, Ludwig Wittgenstein, Gilbert Ryle, Peter Berger, Clifford Geertz, and Erich Auerbach. In addition to this, however, there is another school of postliberal theology, typically called "revisionary theology," which emerges out of the tradition of scholars at the University of Chicago.[14] In its current expression, it embraces various process theologians, such as Charles Hartshorne, Schubert Ogden, John Cobb, David Griffin, Marjorie Suchocki, and David Tracy. This is the strand of postliberal theology that Meland develops from the mid-1930s to the mid-1980s. What is important to note, however, is that fundamental themes from both sides of this Yale-Chicago axis inform the theology of Bernard Meland. They make him, in his dual focus on experience and culture, a resource for a

---

[13] David Ford, ed., *The Modern Theologians: An Introduction to Christian Theology in the Twentieth Century* II (Oxford: Blackwell, 1989), chapters 3-6. See, especially, William Placker, "Postliberal Theology," chapter 6. See, also, Stanley Hauerwas and L. Gregory Jones, "Introduction: Why Narrative?" in *Why Narrative: Readings in Narrative Theology*, edited by Stanley Hauerwas and L. Gregory Jones (Grand Rapids: Eerdmans, 1989), pp. 1-18.

[14] The ignorance of those today who designate themselves as "postliberal" of the postliberal developments among some of the theologians associated with the University of Chicago is apparent in the frontispiece of William Placker, *Unapologetic Theology* (Philadelphia: Westminster Press, 1989). Speaking in the memory of Robert Calhoun, William Christian says, "At one time nearly forty years ago he had been in Chicago as a visiting professor. I asked him what he thought of it. He said, with an air of surprise and puzzlement, 'Those people don't know the Enlightenment is over'." Although the modernism, pragmatism, and scientism of "the Enlightenment" held sway at Chicago for many years, Calhoun clearly knew little of the criticism and revision of the liberal and modern tradition being worked on at the time by one of Chicago's main representatives, Bernard Meland. For a discussion of the differences between these two "schools," see Edward Oakes, "Apologetics and the Pathos of Narrative Theology," *Journal of Religion* 72 (January, 1992): 37-58.

conversation, and a possible convergence, between these two forms of postliberal theology.

Postliberal theology in its "Yale School" variant refers to theologies which offer a new theory of doctrine which reacts against the liberal view of the nature of theology from Schleiermacher through Otto to Tillich.[15] The most influential book in this form of postliberal theology has been George Lindbeck's *The Nature of Doctrine: Religion and Theology in a Postliberal Age*.[16] Liberalism, in his view, is identified as the focus on the "experiential-expressive" dimension of religion in which theology deals with noninformative and nondiscursive symbols of inner feelings, attitudes, and existential orientations. As an alternative to the foundational authority of experience, however, Lindbeck's postliberal theology understands doctrine as communally authoritative rules of discourse, attitudes, and actions. His theory of doctrine is based upon a cultural-linguistic approach to religion and religious language. He offers a regulative view of doctrine in which doctrine does not refer to experience but to rules of usage.

Although Meland does not offer a purely linguistic interpretation of experience and its authority, he nevertheless offers a much richer understanding of experience than is permitted by Lindbeck's typology. Experience, for Meland, is never understood either as source or authority for theology independent of or prior to language, culture, symbol, and myth. There is at the center of his theology a rich interplay of culture, language, and experience, so thoroughly mixed that his concept of experience cannot be described as liberal at all in Lindbeck's sense of the term.

What Meland contributes to the contemporary discussion of postliberal theology is his exploration of the way experience and culture interpenetrate each other in such a fashion that the liberal emphasis on experience, reason, and method is reshaped by the postliberal emphasis on culture, language, myth, and tradition. Meland's theology of the individual, cult, and culture not only corrects the stereotypes that are currently held by revisionary theologians, on the one hand, and postliberal theologians, on the other. He creates a genuine postliberal theology that holds together both experience and culture, and

---

[15] Ford, *The Modern Theologians* II. See Chapter 6, "Postliberal Theology," written by William Placker.

[16] George Lindbeck, *The Nature of Doctrine: Religion and Theology in a Postliberal Age* (Philadelphia: Westminster Press, 1984).

particularly experience and language, as mutually shaping each other. It is through his exploration of the relation of the liberal concept of experience and the postliberal emphasis on culture and language that he makes his major contribution to postliberal theology.

In the current discussion, the distinction has also been made between *modern* and *postmodern* theology.[17] Modern theology is identified with any theology whose agenda is shaped by the Enlightenment. It is dominated by the search for a method which will establish foundations for the certainty of religious beliefs. Rationalism (clear and distinct ideas, necessary ideas, coherent ideas), romanticism (certain states or qualities of consciousness), empiricism (data from the senses), and even fundamentalism (revealed propositional truths) have been shaped by this modern search for certainty through rational coherence, empirical verification, or revelation. Theology could thereby transcend the relativities and uncertainties of historical and cultural traditions by appealing to something thought to be universal or ahistorical. Modernity is defined as this search for founded beliefs beyond the arbitrariness of traditions through a method which transcends historical relativity.

Meland's thought anticipates some of the themes of postmodern theology. Indeed, one can interpret Meland as a liberal theologian who is searching for ways to express and formulate postmodern insights from the point of view of a liberalism that is clearly changing but has not yet emerged into a new era with a new name.[18] His "revisionary liberalism,"

---

17 See, for example, Mark Taylor, *Erring: A Postmodern A/theology* (Chicago: University of Chicago Press, 1984); Thomas Altizer, et. al., *Deconstruction and Theology* (New York: Crossroad, 1982); Robert Bellah, et. al., *Postmodern Theology: Christian Faith in a Pluralist World* (San Francisco: Harper and Row, 1989). For my account of the meaning of the term postmodern, especially as it is expressed in theology, see my "'Postmodernism': Intellectual Velcro Dragged Across Culture?" *Theology Today* (forthcoming, January, 1995)

18 "Recently I have ventured to suggest that one might look upon various contemporary movements of theological expression, movements commonly referred to as 'post-liberal' or 'post-modern', as having initiated a fourth cycle of Liberalism.... However critical I may be toward former cycles of Liberalism, or of strands within the contemporary cycle, such judgments are not to be understood as implying departure from the essential, historical thrust of the liberal ethos." Bernard Meland, "Foreword," in J. J. Mueller, *The Cultural Theology of Bernard E. Meland: Faith and Appreciative Awareness* (Washington: University Press of America, 1981), p. xiv. In his discussion here Meland wants to insist that he remains faithful to "the liberal ethos" in contrast to traditionalism and orthodoxy, but at the same time is concerned to maintain "historical identity and continuity within the Judeo-Christian legacy."

though, is not a return to earlier liberalism; it is a genuine postliberalism. It is, to be sure, in some respects the reverse of the demythologizing project. But it is not a reversion to pre-critical thinking. Rather, it is a postliberal repossession and reconception of the Christian faith in a postmodern context. Yet he has, and we still have, no term that is precise enough to be called anything but the nearly vacant terms, postliberal and postmodern. The postmodern vision is still in the making. The vague and innocuous term "post" is still the most we have to offer. The genius of Meland is that he sees as early at the late 1920s the problem of the decay of liberalism and modernism as few other liberals see it and he spends his life stretching categories and formulating insights in ways few other liberals are both able and willing to do. In the world he creates through allusive language and suggestive image and metaphor, he begins to build a bridge from liberal to postliberal theology.

II. EMPIRICAL THEOLOGY

Bernard Meland is one of the major representatives of empirical theology.[19] The term "empirical," according to Nancy Frankenberry, is used in three ways in empirical theology.[20] First, it refers loosely to a general temperament or *attitude* of the thinker, viz., a tough-minded bias for the stubborn facts of experience. Empirical theology is an effort to develop in theology a spirit of total openness before the entire range of experiential evidence. A theology is empirical if it acknowledges no other final justification for it claims except an appeal to human experience. In empirical theology, knowledge is descriptive of the concrete character of observable data given in experience. Knowledge is ultimately tested for its truth in terms of the evidence supplied by experience.

Second, empirical refers to a *method* of inquiry, a way of getting at and organizing the data of experience that is instrumental, operational,

---

[19] The most comprehensive discussion of the history, meaning, and current status of "empirical theology" is Randolf Crump Miller, ed., *Handbook of Empirical Theology* (Atlanta: Religious Education Press, 1992). See my "History of Empirical Theology," chapter one, for a discussion of the sources and forms of the empirical tradition in theology. For an earlier discussion and evaluation of this tradition in theology, see Bernard Meland, ed., *The Future of Empirical Theology* (Chicago: University of Chicago Press, 1969).

[20] Nancy Frankenberry, *Religion and Radical Empiricism* (Albany: State University of New York Press, 1987), pp. 1-4.

or experimental. An appeal to experience alone in theology does not make one an empirical theologian. Many kinds of theology appeal to experience in their method. Empirical theology has to do with a method of empirical inquiry into the data of experience. Empirical theologians open all theological claims about the data to public inspection and correction. The experimental method of reflection upon the data of common experience designates a theology as empirical theology.

Third, empiricism is an appeal to common human experience in one form or another as the *source* or *justification* for assertions.[21] All knowledge is related to a description of experience, either in the weaker sense that experience provides us with or is the justification of knowledge, or the stronger sense that no source other than experience provides us with knowledge or the justification of knowledge at all. All empirical theologies appeal to experience as the primary source or justification and empirical method as the primary norm for justifying any theological claim whatsoever.

The key to understanding the variety of empirical theologies is to understand what in their view constitutes experience. There are two different ways the term experience can be understood. In classical empiricism, represented by John Locke and David Hume, experience is understood as the perception of ourselves and the world which takes place by means of the five senses, so that experience means sense perception. All knowledge originates in and derives from the experiences of the five senses. Sense experience is the source of knowledge. In order to understand the world we must select certain sensory responses as representative of the world, and our knowledge derives from what is given to us from this source.

No empirical theologian understands experience in this classical sense or any of its contemporary positivistic variants. Theological empiricism moves away from this picture of knowledge derived from or verified by sense experience toward a more inclusive view of experience. Experience is vastly richer and deeper than mere sensation. Sense perception is neither the only nor even the primary mode of experience. Knowledge is derived or justified from a still more elemental awareness

---

[21] The error of empiricism in the history of philosophy was to hope to trace all knowledge to its *source* in experience. Insofar as empirical theology attempts to do this, it becomes problematic. But the appeal to experience for *justification* is another matter, and this is how Meland appeals to experience and is what is left of empirical theology today.

both of ourselves and the world around us. Radical empiricism adds to the five senses an affective or bodily sense of value within an environment. Before we employ the discrimination of our senses, we are already aware of ourselves and our environment as causally efficacious powers mutually interacting with one another.

This newer empiricism attempts to broaden the notion of experience beyond sense experience in two ways. One is to focus on wider modes of experience, such as emotional, volitional, evaluative, aesthetic, and social experience. The other is to stress the givenness and primacy of relations and bodily feelings from which sense experience itself is an abstraction. Experience is the felt, bodily, psycho-social, organic interaction of human beings within an environment. The positivistic concept of experience is a highly selective abstraction from the context and depth of experience as lived.

Theological empiricism, then, is an effort to overcome the sensationalism and reductionism of the classical empirical tradition. This effort at revision results in two distinct ways of understanding experience within an empirical orientation. One is an appeal to the numinous, which stands at the center of Immanuel Kant's critique and informs Frederick Schleiermacher, Albrecht Ritschl, and many of the liberal theologians of Europe and North America. An appeal to experience in the numinous tradition attends more to a particular kind of mystical and religious experience than to experience as such. Empirical theologies emanating from this numinous understanding of experience draw primarily from the modern European philosophical tradition of Kantianism, existentialism, and phenomenology. This line of appeal to experience in theology runs from Schleiermacher through Otto to Tillich.

The other stream is a radical view of common experience, which informs the branch of twentieth century North American empirical theologies shaped by Jamesian, Deweyan, pragmatic, and Whiteheadian understandings of experience. This stream of empirical theology focuses not on numinous religious experience but on a general model of experience in nature. It originates in the Anglo-American philosophical tradition from Locke and Hume to Jamesian empiricism. It culminates in a series of variants within theology designated as process thought and radical empiricism. Here empiricism attempts to work with experience as recorded in history or interpreted by the social sciences, to examine what in lived experience is operational to transform human beings, or to explore the structures of experience. Radical empiricism gives to experience an historicist or social or cultural meaning that is lacking in classical empiricism.

Empirical theology, also, exists in the context of naturalistic principles and a naturalistic worldview. The determination of what counts as "empirical" is, of course, always a highly theoretical matter, as Nancy Frankenberry has argued.[22] Empirical is defined by the particular theory adopted to render experience epistemically accessible in the first place. Any appeal to "experience" is already an effect produced by the particular theory adopted. Charlene Seigfried recognizes this in her description of William James's empiricism.

> In order to understand where the belief in pure, neutral description goes wrong, such concrete or phenomenal description must be distinguished from concretely based interpretive analysis. I will be arguing that James had original insights into both, but did not sufficiently develop them into a coherent theory which would enable him to avoid obvious inconsistencies. In reconstructing such a theory it becomes evident that concrete or phenomenal description attempts the impossible, namely, an unmediated, pure, objective description of things as they are, of reality as it is. Such an unproblematic access to being is impossible in principle because of what concrete analysis discloses. All seeing is "seeing as." Seeing is not passive but always constrained by interests. The context of knowing is the full fact of self-thing-world. Finally, experience always consists of more than what can be explicitly grasped.[23]

All empirical theologians, then, are also naturalists in the sense that they adopt a cosmology derived from the assumptions of evolutionary naturalism and in most cases reinforced by the descriptive generalizations of process philosophy. They believe this world alone is the locus of purpose and value.[24] They relinquish any world of transcendental causes or principles. Reality is the processes and relationships of this world; all theological meaning and truth lies within the natural world. Nancy Frankenberry says empirical theology "presupposes a naturalistic, neo-materialistic worldview in which the basic constituents of reality are energy-events, happenings, or processes.

---

[22] Nancy Frankenberry, "Major Themes of Empirical Theology," in Randolf Crump Miller, ed., *Empirical Theology: A Handbook*, pp. 36-37.

[23] Charlene Haddock Seigfried, *William James's Radical Reconstruction in Philosophy* (New York: SUNY, 1990), p. 17.

[24] See Bernard Loomer, "The Size of God," *American Journal of Theology & Philosophy*, Volume 8 (January & May, 1987), 23-31.

Nature comprises the realm of the experienceable. Matter turns out to be patterning energy and energy is radiating matter, the only 'stuff' of experience. 'Substances' are radically deconstructed into their constitutive processes of becoming, and processes themselves are constituted by energy-events"[25]

This is the framework within which Meland's empirical theology is naturalistic. He attempts to adapt of post-Darwinian naturalistic worldview to Christian theology. As Jerome Stone argues, the adoption of a naturalistic worldview does not proscribe religious symbols, especially symbols of a significant this-worldly transcendence.[26] However, adoption of this naturalistic worldview marks a shift from the resources of salvation derived ultimately from a transcendent deity to a perspective that recognizes nature's grace as emergent within the depths of concrete experience. Theological empiricists are distinctive kinds of naturalists. They reject, on the one hand, the bifurcations and abstractions of modern idealism, and they reject, on the other hand, the reductionistic empiricism and materialistic naturalism of some naturalistic philosophies.[27] They accept the realities of grace that work within the processes of nature to create and redeem value.

---

[25] Frankenberry, "Major Themes of Empirical Theology," p. 37. She sees the major elements of this naturalistic vision as consisting of ten propositions. (1) The conception of nature as co-extensive with 'reality' or the 'life process' and as constituted by spatio-temporal energy-events entails the corollary that there are no disembodied possibilities, ideals, souls, heavens, or gods. (2) In an evolving, ever-unfinished universe of ceaseless creative activity, the fundamental image of nature in terms of interpenetrating fields of forces and organically integrated wholes has replaced that of self-contained, externally related bits of particles and inert matter. (3) Human nature is a factor within and not a mere spectator of it. (4) Nature is both pluralistic and continuous, thus ruling out monisms as well as dualisms. (5) Nature is infinite and inexhaustible. (6) Quality and structure are aspects of all processes and their analysis is at the heart of empirical method. (7) Nevertheless, ultimate reality has a creative character. (8) Value is intrinsic to nature. (9) Transcendence in nature is a function of the nexus of internal relations that comprises the communal ground of all existence. (10) Finally, religious naturalism is a recognition and celebration of the common creaturehood of all beings as attested to in many different fields.

[26] Jerome Stone, *The Minimalist Vision of Transcendence* (New York: SUNY, 1992).

[27] Stone argues that supernaturalists who deny the possibility of significant transcendence within naturalism have most studied earlier naturalists for whom transcendence only applies to ideals. Ibid., p. 107.

III. REALISTIC THEOLOGY

Realism is a loaded term to use in contemporary theology. The reason, primarily, is that the term has two meanings in the history of philosophy, both of which seem to be in conflict with contemporary theological thought. In the earlier history of philosophy, particularly in medieval thought, realism is used, in opposition to nominalism, for the doctrine that universals have real, objective existence. In modern philosophy, the meaning of the term is reversed. It is commonly used for the view that material objects exist externally to us and our sense experience. In the modern discussion realism is opposed to idealism, which holds that no external realities exist apart from our knowledge or consciousness of them, the whole universe being dependent on mind or in some sense mental. It also is opposed to phenomenalism, which, while avoiding idealist metaphysics, denies that external realities exist except as groups or sequences of sensa.

Realism is a term that has also been used in various postliberal theologies. The diverse group of postwar theologians known as "neoorthodox" also call themselves "realists." The term means in part that they are realistic in contrast to utopian in their understanding of human affairs. They are also realists in the more theological sense of emphasizing the "otherness" of God in distinction from the humanistic and subjectivist bent of much of the liberal tradition. There is, however, another group of theologians who are self-consciously working out of the liberal tradition who also call themselves realists. These postliberal or "neonaturalistic"[28] theologians move beyond the mentalism and androcentric orientation of many of their liberal predecessors to insist that there are forces of creation and redemption, assets of judgment and grace, patterns of value beyond the human structure which impinge upon the human structure as resource.

The new theological realists differ significantly from both the medieval and the modern realists. They differ from the older realists in that they reject, in one way or another and to one degree or another, the idealism that lies behind the older concept of realism. Both the neoorthodox and neonaturalists have a basic affinity with modern philosophical realism in their insistence that something "other" than the human equation alone constitutes reality. Most basic to the "new

---

[28] See Bernard Loomer, "Neo-naturalism and Neo-orthodoxy," *Journal of Religion* XXVIII (April, 1948): 79-91.

realism" is the awareness of "realities outside of and other than self-experience, existing independently of it, though engaging it both continuously and in intermittent encounters."[29] Otherness points to what Meland calls "an 'out there' which may not be altered simply by wishful thinking, or evaded by circumvention of human imagination. The fact of another in concourse with the self has become the formidable factor lending depth to self-experience."[30] In neonaturalism "otherness" shifts from a vertical axis to a temporal, horizontal one. Nevertheless, the theme of otherness characterizes both neoorthodox and neonaturalistic realists.

But at the same time neoorthodox and neonaturalistic realists differ significantly from modern philosophical realists in the sense that they reject materialist conceptions of the "outside" world and advocate broader concepts of experience than sense experience. Neoorthodox realists tend toward the phenomenalist view of realism, and neonaturalists tend toward a naturalistic view of realism. But both theological realisms are significant revisions of modern materialistic realism. Neoorthodox theologians extend phenomenalism to include the encounter with the Other in grace through hearing the Word in faith. Neonaturalist theologians extend the concept of experience to include relations of value in experience that are deeper than sense experience.

The point is that postliberal theologies in the twentieth century have been realistic in contrast to the various forms of idealism that informed all the classical liberal theologies.[31] "Otherness" beyond the human equation stands at the center of these postliberal theologies. The neoorthodox version of postliberal realism dominates the theological scene in Europe and North America from the collapse of liberal theology in the twenties to the contemporary versions of it in the Yale School version of postliberal theology. There is, however, a postliberal realism that has more continuity with the liberal tradition in North America, growing out of the revisionary theologies of the Chicago School. This

---

[29] Bernard Meland, *Realities of Faith* (New York: Oxford University Press, 1962), p. 193. See, also, *Fallible Forms and Symbols* (Philadelphia: Fortress Press, 1976), chapter 1, especially pp. 7-10.

[30] Ibid., 196-97.

[31] There are significant but subtle differences here nevertheless. There is an implicit idealism in the dualism of many of the contemporary postliberal narrative theologians. See William Dean, "Humanistic Historicism and Naturalistic Historicism," in Sheila Greeve Devaney, ed., *Theology at the End of Modernity* (Philadelphia: Trinity Press International, 1991), pp. 41-59.

form of postliberal theology arises out of a naturalistic instead of a supernaturalistic framework, thus continuing the naturalistic assumptions that underlie modern science and modern culture. However, it has made such radical revisions of this liberal tradition in its individualist, idealist, and subjectivist emphases that it must be called postmodern when compared to earlier versions.

IV. CONSTRUCTIVE THEOLOGY

There are few theologians about whom there is more divergence of opinion than Bernard Meland. There is disagreement about how to interpret his language, his procedure, and his agenda. What kind of a theologian is Bernard Meland? Part of the difficulty in answering this question lies in Meland's style of thinking and writing. His style is diffuse and indirect. The comment of Joseph Sittler, a colleague of Meland's at the Divinity School, deserves repeating here. "When Meland begins to talk, a gentle mist descends upon the room. Shortly, it envelopes everything in a dense fog. The fog always lifts, but when it does all the furniture has been rearranged!"[32] Meland's thought is rich, complex, and nuanced, making it difficult to describe Meland as a particular kind of theologian or to offer a single key to the interpretation of his thought, including his agenda and his procedure. Thus, Clark Williamson can say about any group of scholars who have been working with Meland's thought that "each is convinced that none of the others rightly interpreted Meland."[33]

One way to approach the theology of Bernard Meland is to ask, as Williamson does, what kind of a theologian is he? Some focus for that question can be provided by eliminating some options. Meland is not a dogmatic or a systematic theologian who is concerned about an explication and systematization of the doctrinal heritage of the Christian church. Nor is he primarily a philosopher of religion who is interested in religion as a system of ideas or the philosophical adjudication of religious ideas and issues. Meland, instead, is a Christian theologian, who is interested in the religious sensibilities, symbols, and practices of historic Christian communities and cultures and in the reconstruction

---

[32] Clark Williamson, "Bernard Meland: What Kind of Theologian?" *Journal of Religion* 60 (October, 1980), 369.
[33] Ibid.

and reappropriation of that broad inheritance of sentiment and symbol for the vitality of contemporary communities and cultures.

If, then, Meland is neither a church theologian nor a philosopher of religion, but a Christian theologian, what kind of Christian theologian is he?[34] One might call him an apologetic Christian theologian in the soft sense of one interested in reducing instead of heightening the dissonance between inherited Christian faith and the sensibilities of modern and postmodern consciousness. In this sense Meland might appropriately be described as a modest apologist for Christian faith. But in the hard sense of the term Meland is not an apologist for Christian faith. He has little interest in establishing Christian faith and life as final or superior or even true in the arena of competition among religious and anti-religious ideas. Furthermore, he has far too much a sense of what Van Harvey calls "the pathos of liberal theology" to be the more aggressive apologist that Schubert Ogden or even David Tracy have been on the current scene. "The pathos of the liberal theologian is that, if he identifies himself too unqualifiedly with modernity, he runs the risk of alienation from the very community his apologetic is to serve. If, on the other hand, he defines his role primarily in terms of classical Christianity, he runs the risk of being an obscurantist, alienated from the modern intellectual community of which he also wants to be a member."[35] Meland's interest is not in establishing the meaning and truth of Christian faith among the faiths and unfaiths competing for the modern person's allegiance. Neither his spirit nor his program is best described as apologetic.

Meland might better be represented as a "theologian of culture," particularly in light of his summit work, his trilogy on theological method.[36] There is also some truth to this designation insofar as

---

[34] In his "letter of application" (my term) to Dean Bernard Loomer on 9 December 1944, for the position in Constructive Theology, Meland says, "I see myself in between the two emphases, somewhat in a liaison role; for I believe I have more of a theological interest than either you or Wieman, and more of a philosophical and metaphysical bent than Pauck."

[35] Van Harvey, "The Pathos of the Liberal Theologian," *Journal of Religion* 56 (1976), 383.

[36] This is the primary focus of the only monograph that has appeared on Meland to date, Mueller, *The Cultural Theology of Bernard E. Meland*. Although Mueller shows an awareness of some of the range of Meland's thought, his study focuses almost exclusively both in resource and structure on Meland's late trilogy on methodology. It thereby ignores Meland's earlier thought prior to his move to the Divinity School,

Meland's thought from the beginning includes experience and culture as well as cult as resource and object of theological reflection. Furthermore, he keeps the role of culture to the forefront of his work throughout a period when most theologians eschew this focus as a hangover of uncritical liberalism (as "christ of culture" or "culture religion"). He maintains this interest both in his earlier years when theology and culture are related almost exclusively in terms of the social and scientific understanding of society, and in the later years when culture includes the arts and humanities as well. This broad focus is present throughout all of his thought.

In his first book he speaks of "our cultural disease" and "the current drift of civilization," and in the 1930s he engages in his first sustained discussion of the spiritual dimensions of culture. However, when the scope of Meland's writings and the shifts in his emphases are explored in detail (see chapter one), it is no more true to say that Meland is a theologian of culture than it is to say he is a theologian of the church or a theologian of individual religious response. The term "theology of culture" does not appear in his writings from 1929-1945. It is after 1945 that he becomes explicitly preoccupied with the meaning of Christian faith as a source of vision and energy in our culture. The first expression of theology of culture as a conscious agenda item is set in his "Some Unresolved Issues in Theology" (1944),[37] and the first elaborate discussion of the relation of religion and culture is his "Genius of Protestantism" (1947).[38] The designation of "theologian of culture" cannot provide the key to his theological agenda.

Others, however, seek to understand Meland's thought and its organizing center through his category of "the appreciative consciousness." Thus J. J. Mueller says that "my own research indicates that the appreciative consciousness is the skeleton key to Meland scholarship which unlocks the various interpretations."[39] Again, there is some truth to this claim, not only in terms of the importance of that concept in *Higher Education and the Human Spirit* and later works, but in

---

as well as the twists and turns in his thought over the years as he revises his interpretation of Christian faith and of liberalism.

[37] Bernard Meland, "Some Unresolved Issues in Theology," *Journal of Religion* 24 (October, 1944): 233-239.

[38] Bernard Meland, "The Genius of Protestantism," *Journal of Religion* 27 (1947): 273-292.

[39] J. J. Mueller, "Appreciative Awareness: The Feeling Dimension in Religious Experience," *Theological Studies* 45 (1984), 62.

terms of the importance of the notion as it appears in earlier works. Closely related, Larry Axel locates the key to Meland's thought primarily in his "elementalism,"[40] and David Tracy finds that "in the Anglo-American empirical (not empiricist) tradition, Meland's work represents the major example of the employment of the art-religion analogy."[41] Clearly, if one takes the traditional Western distinctions between truth, beauty, and goodness to be decisive for the organization of thought, Meland gives the aesthetic a priority over the true (orthodox theology) or the good (liberal theology) as the primary characteristic of faith. But the aesthetic theme, persistent as it is throughout his work, is but one theme within his larger assignment when one reads through the entire Meland corpus from beginning to end.

The strength of each of these suggestions—that it is in the apologetic, the cultural, the appreciative, the elemental, or the aesthetic element of Meland's thought that one finds the skeleton key—is that each does identify a constitutive element in Meland's theology. Each suggestion is strengthened by the fact that these themes are all sources and norms not only in the trilogy on theological method but are employed at each stage of the fifty year development of Meland's thought. The mistake in locating the key to Meland's thought in any one of these themes, however, is that each one significantly cuts out or at least reduces, and so distorts, equally important themes that bear crucially upon the scope and development of Meland's thought in other phases of its development.

An advance is offered by Clark Williamson's suggestion that Meland is primarily "a highly complex dialectical theologian."[42] For all Meland's (and his interpreters's) talk about culture, Meland's primary agenda is constructive theological interpretation and appropriation of a witness of faith, regardless of whether he is talking about it in its individual, cultic, or cultural forms. His purpose and procedure are to offer a more adequate witness of Christian faith as it is conveyed in and bears upon these three vortices as they stand in dialectical relation to each other in a postliberal and postmodern era. His method is a comprehensive dialectic, involving these three centers of witness which weave dialectically an interrelated fabric of testimony to the deeper realities of

---

[40] Larry Axel, "The Root and Form of Meland's Elementalism," *Journal of Religion* 60 (October, 1980): 472-490.
[41] David Tracy, *The Analogical Imagination* (New York: Crossroad, 1981), p. 219.
[42] Williamson, 371, 384, 389.

judgment and grace that speak through the data of culture, cult, and individual experience.

Williamson comes close to what seems to me to be a skeleton key that unlocks the complex and nuanced themes in Meland's fifty years of theological inquiry and reveals how they are held together when he speaks of Meland as "a political theologian."[43] By "political" Williamson means that Meland "deals with and addresses constructive responses to some of the pervasive, critical issues facing the contemporary world."[44] In this sense Meland comes close to being what in the contemporary discussion is called the "practical theologian." Sharing in the legacy of the Chicago School and John Cobb's identification of the task of the theologian,[45] the "political" or "practical" theologian is identified by her concentration on concrete problems. Each of Meland's books addresses a wide range of practical concerns: the shape of worship, a new attitude toward nature, a new personal ethic, criticism of a civilization based on power, making American culture more sensitive, a margin of sensitivity for surviving the nuclear age, an alternative vision of higher education as knowledge for power, coping with secularization, a new vision of the relation of the world's religions. Each of his books addresses the resources of faith to a concrete, practical, political problem facing the individual, the church, and the culture.

Meland never uses the designations "political" or "practical" for himself. He, instead, uses the phrase "constructive theologian." It is the title of the position he assumes when he returns to the Divinity School in 1945. It is instructive, also, in understanding Meland to acknowledge that the book which conveys most successfully the scope of his thought from 1938-1987 is entitled, "Essays in Constructive Theology: A Process Perspective."[46] Meland brings a process perspective to his theology, but that perspective is equally shaped and nuanced by other perspectives as well. These various perspectives contribute to a deeper agenda. His deeper project is a series of essays in constructive theology. "Constructive theology" for him means the effort, supported by a variety

---

[43] Williamson, 371, 387.
[44] Ibid.
[45] John Cobb and Joseph Hough, *Theological Education and Christian Identity* (Chico, CA: Scholars Press, 1985). A similar view is formulated in Don Browning, *A Fundamental Practical Theology* (Minneapolis: Fortress Press, 1991).
[46] Perry LeFevre, ed., *Bernard Eugene Meland: Essays in Constructive Theology: A Process Perspective* (Chicago: Exploration Press, 1988).

of perspectives, insights, nuances, twists and turns, and revisions, to interpret and make available the faith conveyed in the Christian ethos and mythos as a resource for living in an era of the decline of liberalism and the emergence of a postmodern world. His agenda is held together by his effort to reshape the Christian ethos and mythos, especially as it is conveyed in the liberal version of the Christian legacy, as a resource of faith for the cult, culture, and individual in his new context.

His vocation, first, foremost, and always, is to be a constructive theologian. "My own work in the field has centered exclusively in the constructive area.... More recently, I have given attention almost wholly to the constructive task of interpreting Christian faith."[47] Constructive, for him, does not carry the weight of the contemporary constructivist meaning as in the recent work of Gordon Kaufman.[48] This term, also, like the phrase theology of culture, appears late in his writing. But the term accurately describes what he has been doing from beginning to end and what holds his project together in both focus and objective in distinction from dogmatics, systematic theology, apologetics, philosophy of religion, and theology of culture.

It should not be surprising that Meland does not latch on to this designation of his work until he arrives as a faculty member of the Divinity School. His consciousness about method is forged out of the pressures at work on him at the Divinity School following his return to "the Chicago School," represented by Wieman and Loomer as well as the breakup of the Federated Faculty immediately upon his arrival. Indeed, his formal discussion of method does not appear until very late in his work, and in the strictest sense not until his final book. But what he names himself when he assumes his new position at Chicago both describes his work up to that point and posits his agenda for his summit works. Meland understands his work to be directed to the task of constructive theology.

He set out as a constructive theologian to "re-illumine the Christian faith"[49] in the light of the collapse of theological modernism in specific

---

[47] Ibid., p. 14, 15.
[48] Gordon Kaufman, *The Theological Imagination: Constructing the Concept of God* (Philadelphia: Westminster, 1981); *An Essay on Theological Method* (Missoula: Scholars Press, 1975); *Theology for a Nuclear Age* (Philadelphia: Westminster, 1985); *In Face of Mystery: A Constructive Theology* (Cambridge: Harvard University Press, 1993), Part I.
[49] Bernard Meland, *Reawakening of Christian Faith* (New York: Macmillan, 1949), 52.

and theological liberalism in general, and in the light of the new resources available in our culture which both continue to bear the Christian witness of faith and provide new imagery in which to reawaken faith. "What I hope to accomplish is that kind of sensitive selection of the elemental meanings implicit in all the many formulations of Christian doctrine which will disclose what is seminal in the Christian faith, and enable it to become living and compelling in our own time and culture."[50] The task of the theologian is reappropriation and reconstruction of the Christian witness for the concrete problems of living in the postliberal world. "It is ... setting the outreach of faith in an intelligible context such that the language of faith, its hopes and aspirations, become continuous with the reasonable discourse of our culture."[51]

The focus of Meland's thought throughout the fifty years is on the significance of the Christian ethos and mythos for contemporary problems of living. The task of theology is not primarily to resolve conceptual problems but to contribute to the well-being of the individual, the church, and the culture. "Theology is not simply a particular form of methodology; it is a focus of meaning that derives from a conviction that the Christian faith provides a basis for criticism and valuation upon contemporary issues."[52]

His first major sustained description of this constructive task is "A Profile of the Theological Field," where he says directly that by a constructive emphasis he means "a sense of responsibility for the cultural and human implications of their study and a consequent concern for problems and decisions affecting man's destiny."[53] The task of the field is to interpret Christian faith and determine its bearing on the problems of contemporary men and women and upon the issues of modern culture. The constructive theologian lives between the immediate concerns of individual experience within a contemporary culture and the historic witness of Christian faith. The scientific and philosophical concerns of the modernist (1906-1926) and philosophical (1926-1946) phases of the Chicago School must now play a subsidiary role to a constructive

---

[50] Ibid, p. 63.
[51] Ibid, p. 71.
[52] Bernard Meland, "Presuppositions in Religious Education -- An Appraisal," *Journal of Religion* 30 (July, 1950), 217.
[53] Meland, "A Profile of the Theological Field," *The Divinity School News* 24 (1957), 10.

theological task (1945-1966) more consciously directed to problems of faith and belief.

The constructive theologian asks what relevance this heritage has to the serious thought and action of contemporary women and men. Constructive theology, then, deals primarily with "the problematics of faith in the contemporary situation."[54] It has more affinity with historical theology than it does with philosophical theology. "Theology is peculiarly historical in character, more so than philosophy and science. In this respect it is more like the arts and the literary lore of a people, in that it is more or less expressive of a tradition, or of a medley of traditions."[55] The constructive task which works dialectically between heritage and contemporary problematics is basically concerned "with restoring to the witness of faith the stature which its historical structure had attained, but which has been lost to the church and to society through cultural accommodation, sentimentalization, and the attrition that normally comes to it through secularization."[56]

The constructive theologian is like the systematic theologian in that she operates within the circle of faith, but now the circle is widened to include larger orbits of meaning. One can begin with an analysis of culture as a way of getting at the primal witness of faith. But constructive theology includes another strand of inquiry as well, namely, the historical datum, the dimensions of the witness of faith which relate to the historical legacy transmitted through the church and the accumulative thrust of the mythos in culture. In this sense constructive theology includes a theology of culture but it is inclusive of cult and individual as well.

In his last book Meland finally focuses explicitly on his method. Constructive theology focuses theological interest upon the immediate demands and concerns of living as these evoke and convey the realities of faith. Here theology of culture and constructive theology merge, for constructive theology embraces the assumption that faith is not simply a legacy of belief inherited from the past but is a vital response to realities inhering within the immediacies of experience as a resource of judgment and grace. *Realities of Faith*, *Faith and Culture*, and *Fallible Forms and*

---

[54] Bernard Meland, "Response to Paper by Professor Beardslee," *Encounter* 36 (Autumn, 1975), 338.
[55] Bernard Meland, "For the Modern Liberal: Is Theology Possible? Can Science Replace It?" *Zygon* 2 (1967), 167.
[56] Meland, *Realities of Faith*, p. 54.

Symbols form his trilogy on the theology of culture. *Fallible Forms and Symbols* is his book on theological method. But the entire corpus of his writings, from *Modern Man's Worship* through *Fallible Forms and Symbols*, constitutes a fifty year project in constructive theology in a postliberal context.

Meland's constructive theology is a fertile resource for contemporary theological reflection. In addition to the fact that his thought exhibits the metamorphosis of liberal theology throughout the middle half of the twentieth century, the heart of his theology explores problems that are focal in the development of postliberal theology. I conclude by highlighting elements of his thought which are significant for current theological discussion. I believe there are two groups for whom key themes of his thought are an endowment.

1. The first group for whom Meland's thought continues to be important is the current generation of process-relational philosophers of religion and theologians. He is the principal voice in cautioning process-relational thinkers against overreaching the limits of speculative thought. He does this, however, by exploring the character of philosophical thought within the legacy of process metaphysics instead of by appealing to the various forms of antimetaphysical thinking in the twentieth century. Meland calls process-relational thinkers back to the empirical character and sources of their own heritage, avoiding the positivist and deconstructionist negation of all speculative metaphysics while affirming the relative character of every speculative venture.

In addition to representing the empirical orientation of process metaphysical thinking, Meland also claims the socio-historical themes of the long stream of empirical theology in the twentieth century. He thereby keeps the concept of experience in this tradition oriented toward an historical instead of an abstract or abridged meaning. The heart of his theology is the claim that experience in the liberal tradition is more than the autonomous, individualistic, private, and subjective experience of an isolated subject. Experience is social, cultural, and historical to the core. This means that experience in its "basic" or "primal" or "pure" sense includes a community, a tradition, a history, and therefore a complexity that is broader and deeper than merely an impression on the senses or an internal, subjective occurrence within the mind or self. Experience includes language, symbol, myth, and culture in the concept itself. The heart of Meland's theology is the claim that experience, both as it is lived and as it should be constructed metaphysically, includes language, symbol, myth, and culture. The historical context is as much of the experience of the experiencer as is a subjective occurance within the mind or self of the organism.

All process-relational thinkers appeal to language and symbol in their views of experience. But the communal, linguistic, mythical, and historical dimensions of experience have not been as central to their metaphysical constructions of experience recently as it was in the earlier socio-historical phase of empirical theology and as it is throughout the entire scope of Meland's thought. His theology embodies the socio-historical orientation in the concept of experience itself offered at the beginning of the process-relational theology of the Chicago School.[57] Meland is important for the future of process-relational thinking because his socio-historical brand of empiricism enriches the breadth and depth of the process-relational concept of experience and keeps that form of empirical thought faithful to the depth of lived experience in its historical context instead an abstract concept of experience.

2. The second group of theologians Meland's thought is significant for is the postliberal theologians. His rich concept of experience inserts his theology directly into the context of the contemporary postliberal discussion of the historical context and character of experience.

Contemporary postliberal theology has emphasized the intransigent differences between theological methods. These are variously denoted as "experiential-expressive" verses "cultural-linguistic" (George Lindbeck), "hermeneutical-political" verses "grammatical-confessionalist" (David Tracy), or "foundationalist" verses "antifoundationalist" (Ronald Thiemann). These methods all assume a dichotomous split in the relationship between experience and tradition.[58]

Meland's constructive theology undercuts the idea of two polar sources of tradition and experience for theology, which either must be correlated (Tracy) or one is unilaterally triumphant (Lindbeck). Continuing to represent the fundamental assumption of the socio-historical version of the empirical theology of the early Chicago School,

---

[57] See John Cobb, "The Origins of Process Theology," in Leroy S. Rouner, ed., *Meaning, Truth, and God* (Notre Dame: University of Notre Dame Press, 1982), pp. 91-111.

[58] Stephen L. Stell, "Hermeneutics in Theology and the Theology of Hermeneutics: Beyond Lindbeck and Tracy," *Journal of the American Academy of Religion* LXI (Winter, 1993): 679-703.

the given, for Meland, is an organism in an environment. There is an intrinsic reciprocity between culture and experience from beginning to end, so the theologian does not have to correlate two externally related poles or establish the priority (temporal or methodological) of one over the other.

Experience is never "pure experience" (individualistic, subjective, original, underived, autonomous, and foundational). It is always derived from, shaped, and interpreted in a social context, both a natural environment of interrelationships and interdependence (nature) and a cultural environment of language, symbol, and myth (tradition). Neither exists without the other and each is reciprocal with the other. Language arises and develops in the context of an organism encountering a complex environment in experience, and tradition shapes and reshapes the experience of an organism in its (natural, social, and cosmic) environment through language, symbol, and myth. The organism does not have a world without experience and culture interacting to construct a world of organism and enviornment. The resources of faith convey through the interaction of experience and culture the depth of relationships within the natural environment which create, judge, redeem, and fulfill the individual and the society.

Meland's constructive theology is not as "neat" in its dichotomies or polarities as Lindbeck, Tracy, and Thiemann propose in their postliberal methodologies. But his effort to faithfully take account of both experience and language in their interdependence calls for and lays the ground for reconfiguring the interpenetration of experience and tradition. His concept of the appreciative consciousness maintains some features of the liberal idea of experience, viz., the givenness and irreducibility of a relationship between an organism and its (cosmic, natural, and cultural) environment. The world is available to an organism in the depth and wide range of its experience. But that experience is not "given" in the sense that it is an uninterpreted foundation for tradition (language, symbol, myth, art, and science). Tradition is not merely a commentary on some more primordial experience that is expressed through language. Even if methodological neatness is sacrificed in order to be faithful to the complexities of the mutual interpenetration of environment and an interpreting organism, Meland is willing to employ a type of language which coneys the depth, richness, interpenetration, complexity, and ambiguity of what is given in experience and tradition.

One cannot derive a "system" from Meland's constructive theology. Nor can one assign clear and simple meanings to much of his language. Nor does he offer methodological purity. The reason for this goes to the heart of his theology. His constructive theology is an effort to remain faithful in his theological reflection to the rich depth and breadth of the lived experience of the natural and cultural environment. His method and his formulations are meant to bring some intelligibility to the depth and complexity of experience, not as an abstract or isolated source and norm of theology, but as it is lived in history.

When one sees clearly how lived experience stands at the heart of his theology, and that lived experience is richer and more complex than any theories about it, one sees how Meland's thought is a prominent resource for any current theological effort to move beyond the impasse between language and culture, on the one hand, and "pure experience," on the other. In our postliberal context, Meland is one of the most significant voices calling for faithfulness to the richness of lived experience instead of abstractions about "nature" and "history" and "culture" and "tradition" and "God" which are guided by methodological purity or ideological commitments. His constructive interpretations suggest directions the postliberal theologian in a process context can go in interpreting the reciprocity between experience and tradition as they convey the resources of a religious faith.

Bernard Meland: Complete Bibliography of Published Writings

1928

"The Development of Christocentric Theology in America." D. B. thesis, University of Chicago.

1929

"A Critical Analysis of the Appeal to Christ in Present-day Religious Interpretations." Ph.D. dissertation, University of Chicago.

1930

"A Present-day Evaluation of Christian Ethics." *Journal of Religion* 10, pp. 378-93.

"A Recent Reconstruction in German Theology." Review of *Schopfung: Wandel und Wesen der Religion* by Karl Bornhausen). *Journal of Religion* 10, pp. 294-97.

"Why Are Young Ministers' Minds Troubled?" *Homiletic Review* 100, pp. 196-99.

"Why Religion?" *Methodist Quarterly Review* 79, pp. 359-62.

1931

The Christian in Business and Civil Life. Edited with H.Y. McClusky. Board of Publications, Presbyterian Church, U.S.A.

"The Modern Liturgical Movement in Germany." *Journal of Religion* 11, pp. 517-32.

"Must Young Ministers' Minds be Disillusioned?" *Homiletic Review* 101, pp. 275-78.

"Toward a New Appreciation of Jesus." *Open Court* 45, pp. 596-610.

"Toward a Valid View of God." *Harvard Theological Review* 24, pp. 197-208.

"The Worship Mood." *Religious Education* 26, pp. 661-65.

1932

"The Present Worth of Jesus." *International Journal of Ethics* 42, pp. 324-30.

"A Revolt against Modernism." Review of *The Word and the World* by Emil Brunner. *Journal of Religion* 12, pp. 412-13.

"Rudolf Otto and the New Church Worship in Germany." *Homiletic Review* 103, pp. 261-66.

"Trends Toward A United Christendom." Review of *Im Ringen um die Kirche* by Friedrich Heiler. *Journal of Religion* 12, pp. 286-88.

1933

"Frederick Heiler and the High Church Movement in Germany." *Journal of Religion* 13, pp. 139-49.

"Is God Many of One?" *Christian Century* 50, pp. 725-26.

"Kinsman of the Wild: Religious Moods in Modern American Poetry." *Sewanee Review* 41, pp. 443-53.

"Modern Trends in Catholicism." *Unity* 112, pp. 38-40.

"A Psychological Critique of Theism." Review of *God or Man?* by James H. Leuba. *Christian Register* (December 21), p. 830.

"The Religion of Henry Nelson Wieman." *Christian Register* (October 19), pp. 677-79.

"Religious Awakenings in Modern Catholicism." *Open Court* 47, pp. 242-52.

"The Significance of Paul Tillich." *Christian Register* (December 7), p. 797.

1934

"The Appreciative Approach in Religion." *Journal of Religion* 14, pp. 194-204.

"The Development of Cursing." *Open Court* 48, pp. 232-40.

Modern Man's Worship: A Search for Reality in Religion. New York and London: Harper & Brothers.

"Religion: Devotion or Solace?" *Christian Century* 51, pp. 1274-75.

"The Religious Situation." Review of *The Religious Situation* by Paul Tillich. *The Christian Register*, p. 146.

"The Social Ideal of Our Age." *World Unity Magazine* 14, pp. 225-31.

"Visual Trends in Religious Education." *Education* 55, pp. 97-104.

1935

"Contemporary Philosophies of Religion in America." *Proceedings of the Missouri Academy of Sciences* 1, pp. 145-48.

"Mystical Naturalism and Religious Humanism." *The New Humanist* 8, pp. 72-74.

"Religion Has Not Lost Its Hold." *Religious Education* 30, pp. 26-30.

"The Significance of Mystical Experience." Review of *The Mystical Life* by Roger Bastide. *Journal of Religion* 15, pp. 328-30.

1936

American Philosophies of Religion (with Henry Nelson Wieman). Chicago and New York: Willet, Clark & Company; New York: Harper & Brothers, 1948.

"First Principles as Guides to University Education." *School and Society* 44, pp. 648-50.

"The Mystical Adventure." Review of *The Two Sources of Morality and Religion* by Henri Bergson. *Christendom* 1, pp. 195-98.

"Seeing God in Human Life." *Christian Century* 53, pp. 490-92.

1937

"The Faith of a Mystical Naturalist." *Review of Religion* 1, pp. 270-78.

"In Defense of Intuition." Review of *The God Who Speaks* by Burnett Hillman Streeter. *Christian Century* 54, pp. 1107-8.

"The Mystic Returns." *Journal of Religion* 17, pp. 146-60.

"The Quest for God through a New Vision." *The Quest for God through Understanding*, ed. Philip Henry Lotz. St. Louis: Bethany Press, pp. 90-97.

"The Quest for God through Dreams," *The Quest for God through Understanding*, ed. Philip Henry Lotz, St. Louis: Bethany Press, pp. 98-104.

Review of *Our Heritage in Public Worship* by D.H. Hislop. *Journal of Religion* 17, pp. 82-84.

"The Study of Religion in a Liberal Arts College." *Journal of Bible and Religion* 5, pp. 62-69.

"Toward a Common Christian Faith." *Christendom* 2, pp. 388-99.

1938

"Religion Awareness and Knowledge." *Review of Religion* 3, pp. 17-37.

"Theism Philosophically Affirmed." Review of *The Philosophical Basis of Mysticism* by G. Dawes Hick and *The Philosophical Basis of Mysticism* by Thomas Hughes. *Christendom* 3, pp. 454-58.

Write Your Own Ten Commandments. Chicago and New York: Willet, Clark & Company, New York: Harper and Brothers.

1939

The Church and Adult Education. New York: American Association for Adult Education.

"The Criterion of the Religious Life." *Journal of Religion* 19, pp. 33-43.

"The New Age of Christendom." Review of *True Humanism* by Jacques Maritain. *Christendom* 4, pp. 611-15.

"The Present Issue in Christianity." Review of *Revelation*, eds. John Baillie and Hugh Martin. *Christian Century* 56, pp. 156-7.

1940

"Growth Toward Order." *Personalist* 21, pp. 257-66.

"Spinoza and Modern Thought." Review of *The Psychology and Ethics of Spinoza* by David Bidney. *Christendom* 5, pp. 291-2.

"The Spiritual Outreach of the Liberal Arts College." *Religious Education* 35, pp. 219-23.

"Tradition and New Frontiers." *Christendom* 5, pp. 323-31.

1941

"At Home in the Universe." *Contemporary Religious Thought: An Anthology*, ed., Thomas S. Kepler. Nashville: Abingdon-Cokesbury Press, pp. 284-89.

"Beyond Free Mind." *Christian Education* 24, pp. 281-85.

"Comfort of the Stars." *Christian Century* 58, p. 559. (poem)

"Prayer." *Christian Century* 58, p. 616. (poem)

"Some Philosophic Aspects of Poetic Perception." *Personalist* 21, pp. 384-92.

"The Tragic Sense of Life." *Religion in Life* 10, pp. 212-22.

"Why Modern Cultures Are Uprooting Religion." *Christendom* 6, pp. 194-204.

1942

"Anthology of Modern Belief." (Review of *Contemporary Religious Thought* edited by Thomas S. Kepler), *Christendom* 7, pp. 262-64.

"For Self-Realization-Religious Education." *Adult Education Bulletin* 6, pp. 178-9.

"Fragments of Faith." *The Baton of Phi Beta Fraternity* 21, pp. 37-38.

"God, The Unlimited Companion." Review of *Man's Vision of God* by Charles Hartshorne. *Christian Century* 59, pp. 1289-90.

"The New Language in Religion." *Religion in the Making* 2, pp. 275-89.

"Two Paths to the Good Life." *Personalist* 23, pp. 53-61. Reprinted in Chapter 17, pp. 425-432.

1943

"Humanize the University." *Journal of Higher Education* 14, pp. 70-74.

"The Religious Availability of a Philosopher's God." *Christendom* 8, pp. 495-502.

"Response to David D. Henry's Critique of 'Humanize the University'." *Journal of Higher Education* 14 : 394-395.

"The Retreat to Tradition." *Personalist* 24, pp. 40-45.

"Theodore Carswell Hume: His Thought and Work." *Social Action* 9.

"Theodore Carswell Hume: Memorial Address: His Mind and Thought." The Claremont Church (October 31), pp. 8-10.

"Theological Perspective." *Religion in Life* 13, pp. 100-06.
"Three Poems" ("Child by the Sea," "Sea Winds," and "Relinquishment"). *The Baton of Phi Beta Fraternity*, p. 22.

1944

"The Culture of the Human Spirit." *Journal of Bible and Religion* 12, pp. 217-26.
Review of *The Root and Flower of Prayer* by Roger Hazelton. *Journal of Religion* 24, pp. 285-6.
"Some Unresolved Issues in Theology." *Journal of Religion* 24, pp. 233-39.

1945

"The Ascetic Temper of Modern Humanism." *Personalist* 26, pp. 153-65.
"A Christian Apologia." Review of *The Christian Answer*, ed. Henry P. VanDusen. *Christian Century* 62, pp. 1255-56.
"The Creation of a World Culture." *Current Religious Thought* 5, pp. 1-4.
"An Idealist's Preface to Theology." Review of *From Science to God* by Karl Schmidt. *Christendom* 10, pp. 237-40.
"Why Science Needs Theism." Review of *Science and the Idea of God* by William Ernest Hocking. *Christendom* 10, pp. 520-23.

1946

"Education for a Spiritual Culture." *Journal of Religion* 26, pp. 87-100.
"Inner Harvests." *Chicago Theological Seminary Register* 36, pp. 12-16.
"Suffering and Significance." *Religious Education* 41, pp. 37-45.

1947

"The Genius of Protestantism." *Journal of Religion* 27, pp. 273-92.
"Is God Process or Person?" Reply to Charles Clayton Morrison's review of *The Source of Human Good* by Henry Nelson Wieman. *Christian Century* 64, p. 134.
"Philosophy of Religion and the War Years." *Journal of Bible and Religion* 15, pp. 86-89.

"The Range of Our Dedications." *The Divinity School News* 14, pp. 1-4.

Seeds of Redemption. New York: Macmillan.

1948

America's Spiritual Culture. New York: Harper & Brothers.

Review of *The Eternal Gospel* by Gerald Heard. *Chicago Theological Seminary Register* 38, pp. 42-43.

"The Thought of Emil Brunner-An Evaluation." *Journal of Bible and Religion* 16, pp. 165-68.

1949

"The Legacy of a Liberal: A Biographical Study of Raymond Cummings Brooks." *Journal of Religion* 29, pp. 204-19.

The Reawakening of Christian Faith. New York: Macmillan; paperback, New York: Books for Libraries, 1972.

Review of Reports of a Survey of College Reading Materials (Edward W. Hazen Foundation), *Chicago Theological Seminary Register* 39, pp. 37-38.

"A Time of Reckoning — A Editorial." *Journal of Religion* 29, pp. :1-4.

1950

"Presuppositions in Religious Education — An Appraisal." *Journal of Religion* 30, pp. 214-21.

"A Good Not Our Own." *Current Religious Thought* 10, pp. 3-6.

"Integrity in Higher Education." *Religious Education* 45, pp. 7-15.

"Theological Educators in a University Community." *The Divinity School News* 17, pp. 1-7.

1951

"Faith Regenerates the Mind." Review of *Renewing the Mind* by Roger Hazelton. *Christian Century* 68, p. 18.

"On Power and Goodness." *The Divinity School News* 18, pp. 1-6.

"Religion in Higher Education-A Symposium." Comments on Wiley's article, "Native Growth or Import." *Journal of Higher Education* 23, pp. 369-71.

1952
"The Perception of Goodness." *Journal of Religion* 32, pp. 47-55.

1953
"Faith and Critical Thought." *Personalist* 34, pp. 140-50.

Faith and Culture. New York: Oxford University Press. London: George Allen and Unwin, 1955; paperback, Carbondale: Southern Illinois University Press, 1970.

Higher Education and the Human Spirit. Chicago: University of Chicago Press; paperback, Chicago: Seminary Cooperative Bookstore, 1965.

"Interpreting the Christian Faith within a Philosophical Framework." *Journal of Religion* 33, pp. 87-102.

1954
"An Age in Between." *The Divinity School News* 21, pp. 1-7.

"Renascent Protestantism." *Christian Century* 71, pp. 458-60.

Review of *The Realm of Spirit and the Realm of Caesar* by Nicholas Berdyaev. *International Journal of Religious Education* 30, p. 33.

Review of *The Christian Approach to Culture* by Emile Caillet. *International Journal of Religious Education* 30, pp. 37-38.

1955
"American Contributions to Theological Science," *Twentieth Century Encyclopedia of Religious Knowledge.* Grand Rapids, Michigan: Baker Book House, Vol. 2, pp. 1102-04.

"The Chicago School of Theology," *Twentieth Century Encyclopedi of Religious Knowledge.* Grand Rapids, Michigan: Baker Book House, Vol. 1, pp. 232-33.

Review of *Christianity and the New Situation* by E. G. Lee. *The Pastor* 18, pp. 44, 46.

"This Upsurge of Faith." *Christian Century* 72, pp. 561-563.

1956
"The Student-Faculty Spring Conference." *The Divinity School News* 23, pp. 11-14.

1957

"New Dimensions of Liberal Faith." *Christian Century* 74, pp. 961-63.

"A Profile of the Theological Field." *Divinity School News* 24, pp. 9-19.

1958

"A Prayer." *Serampore College Magazine* 13, p. 15.

"Religious Zeal: A Threat to Intellectual Life?" *Christian Scholar* 40, pp. 41-48.

"Together with Differences." *The Divinity School News* 25, pp. 1-6.

1959

"The Christian Encounter with the Faiths of Man," The Resurgent Religions of Asia and the Christian Mission. Chicago: The Center for the Study of the Christian World Mission.

"Huxley at Chicago." *Christian Century* 76, pp. 1429-30.

1960

"From Darwin to Whitehead: A Study in the Shift in Ethos and Perspective Underlying Religious Thought." *Journal of Religion* 40, pp. 229-45.

"Jesus Christ and the Problem of Power." *Encounter* 21, pp. 59-72.

"Who Regardeth the Day." *The Divinity School News* 27, pp. 1-6.

1961

"The Christian Faith and Empirical Method," A Mimeographed Critique of Papers presented by University Educators at Conference of Minnesota Association on Higher Education.

"Theology and the Historian of Religion." *Journal of Religion* 41, pp. 263-76.

1962

"Analogy and Myth in Post-Liberal Theology." *Perkins School of Theology Journal* 15, pp. 19-27.

"A Long Look at the Divinity School and Its Present Crisis." *Criterion* 1 , pp. 21-30.

"The Persisting Liberal Witness." *Christian Century* 79, pp. 1157-59.

The Realities of Faith: The Revolution in Cultural Forms. New York: Oxford University Press, 1962, paperback, Chicago: Seminary Cooperative Bookstore, 1970.

1963

"Modern Protestantism: Aimless or Resurgent?" *Christian Century* 80, pp. 1494-97.

"The Root and Form of Wieman's Thought," *The Empirical Theology of Henry Nelson Wieman*, ed. Robert W. Bretall. New York: Macmillan, pp. 44-68.

Review of *The Impact of American Religious Liberalism* by Kenneth Cauthen. *Church History* 32, pp. 492-93.

1964

"A Post-Retreat Comment to Professor Haroutunian." *Criterion* 3, pp. 11-12.

"How is Culture a Source for Theology?" *Criterion* 3, pp. 10-21.

"New Perspectives on Nature and Grace," *The Scope of Grace*, ed. Philip Hefner. Philadelphia: Fortress Press, pp. 143-61.

"The Self and Its Communal Ground." *Religious Education* 59, pp. 363-69.

"A Voice of Candor." *Religion in Life* 33, pp. 19-27.

1965

"Alternatives to Absolutes." *Religion in Life* 34, pp. 343-51.

"The Critical Stance in Thought." *Personalist* XLVI, pp. 233-244.

"A Critique of Haroutunian's Paper on Theology and the American Experience." *Dialog* 4, pp. 180-87.

"In Response to Dr. Faruqi, 'History of Religion: Its Nature and Significance for Christian Education and the Muslim-Christian Dialogue'." *Numen* 12, pp. 87-95.

"Rudolf Otto," *Handbook of Christian Theologians*, ed. Martin E. Marty and Dean G. Peerman. Cleveland: World Publishing Company, pp. 165-91.

1966

"Narrow is the Way beyond Absurdity and Anxiety." *Criterion* 5, pp. 3-9.

"A New Morality — But to What End?" *Religion in Life* 35, pp. 191-99.

The Secularization of Modern Cultures. New York: Oxford University Press.

1967

"For the Modern Liberal: Is Theology Possible? Can Science Replace It?" *Zygon* 2, pp. 166-86.

"The Mytho-Poetic Dimension of Faith Within Modern Culture." *Criterion* 6, pp. 5-7.

1968

"Credo." *Criterion* 7, pp. 29-32.

"The Structure of Christian Faith." *Religion in Life* 37, pp. 551-62.

"Liberalism, Theological," *Encyclopedia Britannica*. Fourteenth Edition. Volume 13, pp. 1020-1022.

1969

"Can Empirical Theology Learn Something from Phenomenology?" *The Future of Empirical Theology*, ed. B. Meland. Chicago: University of Chicago Press, pp. 283-306.

"The Empirical Tradition in Theology at Chicago," *The Future of Empirical Theology*, ed. Bernard Meland. Chicago: University of Chicago Press, pp. 1-62.

The Future of Empirical Theology, editor. Chicago: University of Chicago Press.

1970

"New Realism in Religious Inquiry." *Encounter* 31, pp. 311-24.

"Response to Citation as Alumnus of the Year." *Alumni* (November), pp. 4-6.

1971

"Analogy and Myth in Postliberal Theology." In *Process Philosophy and Christian Thought*, ed. Delwin Brown, Ralph E. James, Jr., and Gene Reeves. Indianapolis: Bobbs Merrill, pp. 116-27.

"Breaking of Forms in the Interest of Importance." *Criterion* 10, pp. 4-11.

"Evolution and the Imagery of Religious Thought: From Darwin to Whitehead." In *Process Philosophy and Christian Thought*, ed. Delwin Brown, Ralph E. James Jr., and Gene Reeves. Indianapolis: Bobbs-Merrill, pp. 411-30.

"Faith and Formative Imagery of Our Time." In *Process Theology*, ed. Ewert H. Cousins. New York: Newman Press, pp. 37-45.

"The New Creation." In *Process Theology*, ed. Ewert H. Cousins. New York: Newman Press, pp. 191-202.

1972

"The Christian Legacy and Our Cultural Identity." (Working Paper), American Academy of Religion, pp. 22-42.

"History and Nature in the Judeo-Christian Tradition: How Will the Future Be Different?," Religious Reconstruction for the Environment, Proceedings Report from a Post-Stockholm Workshop at Storrs, Connecticut. Faith-Man-Nature Group. November 30-December 2.

"John Milton, Puritan or Liberal." *Encounter* 33, pp. 129-40.

1973

"Language and Reality in the Christian Faith." *Encounter* 34, pp. 173-90.

"Shailer Mathews," *Dictionary of American Biography*. Supplement Three 1941-45, ed. Edward T. James. New York: Charles Scribner's Sons, pp. 514-16.

"The Unifying Moment." Review of *The Unifying Moment: the Psychological Philosophy of William James and Alfred North Whitehead* by Craig R. Eisendrath. *Process Studies* 3, pp. 285-90.

1974

"Grace, A Dimension of Nature?" *The Journal of Religion* 54, pp. 119-37.

"Otto, Rudolf," *The New Encyclopedia Britannica*, pp. 4-5.

1975

"The Mystery of Existing and Not Existing." *Union Seminary Quarterly Review* XXX, pp. 165-75.

"Response to Paper by Professor Beardslee, 'Narrative Form in the New Testament'." *Encounter*, 36, pp. 331-341.

"Daniel Day Williams: A Tribute." *Criterion* 14, pp. 21-22.
Review of *The American Spirit in Theology* by R.C. Miller. *Religious Education* 70, pp. 82-90.

1976
Fallible Forms and Symbols: Discourses on Method for a Theology of Culture. Philadelphia: Fortress Press.

1980
"Prolegomena to Inquiry into the Reality of God." *American Journal of Theology & Philosophy*, 1 pp. 71-82.

1982
"Wieman's Philosophy of Creativity." In *Creative Interchange*, edited by John Boyner and William Minor. Carbondale: Southern Illinois University Press, pp. 15-34.

"Reminiscences and Reflections Concerning Willem Pauck's Years in Chicago." *Criterion* 17, pp. 3-7.

1984
"Reflections on the Early Chicago School of Modernism." *American Journal of Theology & Philosophy* 5, pp. 3-12.

"In Response to My Interpreters." *American Journal of Theology & Philosophy* 5, p. 42.

"In Response to Inbody." *American Journal of Theology & Philosophy* 5, pp. 72-79.

"In Response to Suchocki." *American Journal of Theology & Philosophy* 5, pp. 89-95.

"In Response to Miller." *American Journal of Theology & Philosophy* 5, pp. 107-116.

"In Response to Frankenberry." *American Journal of Theology & Philosophy* 5, pp. 130-137.

"In Response to Loomer." *American Journal of Theology & Philosophy* 5, pp. 144-155.

1987
"Myth as a Mode of Awareness and Intelligibility." *American Journal of Theology & Philosophy* 8, pp. 109-119.

1988

Essays in Constructive Theology: A Process Perspective. Exploration Press. Edited by Perry LeFevre.

1989

"'Ultimate Mystery' and Structured Thought." *American Journal of Theology & Philosophy* 10, pp. 153-157.

INDEX

A
Absolute, the, 101, 104, 133, 139–140, 153, 192, 202
adequacy, judgement of, 112, 135, 195, 199
aesthetics/aesthetic judgement, 124–125, 225
Alexander, Samuel, 36–37
Altizer, Thomas, 195, 214
ambiguity, 28, 79, 110–111, 150, 163, 172, 182, 189–191, 194, 196–198, 203, 209
American Academy of Religion, viii
American-German Exchange student, 15
American Journal of Theology & Philosophy, ix, xi, 14, 69–70, 72, 133, 165–166, 175–176, 178, 184, 191, 218
Ames, Edward Scribner, 17, 19, 148, 177, 182, 192
analogy, 120–121, 136, 147, 153, 160, 182
analytical philosophy, 134
anthropology, 86, 99, 132
apologetics, 223, 225
appreciative consciousness/awareness, xi, 14, 18, 21, 24, 34, 36, 49, 51–53, 55–56, 59–62, 83–84, 115–116, 141, 152, 224, 232
Aquinas, 45
Aristotle, 45, 56
Arnold, Harvey, vii, 143, 148
Auerbach, Erik, 212
Axel, Larry, ix, xi, 9, 19, 35, 50, 131, 177, 185, 225

B
Backus, Burdette, 48
Bacon, Francis, 38, 77
Bangalore, 8, 39
Baptist Theological Union, 2
Barrows Lectures, 38–39
Barth, Karl, ix, 2, 15, 25–27, 29, 36, 113, 162, 212
Baumer, Franklin, 127, 206
Beardslee, William, 110, 168
Becquerel, Henri, 78
Beethoven, 4
Bellah, Robert, 214
Berger, Peter, 212
Bergson, Henri, 14, 49–50, 52, 59, 85, 87, 114–115, 123, 125, 144, 150
Bible, 8, 38, 98, 195
Biltmore House, 6
Bond Chapel, 41
Boodin, J. E., 36
Bracken, Joseph, 109
Brandt, Richard, 87
Brauer, Jerald, viii, 2
Briggs, John, 4
Brown, Delwin, 14, 97, 110, 120, 143
Brown, William Adams, 27, 209
Brunner, Emil, 15, 25, 27, 29–30, 35, 162, 211
brute force, 116, 129, 185–187
Buber, Martin, 36
Bultmann, Rudolf, 101

C
Calcutta, 39
Calhoun, Robert, 212
Case, Shirley Jackson, ix, 13–14
causal efficacy, 89, 127, 132–133, 165, 188, 199
Center for Process Studies, 109
Central College, 20–22, 25
certainty, 134, 139, 152–153, 158, 171–172, 200, 202
Chardin, Pierre Teilhard de, 113
Chicago Daily News, 12
Chicago Presbytery, 17

Chicago School, vii, 2, 10, 13, 15–16, 18–20, 22, 40, 114, 143–145, 148, 153, 181, 193, 209–210, 221, 226–228, 231
Chicago Tribune, 12
Christ, 99, 138
Christendom, 50
christocentrism, 209–210
Christian, William, 212
christocentrism, 209–210
civilization, 91
clarity, 146, 148, 160, 172, 176
Clark Lectures, 33
Clarke, William Newton, 209
classical empiricism, 46, 52
Cobb, John, 19, 21, 71–72, 110, 113, 126, 165–166, 175, 212, 226, 231
cognition, 55–56, 58–61, 65, 118–119, 134, 137, 141–142, 152, 154
cognitive status, 115, 126, 134
coherence, 157, 164–166, 168–171
Collingwood, R. G., 118
Commanger, Henry Stelle, 13
conceptualism, 17, 62, 148, 183
concretion, principle of, 130
Conner, David, 193
constructive theology, 32, 36, 105, 192, 206, 222–233
constructivism, 177–179, 184, 186, 192–193
contextualism, 66–67, 192
covenant, 136, 158, 209
Cranston, Maurice, 206
Creative Passage, 51, 103–104, 112, 130, 152, 155–156, 161, 183, 187–198, 191, 198
creativity, 116–117, 120, 127, 129–130, 162, 168, 186–188, 194
creaturalism, 50, 52, 132
Creel, Herlee, 13
criterion of judgement, 136–138
Crosby, Donald, 176
cultural anthropology, 38, 89, 96, 106, 132, 138, 144, 160
culture, xi, 36, 44, 58, 62–63, 69–70, 73, 76, 86, 89–92, 95–96, 99, 133, 137–138, 142, 208
creatural stance, creaturehood, 14–15, 23–24
crisis theology, 25
Criterion, xi, ix

Curies, 78

D

Danto, Arthur, 76
Darwin, Charles, 77, 85, 128, 219
Dean, William, xi, xiv, 47, 71–72, 76, 109–110, 131, 165, 176–177, 185, 191–192, 195, 200, 221
deconstruction, 71–72, 127–128, 134, 136, 177, 200–201
Deism, 38
depth/depth dimension/depth of sensitivity, 36, 46–48, 56, 68, 76–78, 80, 83–84, 87, 89, 97, 101–104, 110, 112, 117, 124, 131–135, 139, 141–142, 150, 152–156, 159–160, 163, 165, 178, 181, 187–189, 200
depth psychology, 99, 132
Descartes, 38, 43, 75
despair, 167–169, 171–172
Devaney, Sheila, 72, 221
Devenish, Philip, 110–111, 133
Dewey, John, 165, 177, 180, 182, 217
dialectical theology, 28–29, 31–32, 225
discrimination, 59–61
dissonance, 4, 157, 161, 164–165, 168–171, 189
Divinity School, ix, x, xii, 1–2, 10–11, 13–14, 17, 19, 21–22, 24–26, 31, 35–37, 39, 86, 92, 105, 113–114, 143, 145, 188, 206, 223, 227
Divinity School News, 15, 34, 228
dualism, 75–76, 81, 178–179
duration, 88
Durkheim, Emile, 81
Donne, John, 131

E

Eddington, Arthur, 36
Edwards, Paul, 76, 206
Einstein, Albert, 132, 171
elementalism, 15, 23, 36, 50–52, 93, 122, 126, 132, 144, 152, 154–155, 165, 168, 172, 225
emergent evolution/emergence, 14, 36–37, 47, 60, 76–78, 80, 82–83, 85–87, 89, 93, 95, 99, 114–115, 117, 120, 132, 144, 155–156, 187
Emmet, Dorothy, 59

empirical realism, x, 24, 39–40, 44–45, 47, 52, 69–73, 87, 139, 164, 177–179, 184, 187, 195, 200–201, 203, 205, 208, 215–216, 230
empirical theism, 177, 191
empirical theology, viii, 71, 105, 110, 176, 199–200, 215–217
emotion, 49, 116, 151
Encounter, 164, 229
Encyclopedia Britannica, 206
Enlightenment, 30, 38, 43, 139, 205, 212, 214
ethos, 78, 96–97, 105, 133, 228
Evans, Walker, 4
evil, 164–167, 192, 194, 197–198
existentialism, 35, 47, 113, 127–128, 207, 217
experience, 43–44, 65–66, 68–69, 86–87, 90, 105, 117, 137, 141, 200, 213, 216–217, 230–232
experience and language, xi, 44–45, 55, 66–71, 73, 142, 185, 232

F

faith, xi, 24, 34, 36, 38, 86–87, 92–96, 1 05, 115–116, 126, 133, 135, 137, 142, 154, 167, 201
Federated Theological Faculty, 32, 227
Ferm, Vergilius, 76
field theory, 117, 120
Ford, David, 212
Ford, Lewis, 110, 113, 126, 133
forgiveness, 32, 146
forms of perception, 63
Forsyth Auto Manufacturing Company, 9
Fosdick, Harry Emerson, 209
Foster, G. B., 143, 209
foundationalism, 45, 65, 67, 71, 73, 201, 203
frames of meaning, 55, 62–65, 73, 141
Frankenberry, Nancy, x, xi, 45–47, 67, 70–72, 110, 133, 176, 179, 185, 199, 200, 202, 215, 218–219
freedom, 86, 89
fringe of consciousness, 47, 54–55, 61
Frei, Hans, ix, 209, 212
functionalism, 77
fundamental notions, 64, 73, 117–118, 120–121, 143, 147

fundamentalism, 214

G

Garrison, Jim, 195
Geertz, Cliford, 212
Gilkey, Langdon, 164
Gleick, James, 4
God, xi, 37–38, 43–44, 75, 94–95, 130, 132, 138, 153, 158, 165, 168, 170–171, 179–180
God, ambiguity of, 189–192, 195, 197
God as a constructive idea, 177
God as a contemplative idea, 180
God as an imaginative idea, 186
God as a designative idea, 186
God as a gentle working, 186–187
good, 194, 196–198, 225
grace, 84, 94–95, 99–100, 161–162, 229
great chain of being, 127–128
Grenz, Stanley, 113
Griffin, David, 110–113, 126, 165–166, 194, 212

H

Haas, Ernst, 4
Hall, David, 165, 172
Harkness, Georgia, 27
Harnack, Adolf, 25, 209
Harper, William Rainey, 2
Hartshorne, Charles, 19, 33, 37, 109, 113, 115, 147, 149, 151, 153–154, 165, 175, 194, 212
Hauerwas, Stanley, 209, 212
Harvard Theological Review, 182
Havel, Vachav, 205
Harvey, Van, 223
Haydon, Eustace, 19
Hegel, George, 85, 95, 127, 138
Heidegger, Martin, 138
Heiler, Frederick, 5
Herrmann, Wilhelm, 25, 209
Hick, John, 194
Highlands Institute for American Religious Thought, viii
Hiroshima, 32
historicism, 71, 100–101, 105–106, 134, 138–139, 141–142, 177, 200–201
Hodge, Betty Jean, 1
Holmer, Paul, 209
Homewood, IL, 6, 9
Hough, Joseph, 226
Huchins, Robert Maynard, 24, 32

human structure, 80, 85, 155, 158, 176–177
humanism, 48, 82–83, 127–128, 209
Hume, David, 45–46, 75, 216–217
Hume, Theodore, 29
Hynes, William, 13

I

idealism, 56–57, 81–82, 85, 119, 127–128, 201, 220–221
identification, 57–58
Iliff School of Theology, 109–110, 112
immanent, 93, 95–96
Inbody, Tyron, viii, xi, 165, 184–185, 193, 214–215
indeterminacy, 79, 132
India, 39
individuation, 63, 93
intelligibility, 62, 111, 117–120
Interdenominational Student Conference, 13
internal relations, 83, 95, 127, 131, 150

J

James, Ralph, 97, 120, 143
James, William, 11, 19, 37, 47, 52–54, 59, 61, 70, 85, 87–88, 102, 109, 114–115, 123–125, 144, 150, 165, 193, 195, 217–218
Jesse, Jennifer, xii
Jesus, 209–210
Jones, Gregory, 212
Journal of Religion, ix, xi, 8, 28, 31, 33, 64, 145, 163, 165, 167, 201, 209–211, 220, 223–224, 228
judgement, 32

K

Kant, Immanuel, 18, 30–32, 45, 53, 56–58, 61-63, 66-67, 69, 75, 85, 101–103, 128, 178–179, 201, 186, 217
Kaplan, Mordicai, x
Kaufman, Gordon, 43–44, 46, 69, 75, 177–178, 186, 190, 203, 227
Kensington, IL, 5
Kepler, Thomas, 92
Kierkegaard, Soren, 29, 36, 93, 209, 212
King, Henry Churchill, 209
Knox, John, 13
Krafte-Jacobs, Lori, 9

Krikorian, Yervant, 76
Kuhn, Thomas, 212

L

Lamprecht, Sterling, 76
Lane, Belden, 195
Lange, Dorothea,
Langer, Susan, 59
language, 43–44, 62, 64, 66–68, 71, 73, 100, 133, 137, 156–157. 202–203, 208, 232
language and reality, 69, 75, 157, 176, 178, 199
language and experience, 66, 68–69, 72, 202–203
Lee, Bernard, 109–111
LeFevre, Perry, 183, 185, 226
levels of consciousness, 81
liberal theology, 43–44, 75, 128, 207–209, 211, 217, 230
liberalism, 44, 203, 206–211, 214, 220
Lieberman, Archie, 165
limitation, principle of, 65, 84, 100–101, 104, 110, 134, 157, 176, 202
Lindbeck, George, ix, 43–45, 75–76, 20, 29, 211–213, 231–232
linguistic dualism, 75
lived experience, xii, 3, 4, 34, 47–48, 52, 65–67, 69, 73, 87, 109, 117, 122, 124, 140, 146, 148, 150, 155–156, 163, 172, 192–193, 199, 207, 233
Locke, John, 45, 216–217
logos, 158, 161
Loomer, Bernard, ix, 19, 31, 36–37, 26–27, 32, 77, 110, 112, 114, 123, 126, 144, 164, 166, 172, 184, 189, 193, 195–198, 175, 177, 187, 190, 218, 220, 223, 227
Lovejoy, Arthur, 127
Luther, 15, 123

M

Macintosh, D. C., 177
margin of intelligibility, 60, 97, 110, 155, 158, 168, 176, 181, 199
Martindale, Don, 11
Mathews, Shailer, ix, 10, 13–15, 17, 19–20, 177, 182, 192
matrix of sensitivity, 95, 187
Mays, Benjamin, 13

McCormick Theological Seminary, 12, 17
McClelland, Robert, 195
McFague, Sallie, 159
McGiffert, A. C., 19
Meland, Elizabeth Hansen, 6
Meland, Erik, 6
Meland, Margaret, 7, 15, 21, 38
Merleau-Ponty, 38, 40
metaphor, 120, 147
metaphysics, 62, 115, 117
metaphysics and poetry, 121
metaphysics, basis of 117
metaphysics, limits of, 145
metaphysics, nature of, 118
metaphysics, use of, 121
Michigan Agricultural College, 9
Miller, Randolf Crump, viii, 114, 177, 179, 200, 215
Mills College, 26
mind, 53–54, 59–62, 76, 85, 120, 164, 178
modern era, 205–206, 214, 223
modernism, 13–15, 19–21, 210, 214, 228
the More, 3, 47, 52–53, 55, 70, 83, 87, 103, 137, 140–141, 156
Morgan, Lloyd, 36–37
Morrison, Charles Clayton, 26–27
Mozart, 3–4
Mueller, J. J., x, 214, 223–224
Muray, Leslie, xii
Murphy, Arthur, 124
mystery/mysterious universe, 16, 18, 117, 154, 163, 166, 178–179, 181, 193
mystical naturalism/mysticism, xi, 6, 11, 15–17, 21, 23–24, 34, 48–50, 52, 61, 92, 115, 125, 144, 148, 183–184
myth, 34, 36–38, 92, 96, 98, 106, 121, 135–136, 138, 142, 144, 158–159, 161, 209
mythos, 38, 96–99, 105–106, 130, 133, 135–138, 161, 228

N
Nagasaki, 32
National Presbyterian Student Association, 12
nature, 76–79, 81, 86, 94

natural piety, 191, 196–197
naturalism, 21, 45, 48, 50, 52, 76, 80, 83, 85, 100, 177, 181, 191–193, 195, 218–219
naturalistic historicism, 76
naturalistic theism, 183, 190–193, 197–198
neonaturalism, 220–221
neoorthodoxy, 29, 36, 113, 137–138, 162, 201, 208, 211–212, 220–221
neopragmatism, 71, 134, 177
New Creation, 94, 99, 130
New Humanist, 48, 76
New Testament, 97, 101, 138
new metaphysics, 99, 115–116, 119–120, 1124, 132, 134–136, 144, 148
new physics, 47, 78, 120, 125, 132
new realism, 21, 28, 66
New York Times, 205
Newton, Isaac, 64, 77–79, 85, 128, 170
Niebuhr, Reinhold, 2, 12, 26, 27, 29–31, 35, 94, 162
Norway, 5, 8
Norwegian Lutheran Church, 8, 9
novelty, 129, 132

O
Oakes, Edward, vii, 212
objective relativism, 45, 192
Ogden, Schubert, 101, 110, 113, 126, 133, 147, 165–166, 175–176, 212, 223
Olson, Roger, 113
ontological peril, 166, 168
ontology, 111
open awareness, 56–57
orbit of meaning, 39
order, 79
organism/organic/organismic, 70, 78, 93, 115, 117, 120, 130–132, 162–163, 187
otherness, 66
Otto, Rudolf, 15, 46, 52, 213, 217
Oxford Conference 1937, 26–27, 30

P
Pacific Area Conference, 26
pantheism, 184, 189, 191, 196–198
Park College, xi, 10, 13
Pauck, Wilhem, 13, 29, 32
Peden, Creighton, 177, 185, 190, 193

perception, perceptual field, 54–55, 60, 62–65, 75, 116, 133, 146, 151
personalism, 127–128, 209
persuasion/persuasive, 118
phenomenology, 35, 37, 39, 44, 47, 55, 67, 112, 117, 124–125, 127–128, 146, 150, 164, 207, 217
physics, 77–79, 102, 104, 124, 132, 170, 187
Pittenger, Norman, 110, 113
Placker, William, 209, 212–213
Planck, Max, 36
Plato, 105, 136, 160
plurality/pluralism, 148, 180, 182–184
poetry/poetic/poet, 121, 156–157, 159–160
Polanyi, Michael, 39
Poling, James, 190
political theologian, 226
Pomona College, 23–28, 32
Poona, 39
Porter, 4
positivism, 38
postliberal, 200–206, 208–209, 211–213, 215, 230–233
postliberal theology, 202, 206, 208, 211–214, 220–221, 230–231, 233
practical theologian, 226
pragmatism, 14, 21–22, 25, 44–45, 119, 127–128, 139, 152, 165, 185, 200–201, 209, 217
prehension, 127
presentational immediacy, 132
Presbyterian Church, 9, 11–12, 17
primal context, 79–80, 131, 155, 201
principle of concretion, 186
principle of limitation, 100, 155–157
process philosophy/metaphysics, 34, 68, 87, 114, 117, 120, 122, 149–150, 157, 163, 165, 192, 230–231
Process Studies, 21, 165
process theology, 109, 113, 115, 142–144, 146–147, 153, 157, 163–166, 199, 212, 230
process vision, 113, 115, 122, 143
process theology, three types, 109
Proudfoot, Wayne, 46
psyche/psychic energy, 88–89, 93, 95–96, 100, 122
Pullman, IL, 6–7
Pullman Car Works, 6

Purdue University, xi, xiii, 184

Q

Quest, xi
quantum theory, 79, 117, 132, 170

R

radical empiricism, 18–19, 35, 37, 44, 46–47, 52, 54, 65, 61, 67, 85, 102–103, 112, 123, 130, 132, 137, 148, 150, 163, 170, 194–195, 197, 204, 217
Rahner, Karl, 178
Randall, John Herman, 76
Rangoon, 39
rational empiricism, 111, 124, 148, 150, 163
rationalism/rationalistic philosophy, 109–110, 117, 123–126, 146–151, 153, 158–159, 162, 164–165, 169–172, 176, 199, 210, 214
realism/realistic, 15, 18–19, 21, 31, 35–37, 40, 46, 70, 83, 85, 127, 179, 180–181, 184–185, 193, 200–201, 203–204, 208, 211, 220–221
reason, 119, 146–147, 149–150, 153–154, 157–158, 199
redemption, 161–162
Reeves, Gene, 97, 120, 143
Regenstein Library, 1, 2
relations/relatedness, 47, 78, 131
relativity, xi, 14, 45, 77–78, 92, 100–104, 117, 120, 131–132, 134, 147, 202, 207
relativism, 45, 65, 71, 73, 100–102, 105–106, 115, 133–134, 139–140, 142, 192, 202–204
Religion in Life, 8, 79, 98, 120, 190
religious experience, 44, 46, 217
religious adequacy, 196
Religious Education, 49
religious humanism, 48
revisionary theology, 212
Ritschl, Albrecht, 209, 217
Robbins, Wesley, 69
Roentgen, Wilhelm, 78
Rogers, Delores, x
romanticism, 214
root metaphor, 98
Roseland, IL, 8
Roth, John, 194–195

Royce, Josiah, 11
Russellite Movement, 9
Rutherford, Ernest, 9, 78
Ryle, Gilbert, 212

S
Sandburg, Carl, 8
Schoenberg, 4
Schleiermacher, Frederick, 46, 213, 217
Schroder, Widick, 21
Schwab, Joseph, 13
Seaman, Henry, 27
secular/secularization, 98–99, 175
Seigfried, Charlene, 218
sensibilities/sensitivities, 82, 84, 104, 124, 130, 161, 191, 193
sensitive awareness, 84
Sensitive Nature within Nature, 187–188, 197
Shaw, Robert, 25
Shaw, Marvin, 191, 196
Shermis, Michael, xi, 50
Silent Process, 187, 190
sin, 93, 209
Sittler, Joseph, 3, 222
Smith, G. B., ix, 13–16, 18, 21, 23–24, 48, 115, 177
Smuts, Jan, 36–37
social gospel, 7, 10–11
socio-historical method, 19, 21, 114, 144, 210, 230–231
sociology, 10–11, 14
Sontag, Frederick, 194–195
speculative philosophy, 109–111
Speigler, Gerhard, 99
Spencer, John, 21
Sperry, Willard, 31
spirit, 81, 86, 88, 133
stature, 198
Stell, Stephen, 231
Stone, Jerome, x, xi, 71–72, 110, 176, 200, 219
structure of experience, 7, 19, 32, 38, 64, 70, 89, 96, 133, 145
Suchocki, Marjorie, 71–72, 194, 212
suffering, 166–167, 190
supernaturalism, 209–211, 222
surd of insensitivity, 168–170
surplusage of meaning, 61, 82–83, 131, 141, 150, 152

Sutherland, 11
symbolization, 57–59, 62–63, 65, 70, 73
symphonic structure, 3
synthetic ideas, 180
synthetic interpretation, xi

T
Taylor, Mark, 214
temperament, 112, 171–172
term of selection, 198
Theimann, Ronald, 212, 231–232
theism, 181, 191, 197
theodicy, 165–167, 192–196
Theological Studies, 109
Theology Club, 19
Theology Today, 72
theologian, 159–161, 165, 172, 222–223, 226, 228
theology/theologian of culture, 172, 223–224, 229
Tillich, Paul, x, 6, 15, 25, 36, 46, 94, 113, 128, 162, 193, 213, 217
Toulmin, Stephen, 139
Towne, Edgar, 175
Tracy, David, vii, 212, 223, 225, 231–232
tragic sense of life/tragedy/tragic flaw, 7–9, 29, 93, 129, 165–168, 188, 190–191
transcendence, 94–96
trust, 93, 168

U
ultimacy, 35, 99–100, 102–104, 140, 187–188, 201–202, 204
Ultimate Efficacy, 130
Underhill, Evelyn, 195
Union Theological Seminary, 39
United Theological Seminary, xi
University of Chicago, 10–11
University of Illinois, 10
University of Marburg, 15
University Presbyterian Church, 11

V
valuations, 96, 111
van Dusen, Henry, 27
Visser 't Hooft, W. A., 27
Vlastos, Gregory, 13

W

Wagner Car Works, 6
Whitehead, Alfred, 19, 32–33, 36–38, 45, 64–65, 70–71, 73, 91, 102, 109, 113–116, 120–125, 127, 132–133, 135–136, 144–145, 147–151, 160, 163, 170, 182, 217
Whitney, Barry, 194
Wieman, Henry Nelson, ix, 9, 13–24, 27, 32–33, 35–36, 61, 67, 87, 110, 112, 114–115, 144–145, 148, 151, 153, 177, 182, 184, 187, 189, 192–193, 198, 227
Williams, Daniel Day, ix, 31, 36, 40, 90, 92, 110, 113
Williamson, Clark, xi, 95, 113, 222, 225
Willimon, William, 212
Willoughby, H., 9
Wilson, John, 13
Wittgenstein, Ludwig, 209, 212
wonder, 14, 34, 49, 84, 93, 137, 140
World Student Christian Federation, 26–27
World War II, 32
worship, 196–197

Y

Yale School, ix, 209, 212–213, 221

www.ingramcontent.com/pod-product-compliance
Ingram Content Group UK Ltd.
Pitfield, Milton Keynes, MK11 3LW, UK
UKHW041431180426
11947UKWH00007B/383